HARVARD HISTORICAL STUDIES

PUBLISHED UNDER THE DIRECTION OF
THE DEPARTMENT OF HISTORY
FROM THE INCOME OF
THE HENRY WARREN TORREY FUND

VOLUME XXXVIII

HARVARD HISTORICAL STUDIES

GREAT BRITAIN AND THE CYPRUS CONVENTION POLICY OF 1878

BY

DWIGHT E. LEE

Associate Professor of
Modern European History
in Clark University

CAMBRIDGE
HARVARD UNIVERSITY PRESS
LONDON: HUMPHREY MILFORD
OXFORD UNIVERSITY PRESS
1934

TO

MARGARET SHIPLEY LEE

PREFACE

WHILE others are undertaking the task of re-writing the history of the Near Eastern Crisis of 1875-78 either as a European diplomatic episode or as a phase in the development of the Turkish and Balkan peoples, my aim in this monograph has been to trace only a part of the policy pursued by Great Britain in those critical times. I have attempted, therefore, to recount the story of the crisis or the details of British policy as a whole only where explanation has been necessary in order to trace more clearly those threads which eventually went into the pattern of the Cyprus Convention policy.

Any contribution this narrowly restricted work may claim to make either to a synthesis of the crisis of 1875-78 or to a re-interpretation of England's foreign policy is to be found principally in the material drawn from the *Layard Papers* at the British Museum and the *Simmons Papers* in the Public Record Office. These, together with my study of public opinion as expressed in the press, go far to fill up the gaps which still remained after Sir James Headlam-Morley's able summary of the negotiations concerning the Cyprus Convention in his *Studies in Diplomatic History*. They also add important elements to the background and the significance of the British occupation of Cyprus, bringing out as they do the imperialistic hopes and dreams which were closely related to it.

In the preparation of this monograph I have utilized some of the results of research on other aspects of the Eastern Question and particularly on the subject of my doctoral thesis, written at Harvard University under the direction of the late Professor Archibald Cary Coolidge, on "British Policy in the Eastern Question, 1878." While I am grateful to many friends and teachers for their aid and counsel in this earlier work, I take pleasure in acknowledging my greatest indebtedness to Professor Laurence B. Packard of Amherst College who guided and inspired my first studies in this field and introduced me to the archives of London, Paris, and Vienna. He has also most generously lent to me for this study many transcripts and abstracts of documents which have greatly shortened my own labors.

Additional research upon the special subject of this monograph and also assistance in the preparation of the manuscript has been made possible by Grants-in-Aid in 1930 and 1934 from the Social Science Research Council and by the generous co-operation of President Wallace W. Atwood and the Trustees of Clark University. Professor George Hubbard Blakeslee, head of the Department of History and International Relations at Clark, has likewise most kindly aided me in many ways.

To my regret I cannot acknowledge explicitly and fully all of the friendly and generous help extended to me so cordially in England, but I am happy to express my gratitude to Sir George Young, and to Professor Harold Temperley of Cambridge University for helpful discussions of this subject and for aid in the discovery of new material in connection with this and former studies. Professor Henry Donaldson Jordan of Clark University has very kindly read the manuscript and made me his debtor for criticisms regarding style and composition. Also my former students, especially Dr. C. Grove Haines of Syracuse University, and research assistants, Miss B. Eliott Lockhart in London and Mr. Oliver M. Shipley in Washington, have rendered me great aid in preparing this manuscript and collecting material. I genuinely appreciate their services and those extended by the various libraries and archives in which I have worked, particularly Widener Library at Harvard, the British Museum, and the Public Record Office. But most of all I am indebted to Professor William L. Langer of Harvard University for whose encouragement to undertake this work, valuable criticism throughout its preparation, and helpfulness in every way I am sincerely and deeply grateful.

Worcester, Massachusetts   DWIGHT E. LEE
June, 1934

TABLE OF CONTENTS

GREAT BRITAIN AND THE CYPRUS CONVENTION POLICY OF 1878

CHAPTER I

GROPING FOR A POLICY, 1875–77

When the insurrections in Herzegovina and Bosnia re-opened the Eastern Question in 1875, neither the British public nor the Disraeli government was ready to offer an acceptable solution to the ever-recurrent problem of what to do with the Ottoman Empire. The Treaty of Berlin, the Cyprus Convention, and the hopes and dreams of British capitalists and empire-builders at length, in 1878, supplied an answer which had been slowly formulated over the green baize tables of Europe and in the press, the Parliament, and the council chambers of Great Britain. While the Treaty of Berlin represented a compromise of the conflicting European views and aims, the Cyprus Convention between Great Britain and Turkey and the policy and ambitions which it involved were attempts to safeguard and develop what Englishmen considered to be peculiarly British interests.

The ideas and the economic and political factors which helped to determine the policy finally adopted were almost all present from the beginning, but were so incoherent and oftentimes contradictory that for the first two years and a half of the Eastern crisis little progress was made by Great Britain toward agreement upon a goal or the choice of a way to attain it. A review of the character of the Disraeli government and the international situation shows not only the confusion of the time but also the reasons why some alternative to the Crimean War policy of twenty years before, or at least a modification of it, had to be sought.[1]

[1] The latest and best account of the Eastern crisis of 1875-78 is that of William L. Langer, *European Alliances and Alignments, 1871-1890* (New York, 1931), Chs. 3-5. Other useful accounts, though not so recent nor complete are:

Disraeli had been Prime Minister little more than a year when his government was called upon to deal with the troublesome Eastern imbroglio. His fame had been won as the leader of a minority in the House of Commons. His brief periods in government councils had scarcely prepared him for the management of difficult and dangerous crises in foreign affairs, nor had they sufficed to inspire the country, including members of his own party, with entire confidence in his leadership.[2] Yet it very soon became apparent and was generally recognized that Disraeli was the real director of foreign policy and that on the whole he was determined to carry out his platform pledges of a spirited foreign policy and the elevation once more of Great Britain to a high place in the councils of Europe.[3]

By nature, however, Disraeli was not well fitted to apply the policy which he envisaged. His was the role of the imaginative and daring visionary, some would erroneously say Asiatic mystic,[4] whose flair for innuendo and resounding phrase

W. H. Dawson, "Forward Policy and Reaction, 1874-1885," *Cambridge History of British Foreign Policy* (New York, 1923), III, Ch. 2; Mason W. Tyler, *The European Powers and the Near East, 1875-1908* (Minneapolis, 1925); and Rudolf Liebold, *Die Stellung Englands in der russisch-türkishen Krise von 1875-78* (Wilkau, 1930).

[2] W. F. Monypenny and G. E. Buckle, *Life of Benjamin Disraeli* (New and revised edition, New York, 1929), II, 624 and 1515; Lady Gwendolen Cecil, *Life of Robert Marquis of Salisbury* (London, 1922), II, 43-51. A. H. Layard, a political opponent who became one of Disraeli's greatest admirers during the Eastern crisis, wrote of him in 1868: "What an astounding fact—Dizzy Premier. The triumph of jugglery and political immorality. A man whose name is not connected with one political measure either good, bad or indifferent—whose career has been one continuous, cynical contempt of everything honest, upright and true." Letter to G. T. Clark, February 28, 1868 (British Museum, Add. MS., 38,946).

[3] Monypenny and Buckle, II, 615 and 834; B. Holland, *Life of Spencer Compton, 8th Duke of Devonshire* (London, 1911), I, 181; and G. C. Thompson, *Public Opinion and Lord Beaconsfield, 1875-1880* (London, 1886), I, 197, 236, and 240-41.

[4] E. A. Freeman wrote in 1877 that Disraeli was not an Englishman nor even a European, when he talked of the East, but a man "of Asian mysteries, with feelings and policy distinctly Asiatic." While his personality may have given ground for that view, his policies certainly did not and von Bülow seems to be

often obscured his keen perception of the realities in a situation. It was his fondness for the bizarre and fantastic which led him to be distrusted by many of his stolid countrymen, yet no one in his government or England had a more fixed purpose nor a more determined will to achieve his aims. Like Bismarck, Disraeli had chosen the ultimate goal toward which he wished to work, but unlike Bismarck he often left the method of pursuit to be worked out in detail by his colleagues. To say that he had no policy is to confound purpose and method in his work. Though too prone to follow old paths, even in regard to method, he was fruitful in invention and at one time or another suggested much which found its way into the final settlement of the Eastern Question.

Disraeli's policy in Eastern affairs as in every question of foreign relations was to maintain British interests by peaceful means, if possible, but by threat of war if that was absolutely necessary. He consequently cared little for the Turks or the Christians on sentimental or moral grounds, and, for one who had such a firm faith in race, he was singularly untouched by nationalism. Throughout the greater part of his life, England had steadily pursued the policy of supporting the independence and integrity of the Turkish Empire as the means best calculated to secure her interests and it is perhaps Disraeli's greatest mistake that he did not completely and finally abandon that policy. It must be remembered, however, in extenuation of his faults of conservatism that he was an old man with very precarious health. Even so the vigor and at times the originality and perspicuity of his actions were

more nearly correct when he wrote, in connection with the Congress of Berlin: ". . . there was no more English Englishman than Benjamin Disraeli. . . . English—English to the backbone! Every one of his words was meant for the English public. English interests only, English wishes and advantage inspired his acts." E. A. Freeman, "The Relation of the English People to the War," *Contemporary Rev.*, XXX (August 1877), 494-95; and Bernhard von Bülow, *Memoirs*, IV (Boston, 1932), 452-53. Cf. A. Andréadès, "La Politique Orientale Anglaise Avant et Pendant le Congrès de Berlin," *La Vie des Peuples*, VII (1922), 895.

in striking contrast to the inertia and narrowness of view of some of his colleagues.[5]

The man who was best fitted to work with Disraeli, and the only one in any way comparable to him in the cabinet, was Salisbury, Secretary of State for India, and they together, after Lord Derby's withdrawal in 1878, finally shaped the positive policy which England at length adopted. Salisbury combined high intelligence with a willingness to try new methods and strike out upon the unbeaten paths which an objective study of the facts indicated. While he was eager to maintain peace among the European great powers, he detested inactivity and a negative policy, and for that reason, although during the first two years he was as often as not an opponent of Disraeli, he finally swung round to whole-hearted support of his chief and really took the lead in working out practical solutions to the critical problems of foreign policy.[6]

In striking contrast to Disraeli and Salisbury was Lord Derby, Secretary of State for Foreign Affairs until his resignation in March 1878. Everyone agrees upon his hatred of sham, his honesty of purpose, and his stolidity; and everyone equally agrees that he was ill-fitted to formulate and conduct a policy of energy and brilliance because of his over-developed caution and his ingrained aversion to making decisions. Salisbury testified that making a featherbed walk was nothing to the difficulty of overcoming his irresolution, and Shuvalov, Russian Ambassador to England, declared that negotiating

---

[5] Though some of the foregoing interpretation of Disraeli's character and foreign policy will be substantiated by the subsequent pages of this study, much of it has been drawn from the numerous attempts to characterize him, especially: Monypenny and Buckle, II, 873-83, 1495-98, 1511-17 and *passim*; James Bryce, *Studies in Contemporary Biography* (London, 1903), pp. 37-38; [A. H. Layard], "The Early Life of Lord Beaconsfield," *Quarterly Rev.*, CLXVIII (January 1889), 1-42; Frederick Greenwood, "Characteristics of Lord Beaconsfield," *Cornhill Magazine*, New Series, I (November 1896), 589-604; and [Edmond Hippeau], *Le Congrès en Miniature* par Diplomate (Paris, 1878), 32-35.

[6] As in the case of Disraeli, subsequent pages will support much of this interpretation. See especially Cecil, II, Chs. 4 and 5, *passim,* and Monypenny and Buckle, II, 749-50.

with him was comparable to dancing on a carpet to the sound of a pianoforte. While he was willing to admit that in the Eastern Question, the Turkish Empire was virtually done for and the old policy of support no longer possible, he viewed every suggestion for a new solution with distrust, combatting with obstinacy what he regarded as dangerous. There is no doubt that he sincerely and almost passionately desired to prevent England from becoming embroiled in a war in the Near East and it is possible that he is chiefly responsible for preventing it. Also his coolness, caution, and logic often served his government in good stead, but his irresolution and timidity were equally often a real detriment to the prosecution of a desirable new departure.[7]

The other members of the cabinet in their attitude toward the Eastern Question were ranged between the two extremes represented on the one hand by Disraeli and on the other by Derby. At first the conduct of foreign policy was left exclusively to these two,[8] but as time went on and the hopes of immediate peace in Turkey grew dim, uneasiness began to appear in the cabinet as to the policy that England should pursue. The issue which the government at length had to face was how could England prevent Russia from endangering the route to India? Then appeared a "peace" party centering around Derby and a so-called "war" party around the Prime Minister, although it would probably be more accurate to call them the passivists and the activists. Even so, there were almost as many shades of opinion regarding the question of

[7] Unfortunately Lord Derby has not been made the subject of a scholarly biography, but there are two sympathetic short studies of him: W. E. H. Lecky, "Prefatory Memoir," *Speeches and Addresses of XVth Earl of Derby*, Edited by Sanderson and Roscoe. 2 vols. (London, 1894); T. W. Reid, "Lord Derby at the Foreign Office," *Macmillan's Magazine*, XL (June 1879), 180-92. Cf. Cecil, II, 89, 114-15; Monypenny and Buckle, II, 940; Lord Newton, *Lord Lyons* (London, 1913), II, 95, 105, 122, 131-32; Alfred E. Gathorne-Hardy, *Gathorne Hardy, First Earl of Cranbrook* (London, 1910), II, 58; "Home and Foreign Affairs," *Fortnightly Rev.*, XXVI (July 1876), 140-41.

[8] Monypenny and Buckle, II, 887.

what should be done as there were members of the cabinet.[9] Under such circumstances, the policy of the government was often feeble and uncertain.

This situation was but a reflection of the divisions in British public opinion which, frequently ignoring party lines, gave no sure direction to the supposed servants of the public interest. The press displayed all varieties of views from those which were anti-Turk and pro-Russian to the other extreme of pro-Turk and anti-Russian. In between lay expressions of what might be called a neutral view which stressed neither anti-Turkism nor anti-Russianism, but the protection of British interests in a world large enough to accommodate all powers.[10] One reason for this uncertainty and disagreement in 1875 lay in the fact that while England's interests in the Near East were essentially the same as in 1856, two decades had brought changes which tended to give a different interpretation or to place a new emphasis upon old ideas.

First of all, since Turkey had failed to set her house in order and to show that Ottoman rule still constituted a worthy bulwark against the forces of disintegration from within and foreign encroachment from without, British opinion in 1875 was fast drifting toward the idea of accepting and even advocating the dissolution of the Ottoman Empire. "Notorious, palpable, flagrant, ruinous misgovernment must . . . involve in ruin a country with even greater resources and capacities than Turkey" wrote one friend of the Turks,[11] while hu-

---

[9] R. W. Seton-Watson, "Russo-British Relations during the Eastern Crisis. Unprinted Documents," *Slavonic Review*, III (1924-25), 658; Andrew Lang, *Life, Letters, and Diaries of Sir Stafford Northcote, First Earl of Iddesleigh* (London, 1890), II, 105-106; Monypenny and Buckle, II, 1066 and *passim;* and Sir Arthur Hardinge, *Life of Carnarvon, 1831-1890* (Oxford, 1925), II, 351 *et seq.*

[10] See Thompson, I, Chs. III and IV for a thorough analysis of British public opinion regarding the Eastern Question in general and Chs. VI-VIII for a detailed study of the period from 1875 to February 1876.

[11] H. A. Munro-Butler-Johnstone, "Turkish Letters, II," *Pall Mall Gazette,* July 15, 1875, p. 10, reprinted in *The Eastern Question* (For private circulation only, 1875). Johnstone was one of the most consistent and ardent friends of Turkey throughout the crisis of 1875-78.

manitarian as well as economic considerations prompted another writer to declare: "Existing facts must be recognized. The day of Turkish power in Europe cannot be sustained."[12] The *Times* and the *Daily News* strongly advocated that autonomy be granted to Bosnia and Herzegovina and even the *Pall Mall Gazette,* whose opinions are the more noteworthy because of its conservative policy, admitted that this would be the best thing to do even though it would lead, in the end, to the break-up of the Ottoman Empire. While this eventuality should be delayed as long as possible until "time may have brought to light the elements for a more promising solution of the Eastern Question than can at present be discovered," the *Pall Mall Gazette* asserted that few people believed any longer that "if the Turks were judiciously helped they would judiciously help themselves."[13]

Such expressions of opinion multiplied after the Porte virtually admitted bankruptcy by announcing on October 6 that a budget deficit of five million pounds Turkish required a reduction in the payment of interest on its huge debts.[14] The effect of this upon English investors who had put upwards of a million pounds into Turkish bonds and had already been shaken by financial disasters at home,[15] was two-fold. It was

[12] *John Bull,* September 4, p. 601. This weekly had already urged strongly the cause of the "unhappy Christians." See August 21, 1875, p. 568. It is interesting to note that despite the feeling about Turkey, efforts sponsored by Lord John Russell, among others, in August to raise money on behalf of the suffering Herzegovinian insurgents were frowned upon even by the *Times.* The conservative papers thought it an encouragement to rebellion. See summaries of *Times, Post,* and *Daily Telegraph* in *Pall Mall Gazette,* Aug. 30, p. 2. Consul Blunt at Salonica reported that Russell's letter and recent *Times* articles had "given rise to the impression that there was a change in the policy of H. M. Gov't" towards Turkey and Sir Henry Elliot, Ambassador at the Porte, cautioned him to deny that such was the case and pointed out that the views of Russell and the *Times* "met with little approval in England." Elliot to Blunt, Oct. 20, 1875 (F. O. 195/1072).

[13] *Times,* Aug. 23, p. 7; *Daily News,* Sept. 6, p. 4; *Pall Mall Gazette,* Sept. 10, 17, and 24, and October 15, 1875. Quotation taken from Sept. 24.

[14] See Donald C. Blaisdell, *European Financial Control in the Ottoman Empire* (New York, 1929), pp. 1 and 80-84.

[15] See L. H. Jenks, *The Migration of British Capital to 1875* (New York, 1927), pp. 421-24; and *Pall Mall Gazette,* July 10, 1875, p. 3 and July 16, p. 10.

taken as additional proof by those who had voiced a belief in Turkey's downfall that they were right. "We are convinced," declared *John Bull*, "that the Turkish rule in Europe is hastening to a speedy end."[16] The *Times*, in attempting to deny that this episode had changed British views of the Eastern Question and to prove that "unbelief in the possibility of Turkish reform and a healthy detestation of Mohammedan tyranny" were responsible for it, admitted that "of course the act of bankruptcy greatly quickened the feeling of this country."[17]

On the other hand, there were evidences of a philosophical attitude toward the Turkish repudiation. Lord Hammond, in retirement after a long term of office as Under-Secretary of State for Foreign Affairs, wrote to his friend Layard: "We hear less now than we did of indignant Bondholders, who are perhaps beginning to perceive that if Turkey falls to pieces, their hopes of future dividends fall with her. Indeed I hear of some who take the matter very philosophically, and are content to set off the large profits they obtained in former years against their diminished prospects at the present time; and indeed it is contended that with the respite of five years Turkey may be set financially on her legs again."[18] Staunch friends of Turkey were quick to raise old fears of Russia and declare that the action of the Sublime Porte was inspired by Ignatiev, her wily Ambassador, in order to facilitate a partition by which she would benefit most. Or they pointed out that all might yet be well if Turkey could be administered for a few years by a few picked Indian officials or one of those

---

[16] November 6, p. 765. Cf. *ibid.*, p. 759.

[17] *Times*, November 26, p. 7. For similar expressions regarding the effect of the repudiation, cf. *Pall Mall Gazette*, Oct. 21, p. 1; A. J. Wilson, "The Turkish Default," *Macmillan's Magazine*, XXXIII (November 1875), 94; and *The Fall of Turkey* (London, 1875), 21 pp.

[18] Hammond to A. H. Layard, 25 Eaton Place, Nov. 30, 1875 (Add. MS. 38,955, fo. 2). Cf. *Edinburgh Rev.*, CXLIV (Oct. 1876), 546. Lord Derby thought the Turkish bankruptcy had caused less sensation than he would have expected, "being no doubt discounted by popular expectation." Derby to Layard, Private, F. O., Nov. 8, 1875 (Add MS. 39,008, fo. 354).

Pashas who had performed prodigies of good government.[19]
Nevertheless, such opinions were those of a minority in
1875 and there is no doubt that Lord Odo Russell, British Ambassador at Berlin, was correct when he intimated to Bismarck that, judging from the point of view of the press,
"England had fundamentally abandoned her traditional policy"
in the Eastern Question. He was equally correct when he declared that "England had, as always, a life and death interest
in preserving her communications with India."[20]   In this
matter as in the attitude toward Turkey, events of the previous
decade and of the year 1875 had brought about a new situation and re-emphasized an old issue.

The opening of the Suez Canal in 1869 and the constantly
increasing use of it by British shipping had made the Eastern
Question more than ever before one of imperial defense because of the importance this short all-sea route had quickly assumed in the public mind. While the fate of Constantinople
and the Euphrates Valley was still occasionally mentioned as
being vitally connected with the safety of India and the road
to it,[21] Englishmen in 1875 directed their gaze toward Egypt

[19] *Pall Mall Gazette,* October 11, p. 1; Oct. 30, p. 7; and July 5, p. 3;
Morning Post, quoted *ibid.,* Nov. 1, p. 2. It is probably only after the Bulgarian atrocity agitation of 1876 that the full effect of the bankruptcy became
evident and that "investments" joined with "vestments" to denounce the Turk.
The idea of Russian intrigue became a favorite stock in trade of the anti-
Russian propagandists after war broke out in April 1877. For excellent ex-
amples see: Capt. Bedford Pim, *The Eastern Question* (London, 1877), pp.
47-48, and A. Borthwick, *An Address on the Eastern Question* (London, 1878),
pp. 16-17.

[20] *Die Grosse Politik der Europäischen Kabinette, 1871-1914* (Berlin, 1922),
II, 30. Cf. the statement in *Blackwood's Magazine,* CXIX (Jan. 1876), 118:
"England no longer affects to believe in the integrity and independence of the
Ottoman Empire; it is in a condition of moral, financial, and administrative
decay."

[21] See Lepel H. Griffin, "The Present State of the Eastern Question," *Fortnightly Rev.,* XXI (Jan. 1874), 35; Sir R. Alcock, "Inheritance of the Great
Mogul," *ibid.,* XXIV (Aug. 1875), 158; *Pall Mall Gazette,* Oct. 15, p. 9;
Standard, quoted in *ibid.,* Oct. 29, p. 2; "Qui Vive," Letter, *Times,* Dec. 7, 1875,
p. 10; and Butler-Johnstone, *Eastern Question,* pp. 5-7. One reason for the
lack of alarm over Constantinople and the Straits was the fact that Russophobia
was quiescent in 1875 especially after the war scare episode. Cf. "England and

as the real center of British interest and the best compensation for Great Britain in case Turkey should be partitioned.[22] The *Pall Mall Gazette* on November 3 published an article entitled "Egypt for the English" which was the signal for the expression of similar opinions in such politically different journals as the *Standard,* the *Daily News,* and the *Economist* all of which emphasized the importance to England of the Suez Canal and the possibility of guarding it by establishing some form of control in Egypt or at least in the Delta or the Isthmus.[23]

While these views were prompted in part by memory of previous suggestions whenever the dissolution of Turkey had been discussed and more especially by the obvious requirements of England's interests, they were also in line with the expectations raised by the Conservative government under Disraeli and by the exigencies of the international situation. Despite Disraeli's platform pledges his government did not take a prominent part in the early negotiations concerning Bosnia and Herzegovina.[24] The major reason for its modest role at the beginning lay in the fact that England was not in a position to assume the leadership which Disraeli desired.

Russia in the East," *Edinburgh Rev.,* CXLII (July 1875), 264-69, 306; and Thompson, I, 206-08. To be sure it was quick to awaken as already noted above.

[22] See lecture by Thomas Brassey, M.P., *Times,* Oct. 28, p. 6; and M. E. Grant Duff, "England and Russia in the East," *Fortnightly Rev.,* XXIV (Nov. 1875), 606-607. Cf. Lord Dunsany, *Gaul or Teuton* (London, 1873), 271; L. H. Griffin, *loc. cit.,* p. 36; and Frederic Harrison, "Public Affairs," *Fortnightly Review,* XXI (May 1874), 696-97.

[23] *Pall Mall Gazette,* Nov. 3, 1875, pp. 1-2; *Standard,* Nov. 4, p. 4; *Daily News,* Nov. 22, p. 4; and *Economist,* Nov. 20. An excellent summary of opinion on this point is that of Gavard to Decazes, Londres, 19 Novembre 1875, *Documents Diplomatiques Français, 1871-1914,* 1re Série, II (Paris, 1930), 15-19. The Prince of Wales' visit to Egypt on his way to India and his conferring of the Star of India on the Khedive's son was the occasion for the *Pall Mall Gazette* article. In addition to this and the interest in the route to India, the financial condition of Egypt also helped to draw attention to it at this time. Cf. Jenks, *op. cit.,* pp. 319-20.

[24] See Monypenny and Buckle, II, 616; Thompson, I, 197 and 211; Dawson, *loc. cit.,* pp. 91-96; Langer, *op. cit.,* pp. 72-75; and Shuvalov to Jomini, 2/14 Oct. 1875, *Slavonic Review,* III, 426-30.

He himself had been one of the first to realize the change in the international situation which the unification of Germany and Italy had brought about and in 1875 was well aware of England's helplessness in the face of the *Dreikaiserbund*.[25] British public opinion not only recognized the superior power of this group in Near Eastern affairs, if no disagreement developed within it, but was inclined to blame the disturbances there to the intrigues of the "Three Northern Powers."[26] Bismarck's "England has ceased to count in Europe," was quoted regretfully, and the *Times,* in commenting upon the consular mission to the insurgents in August 1875 declared that it was "easy to see the fact that the policy which had been imposed upon the Turkish Government was determined upon by the Three Empires, and that England, France, and Italy have been merely consulted for decency's sake, and have, of course, consented to the inevitable."[27] Under these circumstances the hope for England lay in her sea-power and in acquiring a position, such as Egypt, where that power could be readily exerted in order to guard her most important imperial interest.[28]

[25] Monypenny and Buckle, II, 473-74; 790, 885, and 889-90. Cf. Shuvalov to Jomini, 2/14 Oct. and 30 Oct./11 Nov. 1875, *Slavonic Rev.,* III, 427 and 431-32; and Sir Henry Elliot, *Some Revolutions and Other Diplomatic Experiences* (London, 1922), pp. 201.

[26] *Pall Mall Gazette,* July 22, p. 11; July 28, pp. 1-2 (leading article and summary of *Times* and *Post*); Aug. 23, p. 8; Aug. 24, p. 1; *Daily Telegraph,* Aug. 25, p. 4; Thompson, I, 215-16, quoting *Daily News, Standard,* and *Spectator;* Butler-Johnstone, *Eastern Question,* p. 5; Thompson, I, 252-53. Lord Hammond asserted in connection with Turkish bankruptcy that the Turk would pay "if his dry nurses, the three northern Powers, do not strangle him, which they seem inclined to do. I dread much more their interference, than any efforts of the insurgents, and the only consolation one has is the reflection, that they will themselves not come unscathed out of the web of intrigues which they are engaged in spinning." There was no choice, he believed, between the partition of Turkey and the "assertion of English Supremacy"! Private letter to A. H. Layard, November 17, 1875 (Add. MS. 38,954, fo. 272).

[27] *Pall Mall Gazette,* July 19, p. 11; and *Times,* quoted in *ibid.,* August 26, 1875, p. 8. Cf. Monypenny and Buckle, II, 884.

[28] See "Egypt for the English," *loc. cit.,* and Brassey lecture, *loc. cit.* Butler-Johnstone declared: "Now that France's influence is practically extinct, these three Powers can do exactly what they like on the Continent, provided of course, they are agreed; their power being only limited by the fact of England being still master on the seas." *Eastern Question,* p. 5.

The first significant public pronouncement regarding English policy was therefore listened to with more than usual interest. Disraeli at the Mansion House on November 9 delighted his followers and fulfilled the hopes of the nation when he declared that the interests of the Three Imperial Powers in the Eastern Question were perhaps more direct than those of Great Britain but not more considerable, and that those entrusted with the conduct of British affairs were deeply conscious of the nature and magnitude of British interests and were resolved to "guard and maintain them."[29] "We believe," wrote *John Bull,* "that the speech re-echoes the national sentiment as to this country no longer consenting to be a nonentity in European affairs; . . . Departmental blunders there may have been, but on the broad question of policy, on the unflinching upholding of the national honour, the country knows that it can trust the Government: hence the quiet aspect of politics." While other comments were not exultant in tone, all journals united in approving the words of the Prime Minister with entire satisfaction.[30]

Such was the situation in England and Europe when the government, on November 26, 1875, announced the purchase of the Khedive's shares in the Suez Canal.[31] The comment of the *Times* clearly revealed the prevailing interpretation of this action: "We seem to trace in the business the hand of Mr. Disraeli. . . . It is impossible to separate in our thoughts the purchase . . . from the question of England's future rela-

---

[29] Thompson, I, 235-37; and Monypenny and Buckle, II, 888-90.

[30] *John Bull,* Nov. 13, p. 781; *Pall Mall Gazette,* Nov. 10 and 11, 1875 (leading article and summaries of morning papers).

[31] For the latest account of the purchase, see C. W. Hallberg, *The Suez Canal* (New York, 1931), pp. 231-49. Cf. Halford L. Hoskins, *British Routes to India* (New York, 1928), 459-68; Jenks, *op. cit.,* pp. 320-25; and Monypenny and Buckle, II, 779-91. In view of the prominent part taken by the *Pall Mall Gazette* in calling attention to Egypt, it is interesting to note that the editor, Frederick Greenwood, was among those who suggested the idea of England's buying the Canal shares. Jenks assumes that he may have recommended it as a means of raising the price of Egyptian bonds, but it is also probable, considering his editorials, that he may have stressed its political implications. After all, the two aspects of the purchase are closely related.

tions with Egypt, or the destiny of Egypt from the shadows which darken the Turkish Empire." [32] To a considerable degree, the well-nigh unanimous approval of the purchase is to be explained on the grounds that it seemed to foreshadow a policy of abandoning the independence and integrity of Turkey and at the same time of safeguarding Great Britain's vital interests in a manner compatible with her imperial greatness. *Blackwood's Magazine* pointed out that initiative in the Eastern Question did not rest with England whose hand should be on the Persian Gulf, the Red Sea and the Suez Canal, and that it was a good thing to have a government in power which was conscious of British interests. Indeed the opinion was freely expressed both at home and abroad that England had begun the partition of the Ottoman Empire by an act which indicated her intention of taking Egypt.[33]

But the British government did not follow the policy which the public expected. Instead, Lord Derby proceeded to throw cold water on the whole affair. He declared at Edinburgh in December that England did not wish to establish a protectorate over Egypt and that she had merely obtained additional

---

[32] *Times,* Nov. 26, 1875, p. 7.

[33] "Public Affairs," *Blackwood's Magazine,* CXIX (Jan. 1876), 125; "Home and Foreign Affairs," *Fortnightly Rev.,* XXV (Jan. 1876), 144; "Suez Canal an International Highway," *Quarterly Rev.,* CXLII (Oct. 1876), 451; Thompson, I, 240-43; Hallberg, *op. cit.,* 249-53; Monypenny and Buckle, II, 790-93; G. E. Buckle, *Letters of Queen Victoria.* Second Series (London, 1926), II, 428-30; and *1 Documents Diplomatiques Français,* II, 22-26; Cartoon, "Mosé in Egitto!!" *Punch,* Dec. 11, 1875. There was an undercurrent of opposition in England to the transaction. See: Lang, II, 84-87; Lord Edmond Fitzmaurice, *Life of Granville, 1815-1891* (London, 1905), II, 158-59; and Sir Arnold T. Wilson, *The Suez Canal, its Past, Present and Future* (London, 1933), pp. 51-54. It caused considerable excitement in Syria, where there was a growing party in favor of annexation to Egypt which interpreted the purchase of the Canal shares as a sign of a change in English policy and an additional reason for uniting with Egypt. But when Consul General Eldridge, at Beyrout, asked Elliot, at Constantinople, what attitude he should take toward the movement in Syria, he was told to do all in his power to counteract the impression that the British government had changed its policy as regards Turkey and Egypt, and to be careful not to encourage Syrian aspirations for annexation to Egypt. Copy of Eldridge to Elliot, Beyrout, December 28, 1875; and copy of Elliot to Eldridge, Tel., Constantinople, Jan. 7, 1876 (F. O., 78/2454).

security for a free and uninterrupted passage through that country to India.[34] The press was at a loss how to interpret this declaration from the lips of the Secretary for Foreign Affairs, suggesting that perhaps the speech was intended to hoodwink possible opponents, but asserting that emphasis upon the commercial aspect of the deal could not hide its political import. It was rightly concluded that such utterances would not be taken at their face value by interested powers like Russia and France.[35]

Although the speech also encouraged the belief in a divided cabinet with Disraeli leading an audacious section and Lord Derby a cautious one,[36] later developments scarcely revealed any real disparity between the two in regard to Egypt. Despite Disraeli's announcement in the parliamentary debate over the Canal Shares purchase that he did not recommend it as a commercial speculation but rather as a "political transaction" which was "calculated to strengthen the Empire" he was no more willing than Derby to embark upon further adventures and in fact disclaimed any intention of aggression or redistribution of territory in the Mediterranean.[37]

The action of the government in regard to Egyptian finances likewise disappointed many who had looked forward to active interference in Egypt. The report of Mr. Cave, who had been sent there in November to investigate her financial condition, was withheld from the public in March 1876 in a way which gave rise to the suspicion that the government, out of regard for France and Italy, was repudiating the promises implied in the November transaction. One writer in *Fraser's Magazine* summarized this public feeling by declaring: "There was a cap-throwing and hussaing over it the land through, as an indication that the Tories had at last given us a spirited foreign policy: that we had given the challenge direct to Russia and

---

[34] Monypenny and Buckle, II, 791-93; and Thompson, I, 243.

[35] Thompson, I, 244-47.

[36] *Ibid.*

[37] Speeches of February 8 and 21, 1876, 3 Hansard, CCXXVII, 94-102 and 661. Cf. Monypenny and Buckle, II, 800-01.

Austria henceforth to count with England in their projects for dividing the carcass of Turkey between them. As we interpreted at home so did Europe . . . What, then, has England come to, that she should incontinently slap faces all round, and say with a light laugh, It is nothing?" The *Spectator* of April 1 declared: "Mr. Disraeli will be drowned in the Nile if he does not take care." [38]

There was another side, however, to public feeling which indicates one of the principal reasons for government caution in regard to Egypt. It was pointed out by a few writers in the Conservative press and by members of the Liberal party that the purchase of the shares did not really help to protect British interests. Sir William Harcourt's attitude was summarized by the *Spectator* as follows: "Our power over the Suez Canal and our route to India depend on our command of the Mediterranean. If we have that, shares in the Suez Canal are superfluous. If we have not that, shares in the Suez Canal are no use." [39] This was an indirect way of saying that the balance of power in the Near East was more important to England than the Canal or, perhaps, Egypt, and that the two were but part of one and the same problem, the fate of Turkey.

On this broader question the parliamentary debates in February 1876 showed the power which tradition still exerted over the minds of many who had either participated in the events of the Crimean War period or at least retained a vivid memory of that last crisis.[40] They likewise showed the difference in attitude between the press and men in responsible positions. Uncertainty regarding the attitude toward the Eastern Question which the Liberal party leaders would take caused the

[38] "English Foreign Policy and the Eastern Question," *Fraser's Magazine*, XIII (May 1876), 538-39; and Thompson, I, 250-51, quoting *Spectator* and others. Cf. Langer, *op. cit.*, 255-57.

[39] Quoted by Thompson, I, 247. For similar views, see "Suez Canal," *Edinburgh Rev.*, CXLIII (Jan. 1876), 272; *Fortnightly Rev.*, XXV (Jan. 1876), 142-43; George Campbell, "Our Dealings with Egypt," *ibid.* (Feb. 1876), 157-73.

[40] Cf. *Spectator*, Nov. 4, 1876, quoted by Thompson, I, 162; and Holland, I, 179.

Times to issue a warning against attacking the government on its Eastern policy from a pro-Turkish angle. In the debate on the Address, Granville and Hartington displayed some uneasiness as to how far British co-operation with the other European powers in plans for the reform of Turkey was compatible with the sovereign rights of the Sultan and with England's treaty obligations. The latter hoped that the government would not overstep the limits laid down by Palmerston beyond which intervention in Turkey should not go. Only Gladstone, in a speech which puzzled the Treasury bench, seemed ready to depart, if need be, from England's traditional course of action.[41] The reluctance with which even Liberal party leaders contemplated any departure from the policy of upholding Turkey's independence and integrity was shared by Disraeli and Lord Derby who scarcely wished to take any decisive step toward the partition of the Ottoman Empire.

Lord Derby, who was by nature opposed to an adventurous course of action at any time, refused to consider taking Egypt not merely because of natural hesitancy but because he was sincerely devoted to the cause of peace and feared the consequences of such a policy. As he explained to Russell: ". . . any disturbance of the territorial *status quo* would be unadvisable and dangerous, as one rectification of frontiers could not fail to lead to another, and when a policy of annexation was once entered upon, no one could foresee where it would end."[42] He told the House of Lords that if war could be staved off between Mohammedans and Christians in Turkey, "we should have done a good work for ourselves, for Turkey, and for Civilisation."[43]

Disraeli was always more ready than Derby to take risks in gaining his ends, but, because of tradition and conviction, he still hoped to uphold the treaties and at the same time

---

[41] *Times,* Feb. 7, quoted by Thompson, I, 266-67; 3 Hans., CCXXVII, 22-24, 80-82, and 102-107; and Lang, II, 100.

[42] David Harris, "Bismarck's Advance to England, January, 1876," *Journal of Modern History,* III (Sept. 1931), 450; and Newton, II, 92 and 105.

[43] 3 Hans. CCXXVII, 39-40.

maintain the Empire of England.[44] He was not the man to withdraw from the intricacies of the Eastern Question by the simple expedient of taking Egypt and leaving the rest of Turkey to the tender mercies of the Three Northern Powers. He was too profoundly interested in the affairs of Turkey, too conscious of the dramatic elements in the histrionics of diplomacy as played by Emperors and Chancellors, and too ambitious to win fame for himself to renounce irrevocably the center of the stage even if he thought British interests would permit such a course.[45] In the early months of 1876 he was still feeling his way toward the goal of stage director, but, like Derby, he was also well aware of the complications which might follow any precipitate action on the part of England.

At this time there were not only persistent rumors of Austrian and Russian intrigues but also uncertainty and uneasiness regarding Germany's aims.[46] The deep distrust of Bismarck which had been confirmed by the war scare of 1875 led Englishmen to consider him a conspirator against European peace. His supposed desire for more territory and his position in the *Dreikaiserbund,* thought to be his creation, added a western aspect to the Near Eastern imbroglio.[47] Fundamentally the British government misunderstood Bismarck and were mystified by his overtures to them in November 1875 and January 1876.

[44] Cf. Monypenny and Buckle, II, 881.

[45] *Idem,* II, 886, 903, 956; and Marquis of Zetland, *Letters of Disraeli to Lady Bradford and Lady Chesterfield* (London, 1929), I, 304.

[46] While rumors in October that Austria intended to annex Bosnia had been denied, not only did reports of intentions to occupy Bosnia and create a Bulgarian principality continue through the early months of 1876, but parts of Holmes' Memorandum on the outbreak of the Herzegovinian insurrections, suppressed in the Blue Book, clearly implicated Russia and Austria in fomenting them. The *Times,* October 9, 1875, November 15, 1875, and January 5, 1876; Zetland, I, 296; Russell Memorandum, in Newton, II, 87-90; Loftus Desp. No. 21, St. Petersburg, Jan. 19 (F. O., 65/935); Buchanan Desp. No. 23, Vienna, Jan. 26; Harris-Gastrell to Derby, No. 53, Vienna, Feb. 8, 1876 (F. O., 7/867); and Memorandum by W. R. Holmes, Pera, Feb. 29, 1876 (F. O., 78/2456; and extract in *Parl. Papers,* C. 1531 (1876), pp. 39-41).

[47] Buckle, *Victoria,* II, 391, 406, 408; Monypenny and Buckle, II, 761, 790-91, 893; Newton, II, 88-89, 95-97; and Harris, *loc. cit.,* pp. 447-48.

Bismarck was simply following the current trend of thought in a conversation with Lord Odo Russell on November 29 when he gave his hearty approval to the Suez Canal transaction. He began his remarks by reading passages from a despatch of Count Münster, German Ambassador at the Court of St. James, who praised Disraeli as the greatest leader and parliamentary tactician in the history of England and prognosticated a long life to a government "whose far and clear-sighted policy has known when and how to solve the Eastern Question, as far as English interests are concerned, without bloodshed and through the timely exercise of the arts of peace and high statesmanship." Bismarck then asserted that it was the privilege of friendly powers to lend each other moral support in the attainment of national interests, so long as they did not clash, "but in the present case the interests of England were those of Germany." He had feared a conflict between England and Russia and had advised both Gorchakov, Russian Chancellor, and Shuvalov, the Russian Ambassador in England, to lessen the danger by guaranteeing England's passage to India through Egypt. He hoped that the security of those communications which England had now gained would in the course of time deprive the "inevitable extension of Russia in Central Asia of much of its supposed importance . . . and would facilitate the establishment of those intimate relations between England and Russia which were so essential to the maintenance of peace and the interests of civilization." He therefore gave his most hearty support to the policy which Her Majesty's Government had inaugurated by the purchase of the Suez Canal Shares. Although Bismarck at this time denied that he expected the break-up of Turkey, the implications of his allusion to the policy inaugurated by England were plain.[48]

---

[48] Russell, despatch No. 488, Berlin, Nov. 29, 1875 (F. O., 64/831). The background for this despatch was Russell's exposition on Nov. 12 of a possible partition of Turkey, which Bismarck had been turning over in his mind as early as March. See Newton, II, 87-90; and Hajo Holborn, *Bismarcks Europäische Politik* (Berlin, 1925), 38.

In January he again approached Russell and suggested a frank and close co-operation between the two countries. To be sure he reiterated his belief that the time had not yet come for the partition of Turkey, but at the same time he made no secret of the territorial ambitions of Austria and Russia and his unwillingness to resist them. This overture, although it was welcomed by the Queen and Disraeli who had been on the watch for signs of a rift in the *Dreikaiserbund,* really puzzled the government and the diplomatic corps.[49] Lord Odo Russell was almost alone in believing that Bismarck's professed disinterestedness in the Eastern Question and his desire for peace were sincere. Did he want to establish German along with English influence in the Mediterranean? Did he hope to gain additional provinces for Germany out of the general scramble which would accompany the break-up of the Ottoman Empire? Or did he merely hope to enlist British support in opposing Russia and France?[50]

These queries regarding Bismarck's motives clearly bring out the British distrust which was probably heightened by the uneasiness of France and the coolness of Russia toward the Suez Canal business, attitudes in marked contrast to his own warm approval. The French Foreign Minister, Decazes, told Lord Lyons, the British Ambassador, that the purchase of the Khedive's shares was undoubtedly "calculated to arouse French susceptibilities," and that one great cause for alarm was the chance of its producing a difference between England and Russia which might precipitate events in the Levant. In such an event France might find herself driven to side with one or the other and, since she could not take the same side

[49] Russell despatch, No. 8, Jan. 2, and No. 9, Jan. 3, 1876, published by Harris, *loc. cit.,* pp. 443-48; Buckle, *Victoria,* II, 443-45; Monypenny and Buckle, II, 887, and 892-95. Both the Russian and Austrian Ambassadors were well aware of the way in which rifts in the *Dreikaiserbund* were being awaited in order that England might emerge from isolation. Shuvalov to Jomini, 30 Oct./11 Nov., *loc. cit.,* and Beust to Andrassy, No. 59A, Nov. 24, 1875 (Austrian Archives, Angleterre VIII/88).

[50] Harris, *loc. cit.,* pp. 445-55; Newton, II, 96-97; and Monypenny and Buckle, 924-26. Cf. Langer, *op. cit.,* 75-81.

as Germany, she might have to oppose either Germany and England, or Germany and Russia united against her. While Lyons inferred that, despite annoyance and no little irritation on the surface, the French would avoid any serious difference and make the best of what they could not help,[51] nevertheless, this communication showed plainly that England could not proceed along the lines Bismarck was suggesting in November and January unless she were prepared to disregard France and run the risk of throwing her into the Russian camp.

Reports from Russia were less frank and unequivocal but not less disturbing. Loftus asserted that the purchase of the Canal Shares had created a great sensation. The *Moscow Gazette* denounced it as likely to cause trouble in the east and viewed it as political and not commercial in character. The *Russki Mir,* on the other hand, spoke of it with satisfaction as evincing the possibility of an understanding between England and Russia on the Eastern Question. More significant, perhaps, than the opinions of these two papers was the fact that the ministerial organs and Gorchakov himself evaded the question, although the Brussels *Nord* which was usually inspired from St. Petersburg did say that the Suez Canal was a matter of interest to all Mediterranean countries, especially France, and ought to be a subject of international arrangement.[52]

Although Disraeli might go out of his way occasionally to

---

[51] Lyons despatch, No. 959, Paris, Nov. 30, 1875 (F. O., 27/2116). Cf. Newton, II, 91 and 93-94; Sir Thomas Barclay, *Thirty Years* (Boston and New York, 1914), p. 37; and *1 Documents Diplomatiques Français,* II, pp. 25-35. *The Pall Mall Gazette* reported that the only portion of the French press which was attacking Decazes because he allowed himself to be outwitted was the radical section, particularly Gambetta's paper; issues of Dec. 1, p. 4; and 11, p. 10. See the interesting statement by Dicey in 1878 that "no outcry was raised against this measure, either by the French Government or the French people." Edward Dicey, "England's Policy at the Congress," *Nineteenth Century,* III (April 1878), 792.

[52] Loftus despatch, No. 370, St. Petersburg, Dec. 8, 1875 (F. O., 65/912); Lord A. Loftus, *Diplomatic Reminiscences, 1862-1879* (London, 1894), II, 144-46; "Public Affairs," *Blackwood's Magazine,* CXIX (Jan. 1876), 124; and *Pall Mall Gazette,* Nov. 29, 1875, p. 1.

issue warnings regarding Russia, as he did in the debate on the Royal Titles Bill in March 1876, he was far from wishing to arouse the susceptibilities of France whose obvious desire to co-operate with Russia in Eastern matters he certainly did not want to encourage.[53] His attitude toward France in the war scare episode of 1875 was indicative of the policy which he consistently followed with regard to her in all matters touching Anglo-French relations in Egypt.[54] Derby was even more determined than Disraeli to co-operate with France in the Eastern Mediterranean. Upon every occasion when rumors of an English occupation of Egypt arose, Derby took special pains to assure France that they had no validity.[55] This was equally true of suggestions or rumors which appeared from time to time whenever the partition of Turkey was in the air that England should take Crete or that she was contemplating it.[56]

It is clear therefore that despite the preparation through the press in England for the partition of Turkey and for the occupation of Egypt, and despite what was regarded as the

[53] 3 Hans. CCXXVIII (1876), 500-01; Thompson, I, 272-74; Monypenny and Buckle, II, 466, 906; Seton-Watson, *loc. cit.*, III, 427 and 670-72.

[54] Newton, II, 73; Monypenny and Buckle, II, 793-94 and 930. Cf. Seton-Watson, *loc. cit.*, III, 667 and 680.

[55] Rumors regarding England and Egypt cropped up frequently in 1876 and usually bore evidences of emanating from either St. Petersburg or Berlin. Loftus despatch, No. 7, St. Petersburg, Jan. 5, 1876 (F. O., 65/935); Elliot despatch, No. 57, Constantinople, Jan. 16, 1876 (F. O., 78/2454); Copy of Stanton despatch, No. 115, Cairo, March 31, 1876 (F. O., 195/1103); Prince Chlodwig of Hohenlohe-Schillingsfürst, *Memoirs* (New York, 1906), II, 176; Newton, II, 104-05; and *1 Documents Diplomatiques Français*, II, 28, 39, and 140.

[56] Crete was discussed as a point which England might take almost as often as was Egypt. Elliot despatches, No. 89, Constantinople, Jan. 24, 1876 (F. O., 78/2454); No. 237, February 28, 1876 (F. O., 78/2456); No. 323, March 30, 1876 (*Ibid.*); Stuart Tel., Athens, April 4, 1876 (F. O., 195/1114); and Macdonell despatch No. 65, Berlin, Sept. 21, 1876 (F. O., 64/854). Most of the above reported rumors that British agents were stirring up the Cretans to accept a British protectorate. The last is a report of conversations with General Todleben and other Russian officers who suggested to Macdonell that England take Crete, and is interesting because it coincides with an attempted Russo-British rapprochement.

initial step in that direction by the government's purchase of the Khedive's shares in the Suez Canal, too many factors were weighted against the adoption of such a policy. These were the traditions of English procedure in the East and the uncertainties of the international situation created by the existence of the League of the Three Emperors whose conflicting and uncertain ambitions might lead to a European crisis dangerous to peace. French susceptibilities in Egypt also played some part so far as that country was concerned and Derby's personality was the medium through which all these factors operated effectively to prevent English action.

Consequently the British government supported the plan of reform for Turkey which was drawn up by Count Andrassy and presented to the powers in his note of December 30, 1875, even though they suspected ulterior motives on the part of Austria and Russia.[57] When these proposals failed to satisfy the insurgents, Andrassy, Gorchakov and Bismarck drew up a further plan at Berlin in May 1876, and again asked the other powers to agree to it. Disraeli, however, who resented what appeared to be dictation from the Three Empires, persuaded his hesitant cabinet to reject the Berlin Memorandum on May 19. He feared that it was designed by its authors to pave the way for an intervention in Turkey which would result in the break-up of that Empire and he had now decided to prevent that eventuality if possible.[58] He and his colleagues

---

[57] Monypenny and Buckle, II, 890-92; and Newton, II, 95-97.

[58] Monypenny and Buckle, II, 896-98; Hardinge, II, 329-30; Langer, *op. cit.,* pp. 81-84 and works there cited. The evidence that the principal reason for rejection of the Memorandum was fear of the *Dreikaiserbund's* aims is convincing. Rumors concerning Austrian and Russian desires as noted above at Note 46 were confirmed by a significant conversation between Bismarck and Russell early in April in which the former hinted very plainly that probably "other measures" than attempts at conciliation between Turkey and the insurgents would have to be adopted sooner or later. Shortly before the meeting of the three Chancellors, Beust placed in Lord Derby's hands a despatch from Andrassy stating that "there is an entire agreement between the Governments of Austria, Germany and Russia as to affairs in the East: . . ." Finally the Memorandum itself stated in the first sentence that the three cabinets had been impelled to "resserrer leur entente." It needed only the further reference in

at the same time decided to send the fleet to Besika Bay, just outside the Dardanelles, because they had been led to fear that Russia intended to take advantage of the turbulent situation accompanying the overthrow of Sultan Abdul Aziz in order to gain control of Constantinople and the Straits.[59]

the Memorandum to the taking of "efficacious measures" in case purely diplomatic action failed to complete the picture of imperial designs on Turkey. While Disraeli himself only alludes to this in his plea for rejection of the Memorandum, his action in connection with the fleet was the indirect outcome of his fears. Russell despatch, No. 145, Secret, Berlin, April 5, 1876 (F. O., 64/851) ; Derby to Buchanan, No. 194, F. O., May 4, 1876 (F. O., 7/865) ; and C. 1531, pp. 138-39. Evidences from competent witnesses of British uneasiness and assertions that the rejection of the Berlin Memorandum was due to belief in the existence of a secret understanding are to be found in Langenau to Andrassy, No. 15C, St. Petersburg, May 12, 1876 (Aus. Arch., Russie X/65) ; Monypenny and Buckle, II, 895; Elliot, *Revelations*, 209-11; Gathorne-Hardy, I, 365; Reid (whose article shows signs of inspiration), *op. cit.*, *Macmillan's*, XL, 182-83. See the shrewd comments of Bismarck on England and the *Dreikaiserbund* which fit this period very well: Hermann Hofmann, *Fürst Bismarck, 1890-98* (Stuttgart, 1914), II, 383.

[59] Monypenny and Buckle, II, 898; Gathorne-Hardy, I, 365; Hardinge, II, 329-30; Lang, II, 101-04; and Buckle, *Victoria*, II, 455-56. These last two references which give fear of Russia as the cause of sending the fleet are corroborated by Beust to Andrassy, No. 57A-D, June 16, 1876 (Aus. Arch., Angleterre VIII/88). Although Elliot had been begging for the fleet to be sent to Besika Bay as a "protection to the Christians here, . . ." and himself telegraphed his wish to the Admiral, he reported on May 18 that there was no longer any danger of agitation against Christians, but a possibility of further political complications. What those were he did not say, although he undoubtedly informed Derby privately. Yet the fleet was sent after his telegram of the 18th. Into this situation a story fits very nicely which came to the writer at second-hand through a most reliable source from a former private secretary of Sultan Abdul Hamid. According to it, Midhat Pasha, who was one of the leaders in the deposition of Abdul Aziz, went to Sir Henry Elliot and asked if the British fleet could be brought up to Constantinople in case of need. The latter wished to refer the matter home but thought it could be arranged. The only possible evidence of this is contained in a cancelled draft telegram of May 25 (F. O., 78/2450), which says that H. M. G. rely on Elliot not to let real or assumed alarms of foreigners or other Embassies lead him to infringe the treaty rights of the Porte regarding fleets in the Dardanelles and that he is to report every proposal for bringing ships to Constantinople whether with or without the consent of the Porte. Disraeli objected to this draft on the grounds that it might embarrass the Ambassador. If one reads Midhat Pasha for "foreigner" and Ignatiev for "other Embassies," the situation at Constantinople is clear. The former was afraid of interference with his revolu-

The rejection of the Berlin Memorandum and the despatch of the British fleet to Besika in addition to the deposition of Abdul Aziz and the beginning of the Bulgaria insurrection made the month of May a turning point in the Eastern crisis. Nowhere was this more evident than in England and in English policy. For the first time since the outbreak of trouble in the previous year, England took a leading role in the attempt to bring about peace and reforms in Turkey. For the first time, the dreaded League of the Three Emperors seemed to be confounded. For the first time, the attention of the government and the press was definitely directed toward safeguarding Constantinople and the Straits from the menace of Russian aggression. Henceforth whenever partition was discussed by English ministers and their advisers, it was Constantinople and not Egypt which was uppermost in their minds. They "missed the opportunity of establishing a direct British protectorate over Egypt by vaguely assuming an indirect British Protectorate over Constantinople," declared a critic four years later.[60] For the time being, however, and until the agitation over the Bulgarian atrocities introduced a new element into the situation, public opinion fell in line behind the government.

Just as the bold note struck by Disraeli in his Guildhall speech of the previous November had captured the imagination of the public, so now opposition to the League of the Three Emperors was commented upon with approval. "There is not one of their schemes," declared the *Edinburgh Review*, "which England is not powerful enough to traverse and defeat,

tionary plans, and the latter was offering aid to the Sultan whom he preferred to see remain because he had great influence over him. Of course, the action of both the English and the Russians can be explained reasonably on the basis of the other known facts, but the story about Midhat fits into them and adds another link to the chain of events leading to the dispatch of the English fleet to Besika Bay. Elliot's telegrams mentioned above are: May 9, 10, 11 and 18, 1876 (F. O., 78/2458). See also Captain Fred Burnaby, *On Horseback Through Asia Minor* (London, 1877), I, 16.

[60] P. W. Clayden, *England under Lord Beaconsfield* (London, 1880), p. 192. Cf. Adolphe d'Avril, *Négociations Relatives au Traité de Berlin* (Paris, 1886), pp. 134-35; Monypenny and Buckle, II, 900-04; Langer, *op. cit.*, pp. 83-86; and Hans Rothfels, *Bismarcks Englische Bündnispolitik* (Stuttgart, 1924), p. 32.

if she thinks the time is come for her to take a more active part in the affairs of Europe. The Andrassy Note, to which England gave a qualified assent; the projected note of the Berlin conference, which has fallen to the ground; the intrigues by which Russia acting on Servia, Montenegro, and the Slavonian provinces of Turkey, has brought them actually to war, have all been more or less foiled by the appearance of the British fleet in Besika Bay; not only because that fleet is a powerful armament, but because it is backed by the public opinion of Europe." [61] Even the *Times* reproached the "Imperial Alliance" for acting "with an assumption of exclusive authority, and a forgetfulness, to say the least, of the dignity of the other Powers," and declared that England would not only be taken into account in Europe, but would insist on equality with any power.[62]

Along with this newly found self-confidence, opinion settled more firmly once more into the traditional grooves and stressed the importance of Constantinople to England. *Blackwood's Magazine* declared: "It is of no importance how far the actual dominions of the Sultan are diminished, so long as in alliance with us he continues to hold Constantinople and to command the Bosphorus." Grant Duff's views are of particular interest because of his former position as Under-Secretary for India in Gladstone's government. In opposing a Russian acquisition of Constantinople as "the abomination of desolation" to Europe, he declared: "*We* might, no doubt, seize Candia and Egypt, and hold them so as to keep our way to India clear; but to do so would be an odious necessity, very troublesome, and very compromising in a hundred ways. . . . The presence of Russia in Constantinople would be an unmitigated evil, a constant source of alarm and expense." Arguing that any disturbance of the *status quo* might be inconvenient to England, he asserted that she had a perfect right to send her fleet to the mouth of the Dardanelles "merely to advertise, as

---

[61] "Two Chancellors," *Edinburgh Rev.*, CXLIV (July 1876), 231.
[62] *Times,* July 24, 1876, p. 9.

it were, that we did not intend that anything decisive should be done in those regions without our having our say in the matter." Another Liberal rather regretfully noted that Great Britain was committing herself to the maintenance of the Turks because they were "the best police of the Bosphorus." [63]

The ink with which these sentiments were penned was scarcely dry before news of the severity with which the Ottoman government had attempted to subdue the Bulgarians aroused England to organize a veritable whirlwind of indignation meetings and petitions. Agitation over the "atrocities" reached its height in September about the time that Gladstone placed himself at the head of the movement for the emancipation of the Christians in Turkey by publishing his pamphlet on "The Bulgarian Horrors and the Eastern Question." [64] Much of the perturbation arose at this time because of the belief that while Parliament was not sitting it was necessary by action "out-of-doors" to prevent the government from giving Turkey armed support and force them, if possible, to adopt a sympathetic policy toward her subject Christian population. Disraeli himself had contributed to this belief by his apparent indifference to the fate of the Bulgarians and his insistence at the end of the session that there should be no interference within the Ottoman Empire. [65] While the moderates, among whom the venerable Stratford de Redcliffe was in-

[63] "The Eastern Question," *Blackwood's,* CXX (July 1876), 93; and M. E. Grant Duff, "The Pulse of Europe," *Contemporary Rev.,* XXVIII (July 1876), 357-59. Cf. Arthur Arnold, "Turkey," *ibid.,* pp. 212-14, who admits that in spite of Turkish repudiation of both political and financial promises, the policy of upholding the Turkish power "appears still to be the most popular"; George Potter, "Working Men and the Eastern Question, I," *ibid.* (Oct. 1876), 856-57; Frederic Harrison, "Cross and Crescent," *Fortnightly Rev.,* XXVI (Dec. 1876), 726; "The Conference at Constantinople," *Blackwood's Magazine,* CXX (Dec. 1876), 774-75; *The Dardanelles for England* (London, 1876), p. 8; and Beust to Andrassy, No. 63A, July 14, 1876 (Aus. Archives, Angleterre VIII/88).

[64] For an excellent recent discussion of the moot points in connection with the Bulgarian atrocities, government policy, and British agitation, see Harold Temperley, "The Bulgarian and Other Atrocities, 1875-8 in the Light of Historical Criticism," *Proceedings of the British Academy,* XVII (London, 1931). Cf. Thompson, I, 307-39 and 382-412.

[65] Thompson, I, 373-77, 382-84, and 413. Cf. Lang, II, 102-103.

cluded, definitely demanded the emancipation of the Christians north of the Balkans from Moslem rule, the extremists gave way to such vehement expressons of anti-Turkish sentiment that they were easily accused of encouraging the aggression of Russia and forgetting the interests of England.[66]

The effect of this agitation upon the policy of the government and consequently upon the European situation was undoubtedly of greater significance than the rejection of the Berlin Memorandum and the sending of the fleet to Besika Bay. Lord Derby recognized at once that the pitch to which indignation against Turkey had risen would make it impossible for the government to interfere in case Russia should declare war on Turkey, and believed that knowledge of this fact in addition to Panslavic feeling in Russia would push her into the conflict.[67] Lord Salisbury, Secretary of State for India, concluded that "the traditional Palmerstonian policy" was at an end. Even the Earl of Beaconsfield—to use the title conferred upon Disraeli in August—admitted that now there was no alternative to the policy Great Britain was following except

[66] Thompson, I, 399 and 401-08. It should be noted that even Gladstone did not advocate partition at this time for fear of the "wholesale scramble" which might result from premature abandonment of the principle of territorial integrity, and also that such phrases as "bag and baggage" and Freeman's "Perish India" were twisted completely out of their original meaning in the heat of controversy; 3 Hans. CCXXXI, 201, and Thompson, I, 361. For comments on the effect of the agitation, see, *Edinburgh Rev.*, CXLIV (Oct. 1876), 566-68 and a typical Layard explosion in George Paston, *At John Murray's* (London, 1932), pp. 240-41.

[67] Draft to Elliot, Tel., F. O., Aug. 29, 1876 (F. O., 78/2451); Gathorne-Hardy, I, 367; *1 Doc. Dip. Franç.* II, 89 and 105; and G. de Wesselitsky, *Dix Mois de Ma Vie* (Paris, 1929), p. 266. At the time the fleet was sent to Besika Bay, Derby had warned Musurus Pasha, Turkish Ambassador at London, that public opinion had changed in England since the Crimean War and the Porte must not count upon England for more than moral support in any case; Draft to Elliot, No. 324, F. O., May 25, 1876 (F. O., 78/2450). He still hoped, however, to avoid a Russian occupation of Constantinople and war by upholding the territorial *status quo*; Wolkenstein to Andrassy, No. 79, Sept. 12, 1876 (Aus. Arch., Angleterre VIII/89); and Monypenny and Buckle, II, 934-36. Cf. also *Idem*, II, 905-06; *Times*, July 15, 1876, p. 9; and Sept. 21, p. 6 (Derby and Disraeli speeches).

the partition of Turkey, and he thought it probable that this alternative would have to be adopted.[68]

Events outside as well as the situation within England had brought Beaconsfield to take this view. Not only had no progress been made in the pacification of the insurrections in Turkey, but toward the end of June, Serbia and Montenegro made war upon their Suzerain. The Russian people enthusiastically espoused their cause and the government admittedly did little to restrain the ambitious Balkan princes.[69] At the same time there were evidences that the *Dreikaiserbund* was not so moribund as Disraeli had supposed although his efforts to come to an agreement with Russia met with a good reception.[70] Most disturbing of all the conflicting rumors and reports were those which persistently, week after week, told of Austrian and Russian designs upon Ottoman territory.[71]

[68] Cecil, II, 84-86; Monypenny and Buckle, II, 924 and 940; cf. also, *Idem*, 937, 941-43, 951-52; Gathorne-Hardy, I, 370-71; Zetland, II, 69; Lang, II, 104-05; *Quarterly Rev.*, CLXVIII, 38; and Beust to Andrassy, No. 77B, Sept. 4, 1876 (Aus. Arch., Angleterre, VIII/89).

[69] See Langer, *op. cit.*, 88-92. Loftus reported in June that while Russia would not draw the sword herself, she would withdraw the restraint she had hitherto exercised on Serbia and Montenegro; despatch, No. 281, St. Petersburg, June 21, 1876 (F. O., 65/938. Extract omitting this in C. 1531 (1876), No. 494).

[70] The Reichstadt meeting of the Austrian and Russian Emperors was reported as very satisfactory; Russian newspapers, Gorchakov, Austrian papers, and the *Chargé d'Affaires* in Berlin attested the solidarity of the *Dreikaiserbund*: Loftus, Tel., St. Petersburg, July 11; despatches No. 322, July 17; and No. 329, July 19, 1876 (F. O., 65/938); Buchanan despatch, No. 505, Vienna, July 26, 1876 (F. O., 7/872); and Macdonell, Tel., Berlin, August 28, 1876 (F. O., 64/854). The British government was trying out Germany and Russia for possible understandings at different times in the summer and autumn. See Langer, *op. cit.*, pp. 100-02; Buckle, *Victoria*, II, 477-78; Monypenny and Buckle, II, 942-43; Seton-Watson, *loc. cit.*, III, 669-77; *1 Doc. Dip. Franç.* II, 71-73; and Boker to the Secretary of State, No. 84, St. Petersburg, Sept. 28, 1876 (U. S. Dept. of State, Russia, Vol. 30). This last despatch acclaims an understanding between Russia and England, and reads as if Boker had received his information from Loftus.

[71] These reports differ from those early in 1876 in being more numerous and more explicit as to facts and dates. Throughout July and August a newspaper discussion about the annexation of Bosnia was carried on in Austria. Loftus, Tel., July 1; despatches No. 343, Aug. 2, and No. 386, Aug. 29, 1876 (F. O.,

The climax was reached in late September and early October when Russia openly proposed that in case the Sultan did not accept reforms Austria should occupy Bosnia, Russia enter Bulgaria, and all the powers join in a naval demonstration at Constantinople. This was shortly followed by the news that the Russian army was being prepared for an immediate attack on Turkey, and renewed advices from Germany that everyone should take a share of the Ottoman Empire and be happy.[72] No wonder that Beaconsfield and his cabinet believed nothing could now prevent the final solution of the Eastern Question even though Russia withdrew her disturbing proposal and failed to march across the Pruth.[73]

While Derby participated in negotiations which brought

65/938 and 939); Draft to Buchanan, No. 347, Aug. 5, 1876 (F. O., 7/866), asking to observe any signs of an increasing disposition on the part of Austria to adopt a policy of annexation; Buchanan, despatches No. 475, July 15; Nos. 480 and 484, July 17; No. 486, July 18; Nos. 510 and 513, July 27; No. 519, July 29 (F. O., 7/872); No. 529, Aug. 1; Nos. 530 and 537, Aug. 8; and No. 663, Vienna, Sept. 28, 1876 (F. O., 7/873). Some of the above despatches contained denials of annexationist ambitions, but the English did not trust Andrassy. See Eduard Wertheimer, *Graf Julius Andrassy* (Stuttgart, 1913), II, 315-18 and 335. On the other hand, Andrassy asserted that the only alternative to reform was the complete solution of the Eastern Question and suggested that public opinion in England would no longer oppose a Russian armed intervention in Turkey; Buchanan, despatches No. 578, Aug. 30 and No. 589, Sept. 2, 1876 (F. O., 7/873). Cf. *Blackwood's Magazine*, CXX (Nov. 1876), 648; and *Contemporary Rev.*, XXIX (Dec. 1876), 166-68.

[72] S. M. Goriainov, *Le Bosphore et les Dardanelles* (Paris, 1910), 322-24; Buchanan despatches Nos. 664 and 667, Sept. 29 and 30, 1876 (F. O., 7/873); Gathorne-Hardy, I, 372-73; and Monypenny and Buckle, II, 950-51. News reached London regarding the Russian army on October 5th or 6th; Loftus despatch No. 464, Oct. 5; Tel., Oct. 10; and No. 478, Oct. 11, 1876 (F. O., 65/941). On Germany: Buchanan Tel., Vienna, Oct. 6, 1876 (F. O., 7/874); Russell, despatches No. 432, Berlin, Oct. 7 and No. 472, Berlin, Oct. 23, 1876 (F. O., 64/855).

[73] The Russian proposal was strongly opposed by Austria and England, although Derby declared that an Austrian occupation of Bosnia was a matter of indifference to Great Britain. He felt compelled to advise against it, however, because of the encouragement it would give for similar steps in Bulgaria. Beust almost immediately suggested that England and Austria should come to an understanding. Beust to Andrassy, Tels., No. 96 and 98, London, Oct. 9; and Report No. 91A-B, Oct. 10, 1876 (Aus. Arch., Angleterre VIII/89).

about the arrangement of an armistice between Turkey and her rebellious subjects and prepared the way for the Conference of Constantinople to meet in December, Beaconsfield turned his attention to the problem of how best to uphold the independence and integrity of Turkey and safeguard British interests. His real preoccupation was with the fate of Constantinople which he now regarded as "the key of India." He repudiated the idea of taking Egypt which Bismarck was again suggesting in October and November and professed to be more interested in Asia Minor. "What he wants," recorded Hardy, "is a Malta or Gibraltar which could prevent the Black Sea being a constant threat to our maritime power in the Mediterranean." The most pressing immediate problem, however, was to provide for the defense of Constantinople against the inevitable Russian attack and he put the War Office to work on a series of studies and plans which led eventually to the occupation of Cyprus as the *place d'armes* from which to protect the route to India.[74]

Captain Ardagh, a British officer who was observing the war with Serbia from the Turkish side, was hurried back to Constantinople early in October to survey and prepare a project for the defense of that city. Before the end of the month the War Office decided to send out Colonel Robert Home of the Intelligence Department with a group of officers to take over and complete as secretly as possible the work begun by Ardagh. Home's group were "to examine a defensive position extending across the Thracian peninsula to the west of Constantinople from the Black Sea to the Sea of Marmora, to design the works requisite for its defence, and to report on the force necessary for their occupation, on the best land-

---

[74] For the negotiations, see Langer, *op. cit.*, pp. 99-105; and Dawson, *loc. cit.*, III, 107-10. For Beaconsfield's proposals, see Monypenny and Buckle, II, 924, 947, 955-56, 970-78; Gathorne-Hardy, I, 372-74, 376-77. Cf. Cecil, II, 113; Hardinge, II, 346-48; and Tyler, *op. cit.*, p. 77. Even Lord Derby thought England might have to occupy Constantinople; Buckle, *Victoria*, II, 503. Cf. *The Dardanelles for England*, p. 8, and *Pall Mall Budget*, Oct. 14, 1876, p. 15. Public opinion at this time swung between hatred of Turkish misgovernment and fear of Russian aggression. See Fitzmaurice, II, 166.

ing place for that force, on the means for hutting, etc.; in fact
on all matters required to be known by the authorities in England in the event of a British force being sent to hold that
position, and as no British force would be secure in that position unless the command of the Dardanelles was assured they
were also to report on the means to be adopted for securing
the Peninsula which encloses the Straits on their western side."
As time passed, this original aim was greatly modified and extended by Lord Salisbury and Sir Henry Elliot at the Conference of Constantinople.[75]

Lord Salisbury, who was chosen as first British Plenipotentiary to the Conference, had become convinced that England
should adopt a policy of co-operation with Russia in order to
bring about reforms in Turkey. His conversations with Bismarck, Andrassy and the foreign ministers of France and
Italy whom he visited in November on his way to the East
confirmed him in this view and in his opinion of the hopeless-
ness of upholding longer the integrity of the Ottoman Empire.[76]

Upon his arrival at the Conference early in December, he

---

[75] Lady Ardagh, *Life of Major-General Sir John Ardagh* (London, 1909),
p. 42; *Strictly Confidential. Reports and Memoranda Relative to Defence of
Constantinople and Other Positions in Turkey, also on Routes in Roumelia*
(0631). Printed at the War Office, 1877 (F. O., 358/1). Home's instructions are
dated October 29, 1876, and signed by J. L. A. Simmons, Inspector-General of
Fortifications, under whom Home was put for this work. The quotation is
taken from Simmons Memorandum, Feb. 10, 1877 (*ibid.*). Home was accompanied by Captain Fraser, Lieutenants Cockburn and Chermside and was
reinforced in the field by Captain Ardagh, and in December by Captains
Grover and Anstey and Lieutenant Hare. Russia was not unaware of Beaconsfield's plans and Home believed that Ignatiev set spies to watch him. *Grosse
Politik*, II, 83; and Home to Simmons, Private, Dec. 28, 1876 (F. O., 358/1).

[76] Cecil, II, 94-107; Monypenny and Buckle, II, 974-80; H. S. Edwards,
Sir William White (London, 1902), p. 117; *Die Grosse Politik*, II, 123-25.
Salisbury's visits to the principal capitals of Europe were interpreted by some
as a search for allies. If it is understood that the word "allies" means friendly
powers who would support England's policy, there is ground for the correctness
of this view. The American Minister at Vienna declared: "Personally I am led to
believe from what I see, that the question will narrow itself down to this:
Can England find allies. If she can and the tone of the various cabinets is such
as to encourage Lord Salisbury, she will probably stand out on the Article of
the guarantee which Turkey is to give, and we shall have war." Beale to

at once came to an agreement with Ignatiev, much to the disgust of Sir Henry Elliot, British Ambassador and second plenipotentiary, and of Beaconsfield who complained that Salisbury seemed to forget his main object at the Conference which was to keep the Russians out of Turkey. Once the two first plenipotentiaries of England and Russia were in accord, it was an easy matter to formulate a set of conditions providing justice and security for the Christians of Turkey. But the Porte now became obdurate and wrecked the work of the Conference by resolutely refusing to accept the measures which the representatives of Europe had drawn up.[77] Despite this failure, which he had more than half expected, Lord Salisbury concluded that the Conference had done good because it had made it impossible for England to spend any more blood in sustaining the Turkish Empire and he hoped that it would "make English statesmen buckle to the task of devising some other means of securing the road to India."[78]

This task he had already inaugurated with the aid of Colonel Home who kept in close touch with him as well as with Sir Henry Elliot throughout the meetings of the Conference. Home was a man of varied experience who had, among other things, served with the Royal Engineers in the Crimean War and in Canada, helped to develop the Intelligence branch of the War Office and commanded the Engineers in the Ashantee Expedition under Wolseley. Endowed with good sense, imagination, and an honorable and upright character, he came to be one of Beaconsfield's and Salisbury's closest and most trusted advisers in the later phases of the Eastern crisis. He was just the man to appeal to them both, for, as one who knew him wrote: "He belonged to a class—a well-known one among

---

Secretary of State, No. 17, Vienna, December 1, 1876 (U. S. Archives, *Austria,* Vol. 24). Home speaks of Salisbury "going round Europe looking for allies." Private to Simmons, Jan. 16, 1877 (F. O., 358/1. See appendix).

[77] Cecil, II, 107-23; Monypenny and Buckle, II, 979-86. For the whole story of the Conference which came to an end on January 20, 1877, see Langer, *op. cit.,* 105-109; Dawson, *loc. cit.,* III, 110-15.

[78] Cecil, II, 122.

English officers who have done individual work among half-civilized races, the class of which Gordon was the supreme type—who combine great practical ability in administration and fighting with a strongly imaginative idealism. . . . Such men are very often strongly convinced imperialists, England having in their eyes a special mission to bring light to the dark corners of the earth." He could turn from a discussion of the most practical political and strategical detail to a map and point out what he believed would prove to be the battleground of Armageddon, or after a day in the mud and slush of Constantinople's environs write to the first secretary of the Embassy a historical sketch of that city's defences since the days of Belisarius "because the history of these places adds so much to their interest." His private letters to General Sir J. L. A. Simmons are invaluable not only for a study of the Conference of Constantinople but also for further evidence of some of the ideas upon which the settlement of 1878 was finally based.[79]

After more than a month spent in or near Constantinople, Home was not only convinced that Russia intended to make war on Turkey, but that the attack was imminent. He believed that this would be followed by another massacre of Christians, by atrocity meetings at home, and the carrying out of Gladstone's "bag and baggage" policy. Austria would throw in her lot with Russia and seize Bosnia and Herzegovina. Under the circumstances the country which had an army ready would profit and that country would be Russia. Home did not agree with those—among them, Sir William White— who wanted to occupy Constantinople and hold it against the Turks and the Russians, "annex it in short," for that would require 60,000 men, cost twenty-five or thirty millions, and place England in much the same position as France had oc-

[79] Quotations from a private collection and Home to Jocelyn, Dec. 19, 1876 (F. O., 195/1116). See *Dictionary of National Biography*, XXVII, 238-39; Cecil, II, 214-15; and Frederick Greenwood, "Characteristics of Lord Beaconsfield," *loc. cit.*, pp. 593-95 (erroneous in details regarding Home's work for Beaconsfield).

cupied in Rome. Her prestige would suffer when the city was abandoned. He therefore suggested another plan: "to seize Crete, Egypt or Rhodes, or all these." For various reasons he preferred Rhodes and thought that England should get 10,000 men ready to take it at once. In any case, he concluded, it would be impossible to occupy Constantinople except as the friend or ally of Turkey.[80] But on December 26, Home wrote to Simmons that the Sultan's military forces were such that "you must be very careful not to get England embroiled in a war with Turkey alone for an ally; God help us if this be the case." England should not waste her power backing a falling Empire. "I think the time has come to cut it up, and let us have our share of it."[81]

Home's views were apparently not unheeded at Constantinople, for in January, when the immediate danger of a Russian attack was proved exaggerated, but when intrigues were rife, British prestige lowered, and the Conference seemed doomed by Turkish obstinacy, Lord Salisbury and Sir Henry Elliot both "expressed themselves very strongly that it was absolutely requisite (looking to future complications that might possibly arise) that the country should be completely examined, more especially those portions which may in the future be of importance to British interests." In accordance with these views Salisbury issued new instructions for the

[80] Home to Simmons, Private (Constantinople), Dec. 20, 1876 (F. O., 358/1. See appendix). Salisbury on the same day asked the cabinet to decide at once what course to pursue if the Turks refused the terms given them, because Russia was ready to declare war on January 6. Salisbury to Derby, Tel., Dec. 20 (F. O., 78/2675). In a private letter of Dec. 13 (F. O., 358/1), Home wrote as if England were definitely planning to occupy Gallipoli, and thought that if they calculated that it would take Russia sixty-four days to march from the Pruth to Constantinople they would be safe and would have "time to turn ourselves round, sweep the hearth, and boil our kettle before we are molested." Cf. also Home to Jocelyn, No. 8, Constantinople, Dec. 17 (F. O., 195/1117), and to Simmons, Dec. 28, 1876 (F. O., 358/1).

[81] Home to Simmons, Private, Constantinople, 26/12/6 (F. O., 358/1). Simmons agreed with this view and had already stated it in a memorandum which may also be responsible for Beaconsfield's allusions in November to Asia Minor; Memoranda, October 30, 1876 (F. O., 358/2); and Jan. 9, 1877, *Reports and Memoranda* (0631), pp. 3-5, and 100.

military mission, which were contrasted by Home with those drawn up in England as follows: "They were drawn up with the view of obtaining such information as might be useful if Her Majesty's Government were to determine to deny the city [Constantinople] to a Russian army. The instructions received at present point rather to the obtaining of such information as may enable Her Majesty's Government to seek for and select suitable compensation should extensive territorial changes take place in the East." Also, thought Home, the information might enable England to help maintain the *status quo,* if that were possible. Home proposed to examine and report on Bourgas, the Balkan passes, Varna, Pravadi and Shumla, the line of the Danube, Roumania, Rhodes, Cyprus, "certain points connected with Egypt," the defensive line between the Gulf of Ismid and the Black Sea, Trebizond, and the defenses of Kars and of Erzeroum.[82] Thus he and his officers without entirely abandoning the idea of defending Turkey against Russia were to explore the ground for English acquisitions in the Near East.

Home's program caused uneasiness in England whence successive orders were sent out cancelling his plans. Simmons thought that since the examination of Rhodes, Cyprus and Egypt looked rather toward compensation for England than toward the original object of the mission, officers could be sent as well from England as Constantinople to examine those places, if that seemed desirable. A telegram was sent on February 3, countermanding this part of the plan, but did not arrive before Captain Ardagh had embarked for Alexandria. News of the work of the officers had begun to get about and a question was asked in Parliament concerning their activities. This, coupled with knowledge of the growing suspicions of the Turks who were beginning to mistrust that England was joining with Austria and Russia in a partition of Turkey, prompted

---

[82] Home Report, No. 17, Constantinople, January 15, 1877, and copy of Salisbury Memorandum, Jan. 15 (F. O., 358/2). Cf. Home to Simmons, private letters, Jan. 15 and 16, 1877 (F. O., 358/1); and Salisbury to Derby, Secret Desp. No. 130, Constantinople, Jan. 16, 1877 (F. O., 78/2676).

a call, sent out on February 7, for all officers to return home immediately. One of the group, Captain Fraser, had already gone to Batoum but Home ordered the others to return by different routes, one by way of Odessa, others through the Balkan passes, Home himself planning to visit Varna, Shumla and Ruschuk. All were to keep their eyes open and, as he explained it: "Of course all will be urged to reach home as soon as possible, but the trains in the country are very difficult indeed to manage." It is obvious that despite orders he hoped to accomplish many of his aims.[83]

Aside from the drawing up of plans and estimates for the fortification of the Buyuk-Chekmedje-Derkos lines to guard Constantinople and the lines of Bulair across the neck of the Gallipoli Peninsula, Home memorialized the War Department and wrote privately to Simmons concerning both the military and the political policy which he believed England should follow in case of a Russo-Turkish war and the consequent fall of the Ottoman Empire. He took for his point of departure the view expressed in Lord Salisbury's dictum that England would not fight for the Turks but for Turkey, or, as Salisbury explained, she would not fight for the Bosphorus but for the Dardanelles and the Persian Gulf. Home himself made a slightly different approach to the problem: England might maintain Turkey at the expense of enormous blood and treasure, but what good would that do? She had better leave Turkey to her fate and seize upon some place that would be of use to her "such as the Dardanelles and Cyprus."[84]

As far as the Dardanelles were concerned, he believed that England could control this passage by fortifying the Asiatic as well as the Gallipoli side at a cost of £2,632,000 and a peace

[83] Simmons Memorandum, Jan. 22; Simmons, draft telegram, Jan. 23; Home to Simmons, Private, Constantinople, Jan. 22; copy of Jocelyn Tel., forwarding Home to Secretary of State for War, Feb. 1; Simmons Memorandum, and draft Tel., Feb. 3; Simmons to Home, Tel., Feb. 7; Home to Simmons, Private, Constantinople, Feb. 8, 1877 (F. O., 358/1); 3 Hans. CCXXII, 161 and 259.

[84] Home to Simmons, Private, Jan. 16, Jan. 22, and Feb. 8, 1877 (F. O., 358/1). See appendix for the first and last of the letters.

time garrison of 4,000 men to be increased to 20,000 in war time. By taking additional land on the Asiatic and European sides of the Strait, half the taxes exacted by the Turks would pay the annual cost of a military establishment. He expatiated upon the "moral and political advantage" to be gained by such an occupation: "The sight of a mixed population of varied creed and race well governed and in a happy flourishing condition and the contrast that would be afforded between those under British rule and those outside the pale would be very great." The disadvantage of taking Gallipoli as a material guarantee or compensation was that it would be a continental possession close to the frontier of what might be a great military power, namely, Russia, at Constantinople.[85]

In order to justify his recommendation regarding Gallipoli, Home declared: "There is perhaps no portion of the Turkish Empire, the future of which is so important to Great Britain as the Dardanelles. If these Straits be held by England, or a power friendly to England, the Bosphorus is of comparatively small importance." There was only one case in which the possession of the Bosphorus would give Russia an advantage even if the Dardanelles were denied to her and that was the seizure in addition to Constantinople of Turkish Armenia. "Holding Armenia and the Kurdish mountains Russia could threaten the head of the Persian Gulf *via* the valleys of the Euphrates and Tigris." He was convinced that Russia intended to fight her coming war with Turkey chiefly in Asia, but was relieved to find that the Turks were doing their best to fortify Batoum, one of the necessary stages on the Russian march toward Erzeroum and Armenia. In support of his contention regarding the theater of the coming war, he quoted at length from a pamphlet of Baron Kuhn von Kuhnenfeld, late Austrian war minister, which became one of the principal sources of inspiration for those who preached during the succeeding months of Russian designs upon Mesopotamia and the Persian Gulf. Home did not at this time, however, de-

[85] Home Memorandum [Jan. 12, 1877] (F. O., 358/2. See appendix).

velop a line of defense against this menace, perhaps because he hoped the Turks would be able to hold Batoum.[86]

Simmons agreed with him in regard to the importance of Turkish Armenia to England and Russia's intention there, but he could not agree with him about the desirability of attempting to seize the Dardanelles. In the first place, he believed that Home's estimate of both the cost and the number of men which would be required was far too low. Furthermore, since there were no good harbors on the Gallipoli Peninsula, it would be necessary to seize some other place on which a naval base could be built, and this he presumed was the reason for wishing to examine Rhodes and Cyprus. He agreed that the military advantage which Russia would gain by possession of the Bosphorus would be nullified if England controlled the Dardanelles but concluded that Home's plan should be contemplated only after the most serious consideration.[87]

Home's final impressions and suggestions regarding the political aspects of Turkey's future and of England's policy, whether or not they met with the approval of Simmons, were in accord with the growing convictions of most Englishmen in close touch with the Near East. Home declared that he was leaving the country "strongly imbued with the opinion that no reforms, no constitution will make a nation or a country here."

[86] Home, "Memorandum on the Dardanelles," Feb. 3, and Report No. 23, Feb. 10, 1877, *Reports and Memoranda* (0631), pp. 130-31 and 174-75.

[87] Simmons Memorandum, Feb. 2, 1877 (F. O., 358/2). His insistence that England must have a secure naval base was founded upon a generally accepted principle among army experts and was essentially the reason for seeking the *place d'armes* upon which Beaconsfield later insisted. In 1870 Simmons wrote that if the powers bordering the Mediterranean were all friendly, it was probable that Great Britain would have no difficulty in obtaining supplies for a force sent to assist Turkey, but "if there were much war risk attending sea transport outside the Dardanelles, this would become questionable." So long as Russia remained inside the Bosphorus, the war risk in 1877 was likely to come only from France whose Mediterranean fleet was regarded by the British attaché at Paris as stronger in some respects than England's and whose policy was none too certain. Simmons Memorandum to Cardwell, Dec. 14, 1870 (F. O., 358/2); and Lyons, despatches No. 542, Paris, June 26, and No. 639, Paris, July 31, 1877 (F. O., 27/2240).

From his point of view, conditions in Turkey were so rotten and the recuperative power in the nation so reduced that nothing short of a protectorate exercised by an outside power would make Turkey "go straight." England could undertake it if she were given ten years and allowed by the other powers to do so. She should face the issue squarely, whether or not Turkey was worth maintaining, and make her decision regardless of such sentimental considerations as the word "ancient allies" and religious questions, which had hitherto prevented her from adopting a policy of any kind. He summarized his views by saying:

> "Can England put things right? Undoubtedly she can. But she will not.
> "Can Russia put things right? Undoubtedly she cannot. But she is quite ready to try. Such is the state of affairs.
> "It is all very well to blame our envoys but no envoy can make matters straight, when the Trumpet gives an uncertain sound.
> "Blame not Sir Henry Elliot, nor Lord Salisbury. But blame the people of England who boast that they rule themselves, that the Prime Minister is but their servant. How can he go straight if they don't know their own mind?" [88]

These letters and memoranda confirm the impression that at the time of the Constantinople Conference, Salisbury wanted to adopt a policy of accepting the partition of the Ottoman Empire. His remarks and the plans and suggestions worked upon and reflected by Home contain the germ of what became the Cyprus policy, including as they did not only the effort to establish a base of operations in the Eastern Mediterranean both as a means of guarding British interests and as compensation for the gains of others, but also the idea of a protectorate over Turkey in order to make her reform. Omitted from the discussion at this time was the economic angle of the later policy in Asia Minor whose political and military importance to England, however, was beginning to be prominently noted.

Although Home's private letters to Simmons probably were never perused by Beaconsfield, many of his opinions were being reflected in the press, and were no doubt discussed by

[88] Home to Simmons, Private, Constantinople, Feb. 8, 1877 (F. O., 358/1).

Salisbury on his return.[89] Whether influenced by them or merely by the situation during and following the Conference, the Prime Minister began watering down the traditional concepts of the independence and integrity of the Ottoman Empire in such a way as to make it appear admissible for the Sultan to lose some provinces and permit supervision of internal reforms. At the same time, while Beaconsfield admitted that if war began it would end in partition and thus compel England to seize something in order to secure her imperial unity,[90] his efforts were still directed toward the prevention of war. This appeared to him and his colleagues an imperative and perhaps attainable goal, because Russia seemed to be anxious for a "golden bridge" across which she could retreat from her previous bellicose attitude toward Turkey and it looked to the English as if Bismarck were preparing to attack France if Russia were entangled in the East.[91]

Instead, therefore, of attempting to formulate a definite Near Eastern policy such as Salisbury and Home desired, the British cabinet devoted their energies to the discovery of means by which peace could be maintained between Russia and Turkey and on the larger issue of what was eventually to be done about the obvious decay of Ottoman power they seemed to adopt Derby's motto, to "wait, say little, and pledge our-

[89] See "The Conference at Constantinople," *Blackwood's Magazine*, CXX (Dec. 1876), 774; H. M. Havelock, "Constantinople and Our Road to India," *Fortnightly Rev.*, XXVII (Jan. 1877), 120-23 and 129-30 (Advocates keeping Straits closed to Russia or taking one side of the Dardanelles or Crete); [A. H. Layard], "The Eastern Question and the Conference," *Quarterly Rev.*, CXLIII (Jan. 1877), 300-02 (Mentions Besika Bay, Cyprus, Crete, and Egypt as places from which England might intercept a Russian dash on Suez from Constantinople); and "Crete," *Blackwood's Magazine*, CXXI (April 1877), 431 and 454.

[90] Monypenny and Buckle, II, 989, 992-94, 998; and 3 Hans. CCXXXII, 711-12.

[91] Monypenny and Buckle, II, 984; Hardinge, II, 350-51; Loftus, II, 203; Cecil, II, 127-29; Newton, II, 107-108; Goriainov, *op. cit.*, pp. 339-40; and Charles Gavard, *Un Diplomate à Londres, 1871-1877* (Paris, 1895), p. 314. For an exposition of the war scare of 1877 and the negotiations for keeping peace between Russia and Turkey, see Langer, *op. cit.*, pp. 109-17, and references there cited.

selves to nothing." [92] The result of their endeavors was the
London Protocol of March 31, 1877, recapitulating the list of
reforms which the concert of Europe again asked Turkey to
accept and put into effect. When this was refused by the
Porte, Russia on April 24 entered upon the long discussed war
with Turkey. The question of the attitude and course of action
Great Britain was to take could no longer be put off with im-
punity, but both public opinion and the cabinet were still so
divided that for another ten months the government could do
little more than wait upon events. After all the groping and
stumbling of more than a year, only one thing was plain,
that England wanted peace and no repetition of the Crimean
War.[93] There was still the possibility, however, that she could
be aroused to safeguard her imperial interests in some other
way and Beaconsfield with the aid of enthusiastic assistants
energetically began educating his colleagues and the public
to an appreciation of those interests and how to protect them.

[92] Newton, II, 107; and 3 Hans. CCXXXII, 3-4, 37-42, 54-55, and 105-11.
Salisbury made an attempt during the spring to get the cabinet to substitute for
England's traditional policy a bold initiative in partition, but without success.
See Cecil, II, 130 and 134-35.

[93] This feeling became very apparent after the Russo-Turkish war broke
out, but had been clear since the time of the Bulgarian atrocities agitation. See
Cecil, II, 131; "Turkey and Russia," *Edinburgh Rev.*, XCLV (Jan. 1877),
279-84 (Quotes Duke of Wellington's policy in 1826-28 with approval as
applicable to existing conditions) ; and Reid, *loc. cit.*, p. 187.

CHAPTER II

CONSTRUCTING A POLICY, APRIL 1877 TO JUNE 1878

EVEN before the outbreak of the Russo-Turkish war, Beaconsfield took a step of great significance for British policy in the East by sending Austen Henry Layard to the Sublime Porte in the place of Sir Henry Elliot who had returned home when the Conference of Constantinople broke up.[1] It was Layard, more than any other single individual at home or in the foreign service, who brought to the attention of the government and the British public the subject of Asia Minor and its relation to British interests and especially its connection with the route to India. His name, moreover, became inseparably linked with the revival of the traditional policy toward the Ottoman Empire and with the attempt at its reform which was undertaken after the Congress of Berlin.

His interest in the Near East dated from his early travels through the Balkans and Asia Minor in 1839 when he wandered almost a vagabond among then little known peoples and scenes. He was subsequently employed by Lord Stratford de Redcliffe in both diplomatic and archeological work and in the latter field made himself famous as the discoverer of Nineveh. Becoming a member of Parliament as a follower of Palmerston, he was made Under-Secretary of State for Foreign Affairs in 1852 and again in Palmerston's last ad-

---

[1] Layard's temporary appointment was announced on March 30, 1877, the day before the signature of the London Protocol, although his instructions were dated April 13. The Constantinople embassy had been left in charge of Mr. Jocelyn after the simultaneous withdrawal on January 22 of all ambassadors as a protest against Turkey's refusal of the terms drawn up at the Conference of Constantinople. Layard's definite appointment as Ambassador was made at the end of 1877 when Sir Henry Elliot was sent to Vienna. See *Times*, March 30, 1877 (leading article); Draft to Layard, No. 1, F. O., April 13 (F. O., 78/2559); Cecil, II, 125; and Sir Henry Elliot, *op. cit.*, pp. 293-94.

ministration. Later he served for a short time under Gladstone as head of the public works department and finally went as ambassador to Madrid in 1868 whence he was summoned in March 1877 to take the post at Constantinople.[2]

Layard regarded himself as still a Liberal in 1877 although he vehemently repudiated Gladstone and his agitation of 1876, claiming that he and his followers had departed from the tried and true principles of Palmerston in regard to the Turkish Empire and British interests. "It did so happen," Layard explained, "that my opinions on the 'Eastern Question' were, in many respects, in accordance with those of Lord Beaconsfield, or rather, I would say in accordance with those of the greatest statesmen who have hitherto directed the Foreign Affairs of this country, and whose policy . . . he was resolved not to abandon." Briefly he believed that England should support Turkey, aid her by diplomatic pressure to reform in the interests of both Christians and Mussulmans alike and thus continue to guard the route to India by maintaining the Sultan's rule over Constantinople, the Straits, and Armenia. Despite his own denials of the fact, his judgment was much influenced by his passionate prejudices in favor of the Turks whom he almost invariably regarded as gentlemen of the best intentions and against the Russians whose diplomats, he once remarked, were "trained to habits of deception and dissimulation." But quite apart from the merits of Turks and Russians, and above everything else, he believed that England should adopt a clear, precise and energetic policy and stick to it with firmness and determination.[3]

[2] See A. H. Layard, *Nineveh and its Remains* (London, 1849); *Discoveries among the Ruins of Nineveh and Babylon* (London, 1875) and *Autobiography and Letters from his Childhood until his Appointment as H. M. Ambassador at Madrid* (London, 1903), 2 vols. His unpublished memoirs of his ambassadorships at Madrid and Constantinople are deposited with his other papers at the British Museum (Add. MSS. 38,930-38,938). Cf. Monypenny and Buckle, II, 757-59 and 1007; and W. S. Blunt, *Secret History of the English Occupation of Egypt* (London, 1907), p. 89.

[3] Layard, *Memoirs*, IV (Add. MS. 38,934), fos. 24-26, 96-109; and private letter to Sir William Gregory, Nov. 30, 1876 (Add. MS. 38,949, fos. 162-63).

Not only because he was "a fighting diplomatist and possessed the rare quality of knowing what he wanted," but also because of his experience in handling Orientals, Layard was well-fitted to take the position at Constantinople. Moreover, if his German colleague is to be credited, he was a man with the additional quality for which Lord Beaconsfield was looking at this time, "not one too scrupulous."[4] Layard was probably right in believing that his choice was due entirely to Lord Beaconsfield, for Derby was hesitant about sending him even though his friends, including Lord Hammond and Lord Cowley, former Ambassador at Paris, had been pressing his suitability for the Ambassadorship upon the Foreign Office.[5] Considering his reputation and well-known views on Eastern affairs, it is not surprising that his appointment just

His views before his appointment were ably set forth in "The Eastern Question and the Conference," *Quarterly Review,* CXLIII (Jan. 1877), 276-320. Cf. also the Duke of Argyll, *The Eastern Question* (London, 1879), II, 24-25; and Buckle, *Victoria,* II, 527.

[4] Quotations from Newton, II, 138; and Zetland, II, 114-15. Reuss, whom Bismarck sent to Constantinople shortly after Layard's appointment, is reported as saying: "Er ist noch unzuverlässiger und lügenhafter wie Ignatiev. Die Türken können ihn nicht leiden, und er schimpt auf sie, dass sie jetzt nicht mehr tun wollen, was er ihnen rät. . . ." J. M. von Radowitz, *Aufzeichnungen und Erinnerungen.* Edited by Hajo Holborn (Stuttgart, 1925), I, 367. Beaconsfield himself at one time distrusted Layard (Monypenny and Buckle, II, 757), and certainly Layard was not an easy man to get along with. Lady Palmerston is said to have remarked that they were thankful to Layard for bringing Nineveh to light, but not Nineveh for bringing Layard to light; L. Raschdau, "Aus dem Literärischen Nachlass des Unterstaatssekretärs Dr. Busch," *Deutsche Rundschau,* CXLI (1909), 363.

[5] *Grosse Politik,* II, 144; Monypenny and Buckle, II, 921; Layard, *Memoirs, loc. cit.;* Morier to Layard, Private, Munich, May 23, 1876 (Add. MS. 39,010, fo. 69); Hammond to Layard, Private, Dec. 16, 1876, Jan. 12 and 25, March 12 and 19, 1877 (Add. MS. 38,955, fos. 75, 85, 95, 101, and 109); and Cowley to Layard, Private, Jan. 28 and Feb. 26, 1877 (Add. MS. 39,011, fos. 76 and 178). Layard claimed that he had not sought the appointment and, in fact, he had written to a friend in March that he thought his "supposed 'Turkish proclivities'" stood in his way and that "Gladstone and Co. would be frantic if I were sent to Constantinople." He added that he would be well content to be sent to some small post in Europe where he could be quiet and his wife could have good health and some amusement. Layard, *Memoirs, loc. cit.,* and letter to Clark, Madrid, March 12, 1877 (Add. MS. 38,946, fos. 154-55).

on the eve of the Russo-Turkish War caused uneasiness among those who thought the government had definitely abandoned a pro-Turkish policy, and was welcomed by all Turkophils and by those who were fearful lest British interests were being jeopardized by the absence of an able representative at the Turkish capital. The *Times* condoned his appointment on the latter ground, while the Porte telegraphed that the Sultan "was very sensible of this delicate mark of attention on the part of the English government." [6]

Layard was given no definite instructions regarding his mission to Constantinople other than to prevent the war if possible and make plain to the Sultan his loss of sympathy and friendship in England because of misgovernment and atrocities. He inferred, however, from what he was told by Beaconsfield—"with whose broad and statesmanlike views" he was greatly impressed—that while England could not give any material assistance to Turkey because of Gladstone's agitation, yet the Prime Minister was not prepared to witness the downfall of the Turkish Empire and the occupation of Constantinople by Russia. If the Turks were able to defend themselves and gave proofs of their ancient courage and devotion, there was a fair prospect of a change in English opinion toward them. This might enable the government to follow a more decided policy and to interfere in such a way as to prevent Russia from an advance on the Bosphorus. "But he impressed upon me," writes Layard, "the great importance of giving no

---

[6] Thompson, II, 179; P. W. Clayden, *England under Lord Beaconsfield* (London, 1880), p. 327; Stephen Gwynn and G. M. Tuckwell, *Life of the Right Honorable Sir Charles W. Dilke* (New York, 1917), I, 208; *Grosse Politik*, II, p. 144; Seton-Watson, *loc. cit.*, V, 417; and *Times*, March 31, 1877, leading article. Cf. *Edinburgh Rev.*, CXLV (Oct. 1877), 562, which spoke of Layard as a "man of very advanced and decided Liberal opinions." Lady Stratford de Redcliffe wrote Layard that she and her husband hoped Layard would arrive in time to persuade or force the Turks to do what was best for their own interests, and Granville reported Ellenborough's remark to Layard that "you knew better how to deal with Orientals than any one he knew," but for himself warned: "Do not get us into another Crimean War." Lady Stratford de Redcliffe letter, April 10, and Granville letter, April 19, 1877 (Add. MS. 39,012, fos. 34 and 84).

encouragement to the Sultan or his Ministers to hope for material aid from his Government at any time or under any circumstances."[7]

After his arrival at Constantinople on April 20, Layard kept in close touch by private letter with Beaconsfield, Derby and Lord Tenterden, Permanent Under-Secretary of State for Foreign Affairs, but to judge from his correspondence both official and unofficial he was given very little positive guidance and was left, as Lord Hammond expressed it, "unfettered" to do what he thought was best.[8]   After his failure to avert war, he concerned himself with the two principal objects which were also uppermost in Beaconsfield's mind: to restore English influence at the Porte to the position held at the time of Lord Stratford de Redcliffe and to prevent Russia from breaking up the Ottoman Empire.   His method of achieving the first of these was to gain a personal ascendancy over Sultan Abdul Hamid II whose "charm of manner and bearing," humor, quick understanding, kindness, simplicity and good intentions, Layard never tired of attesting.   The friendly and even intimate relationship which Layard believed he had established with the Sultan by the end of the summer of 1877, he hoped would also help to achieve the second of his aims.[9]

This was a much more difficult task not only because of the suspicions entertained toward England by the Turks but also because of the equivocal policy which the English government was compelled to adopt in view of the divisions of opinion in

[7] Layard, *Mem.*, IV, fos. 87-88. Cf. *Idem, op. cit., Quarterly Rev.*, CLXVIII, 39.

[8] Hammond to Layard, Private, Aug. 20, 1877 (Add. MS. 38,955, fo. 161). Layard describes his interviews in London and his trip to Constantinople in *Mem.*, IV, fos. 87-97.

[9] Layard, believing he had the support of the Duc Decazes whom he interviewed at Paris on his way to Constantinople, persuaded the Porte to appeal to the powers on the basis of Art. VIII of the Treaty of Paris, but it was not done till the 24th and came too late. Layard, *Mem.*, IV, fos. 93-95; and despatches to Derby, April 25, 1877 (*Parl. Papers*, "Turkey No. 25 (1877)," Nos. 206 and 207). Layard describes the Sultan and his relations with him at various places in his *Memoirs*, notably at IV, fos. 103-104; and V (Add. MS. 38,935), fos. 166-67. Cf. Monypenny and Buckle, II, 1051.

the country and the cabinet.   Although Layard felt it necessary to make the Turks "understand that tho' we cannot help them, we are not disposed to deal with them unjustly and to give aid to their enemies" and in so doing overstepped the bounds of strict neutrality and gave them false hopes of English aid,[10] nevertheless he never minced words with the Porte about the necessity for punishing the perpetrators of atrocities, instituting reforms and arranging a satisfactory settlement with its creditors.   At the same time he did all in his power by means of private letter and official despatch to support Beaconsfield at home in his plea for an energetic British opposition to Russia's southward advance in both Europe and Asia Minor.

While the outbreak of the Russo-Turkish war had emboldened the small group of Turkophils in England to take an attitude of unveiled hostility toward Russia, few people really wanted to go to war.   On the other hand, only a few among the opposition in Parliament followed Gladstone in his expressed pro-Russian and anti-Turkish sentiments and nearly everyone recognized that Great Britain had serious interests at stake in the Near East which ought to be safeguarded.[11]

[10] For Turkish suspicions and quotation, Layard to Derby, Private, June 6, 1877 (Add. MS. 39,030, fo. 28). Some of the Turks became very bitter because of the false hopes of British aid which they believed Layard had given out. See the interview with Server Pasha in *Daily News*, Feb. 7, p. 5, and March 14, 1878, p. 5; and G. Hanotaux, *Histoire de la France Contemporaine, 1871-1901* (Paris, 1908), IV, 296. Layard cannot be held responsible, however, for all encouragement given the Turks, for when he arrived at the Porte he found that Butler-Johnstone, who had caused trouble during the Conference of Constantinople, was still there using his influence as an M. P. and his money lavishly in the Turkish cause. Layard claims that he never saw him and that his counsels were sometimes listened to in preference to the Ambassador's. Layard, *Mem.*, IV, fo. 145. Cf. Cecil, II, 111; Seton-Watson, *loc. cit.*, IV, 454; and Wertheimer, II, 380.

[11] Thompson, II, 183-208; Raschdau, *op. cit.*, *Deutsche Rundschau*, CXLI, 212; Seton-Watson, *loc. cit.*, V, 415-16; Gwynn and Tuckwell, II, 220-23; Monypenny and Buckle, II, 1049; *Times*, April 19 and 20, May 2, 3, 4, 5, 11, 12, 15 and 17, 1877, leading articles. Cf. for radical party opinion: Leonard Courtney, "Our Eastern Policy," *Fortnightly Rev.*, XXVII (May 1877), 603-26; for moderate party opinion: Lord Stratford de Redcliffe, "Turkey, II," *Nineteenth*

The question upon which most disagreement arose was how to do it. Beaconsfield at once proposed to declare to Russia what interests Great Britain would be ready to defend and at the same time to seize some place in the East, the Dardanelles or some other point near the danger line, and hold it as a "material guarantee" of Russia's good behavior. He further believed that there was no time to waste because General Simmons, obviously basing his calculations upon the conclusions of Colonel Home, informed the government that Turkey would be too weak to resist Russia and that the Russian armies would probably reach Gallipoli in twelve or thirteen weeks and Constantinople in two weeks more from the time they crossed the Danube.[12]

Although the cabinet did not want to permit British interests to be endangered, they did want to avoid committing themselves to a policy which might lead to war. Since the members of the "peace party" consisting at this time of Derby, Salisbury and Carnarvon, suspected that Beaconsfield wished to engage England in the Eastern conflict, they sought to check what they regarded as his ambitious designs.[13] In this they were aided by several troublesome factors inherent in his proposals. The problem of taking a material guarantee such as the Gallipoli peninsula was not a simple one. According to

Century, I (June 1877), 750; Julius Vogel, "Greater or Lesser Britain," *ibid.*, I (July 1877), 810; and "Turkey," *Quarterly Rev.*, CXLIII (April 1877), 599-600. As late as August, 1877, Mr. Pierrepont, American Minister at London, declared: "The signing of the Protocol ended all talk about Treaties, the speeches of Lord Salisbury after his return from Constantinople destroyed all respect for the Turkish Government; and the reports of trusted correspondents of the newspaper press, aided by Mr. Schuyler and largely confirmed by Mr. Baring, have so awakened the conscience, the humanity, and the sense of outraged justice in the British nation that war to support Turkey is just as impossible as war to restore slavery." While this is a slightly exaggerated statement, it sums up the "peace party" point of view accurately. Pierrepont, No. 219, London, August 15, 1877 (U. S. Archives, *Great Britain*, vol. 133).

[12] Buckle, *Victoria*, II, 529-30; Cecil, II, 139-40; Gathorne-Hardy, II, 18-19; Monypenny and Buckle, II, 1005-6; and Simmons, Confidential Memorandum, April 19, 1877 (F. O., 78/2664 and 358/2).

[13] Monypenny and Buckle, II, 1010; Hardinge, II, 352-54; Cecil, II, 135-37; and Seton-Watson, *loc. cit.*, V, 416-17.

Simmons it had to be done in one of three ways: either with Turkey's consent, which virtually meant an alliance with her; or in opposition to Turkey and in agreement with Russia; or in opposition to Turkey but without the agreement of Russia. Few in the cabinet or the country would agree to an alliance with Turkey and Lord Salisbury was categorically opposed to it. The second alternative was out of the question for Beaconsfield and the Queen who was now thoroughly aroused to what she regarded as the menace of Russian aggression. The third would be a hazardous venture. It looked to Lord Derby too much like seizing territory. Simmons warned that it might lead to riots in Constantinople and compel England to interfere there, or, on the other hand, it might encourage a Russian attack which would compel England to undertake very extensive and costly fortifications. Finally, England must know definitely whether the Mediterranean powers were certain not to interfere, since the *Alabama* had shown what a single cruiser could do to interrupt communications by sea; and in any case England should secure the alliance of another nation such as Austria before she undertook measures of opposition to Russia.[14]

Nevertheless, Secretary of War Hardy and the Lord Chancellor, Cairns, came out so strongly in favor of taking Gallipoli that the peace party was startled and aroused to vigorous protest against it. The result of the cabinet conflict was the adoption of a compromise policy. They agreed to declare their views of the Russian manifesto which preceded the declaration of war and to define their interests leaving the question of when and how to guard them by active measures open for the future to decide.[15] A despatch of May 1 therefore pointed

[14] Simmons, Memoranda of April 19, May 2 and May 11 (F. O., 358/2); Monypenny and Buckle, II, 1004; Cecil, II, 139-40; and Buckle, *Victoria*, II, 530-31. France was an uncertain factor in the Mediterranean at this time and Italian aims were under suspicion. See Newton, II, 112-13 and Sir Frederick Ponsonby, *Letters of the Empress Frederick* (London, 1929), pp. 150-51.

[15] Buckle, *Victoria*, II, 532-36; Hardinge, II, 354; and Gathorne-Hardy, II, 21.

out that England could not accept Russia's declaration that by coercing Turkey to give good government to the Christians the Tsar was acting in accordance with the sentiments and interests of Europe. Russia had separated herself from the concert of Europe, the English despatch explained, and was contravening the stipulations of the Treaty of 1856. In a note of May 6 to the Russian government, they defined the British interests which Russia was called upon to respect. These were the Suez Canal, Egypt, Constantinople, the Straits, and the Persian Gulf.[16]

Taken together these two documents showed that Great Britain would not acquiesce in a Russian settlement of the Eastern Question and defined the conditions upon which her neutrality was to rest. They satisfied the "peace party" but not Lord Beaconsfield nor Mr. Layard who were stimulated by the events of the next two months to attempt more active measures. Before the end of May, the Russians captured Ardahan in Armenia although their progress on the European side was so slow that they did not cross the Danube until June 27. What was much more alarming in June was the diplomatic situation.

First of all, Russia refused to promise that she would not occupy Constantinople if military necessity required it. This information was accompanied and followed by dire predictions on the part of British agents regarding Russia's intention of gaining control over Constantinople and the passage of the Straits.[17] The determination to partition Turkey

---

[16] See *Parl. Papers*, "Turkey No. 18 (1877)," No. 2 for the despatch of May 1; and *ibid.*, "Russia No. 2 (1877)," No. 1 for that of May 6. The rough draft of the latter (F. O., 65/986) was almost entirely rewritten in Derby's own hand and is rather exceptional in that respect. Cf. Seton-Watson, *loc. cit.*, V, 421-22.

[17] *Parliamentary Papers*, "Russia No. 2 (1877)," No. 2, and "Turkey No. 15 (1878)," No. 1; Loftus, Tel., St. Petersburg, May 21; Desp. No. 267, May 23; No. 307, June 11 (F. O., 65/966); Desp. Nos. 329 and 330, June 20 (F. O., 65/967); Buchanan, Tel., Vienna, May 27; and May 29 (F. O., 7/901); Layard, Tel. No. 161, Therapia, June 11 (F. O., 78/2598); Paget, Desp. No. 265, Siena, June 30 (F. O., 45/313). Cf. Monypenny and Buckle, II, 1012; and *Edinburgh Rev.*, CXLVI (July 1877), 260.

seemed only too well proved by the suggested terms of peace communicated by Count Shuvalov to Lord Derby on June 8 when Russia proposed autonomy for Bulgaria, extensions of territory for Serbia and Montenegro, compensation for herself in Bessarabia and Batoum, and additional territory for Austria, if she wanted it, in Bosnia and Herzegovina. Bismarck again urged England to take Egypt and so generally were proposals for a division of the spoils being discussed in the press and diplomatic circles that even the French Foreign Minister, probably to test British aims, tentatively suggested a joint Anglo-French occupation of Egypt and Syria with Crete and Cyprus as advanced posts.[18] Finally Derby's failure to obtain Austria's co-operation in opposing a Russian march on Constantinople emphasized the strength of the Three Emperors' League and England's isolation, already patent not only to the government but to the public as well. As Derby himself wrote to Layard, Germany was "wholly Russian," no help was to be expected from France nor Italy, and the influence of Russia over Austria was "undoubtedly very great."[19]

[18] *Parl. Papers*, "Turkey No. 15 (1878)," No. 1; Seton-Watson, *loc. cit.*, V, 426-27; Russell, Desp. No. 211, Berlin, May 19 and No. 221, May 27 (F. O. 64/878); Lyons, Tel. and Desp. Nos. 474 and 476, Paris, June 7 (F. O., 27/2239). As at every previous occasion when partition plans were being discussed, an English occupation of Egypt was very much in the air not only in diplomatic circles but in the press as well. See *Grosse Politik*, II, 149-50, and 152-58; Thompson, II, 212-13; Edward Dicey, "The Route to India," *Nineteenth Century*, I (June 1877), 665-85; *idem*, "The Future of Egypt," *ibid.*, II (Aug. 1877), 3-14; W. E. Gladstone, "Aggression on Egypt and Freedom in the East," *ibid.*, pp. 149-66; "The Khedive's Egypt and Our Route to India," *Blackwood's Magazine*, CXXII (Oct. 1877), 477-90; Englishman, *England in Egypt* (London, 1877), 14 pp. This pamphlet may have been written by "one Bright" to whom Beaconsfield refers in a letter to Layard of November, 1877 (Monypenny and Buckle, II, 1123-24). A "Frenchman" told the American Minister in Berlin that Salisbury and Carnarvon were disposed to listen to overtures regarding Egypt, but that Derby showed no favor toward them and Beaconsfield opposed them, Davis, Desp. No. 726, Berlin, July 25, 1877 (U. S. Archives, *Germany*, Vol. 22). Cf. Buckle, *Victoria*, II, 546 and 549; and Cecil, II, 145-46.

[19] Derby to Layard, Private, June 14, 1877 (Add. MS. 39,013, fos. 100-101); Monypenny and Buckle, II, 1015-16; Buckle, *Victoria*, II, 539-42; *Grosse Politik*, II, 158; *Revelations from the Seat of War* (London, 1877), pp. 90-91; *Pall Mall Gazette*, Sept. 28, p. 1, and Oct. 25, 1877, p. 1.

Even before the cumulative effect of these various factors was fully appreciated, Beaconsfield's uneasiness led him to inaugurate a secret correspondence with Layard on June 6. The latter had asked on April 24 if he should persuade the Sultan to invite the British fleet to Constantinople in accordance with the treaty of 1871, but had been informed that such a move would be inexpedient under existing circumstances.[20] A month later, Lord Augustus Loftus, Ambassador at St. Petersburg, urged that England should occupy Constantinople and the Dardanelles in order to aid in the satisfactory conclusion of peace. Both Bismarck and Andrassy professed to see no harm in such a step.[21]   Beaconsfield now took up both ideas and asked Layard if there was any possibility that the Porte might ask England for the presence of the fleet at Constantinople and a military occupation of Gallipoli for the duration of the war. His idea was to remain neutral and take such action on the excuse of requiring a material guarantee for the observance of existing treaties. It is obvious that he had not accepted the defeat of his first proposal at the hands of the cabinet and was supporting the views of Home rather than those of Simmons regarding the feasibility of such a plan.[22]

[20] Monypenny and Buckle, II, 1013; Layard, Tel., Constantinople, April 24 (F. O., 78/2597) and Draft to Layard, Tel., F. O., April 25, 1877 (F. O., 78/2559).

[21] Loftus, Desp. No. 267, May 23 (*loc. cit.*); Russell, Desp. No. 221, Berlin, May 27 (*loc. cit.*); and Dwight E. Lee, "Unprinted Documents. The Anglo-Austrian Understanding of 1877. II." *Slavonic Rev.*, X (Dec. 1931), 451-53. Reuss, German Ambassador at the Porte, believed that Russia would take no offense at an English occupation of Gallipoli if it were done "firmly but courteously," and Admiral Hornby, in command of the Mediterranean squadron, also advocated it. See Mrs. Fred Egerton, *Admiral of the Fleet Sir Geoffrey Phipps Hornby* (London, 1896), pp. 213 and 216-18.

[22] Monypenny and Buckle, II, 1014-15. Cf. Harold Temperley, "Disraeli and Cyprus," *English Historical Rev.*, XLVI (April 1931), 274-75. Layard had warned Tenterden that England should look to the protection of the Gallipoli Peninsula since the Turks had no reserves at Adrianople and they had just begun to fortify the lines of Buyuk Chekmedje; Layard, Private, Therapia, May 23,

By the time Layard received this letter Russia's suggested peace terms, which he had himself believed should be sought as a test of Russia's real intentions, had been communicated to him and seemed to reveal the worst of his anticipations. He therefore telegraphed to Beaconsfield on June 18 that the fleet should be sent to the Bosphorus and Gallipoli should be occupied, although the latter was much more important to England because it could be taken by Russia at a "dash" while Constantinople could not. He thought that he could get the Sultan to agree to both proposals but did not dare even hint at the subject until he knew that the government had decided upon it.[23] In a private letter to the Prime Minister on June 20 and a formal despatch of the 19th, Layard developed his views at great length.

In the former, he declared that the only way to insure the *status quo* and the English control of the situation which Beaconsfield desired was to tell Russia distinctly and decidedly what Great Britain would allow her to do and that she was prepared to take measures at once to prevent her doing more. Then, urged Layard, the government should make up its mind to what it would do. While he thought that Beaconsfield was the best judge of how far public opinion in England would let the government go, and that the attitude of the Great Powers must be kept in mind, he suggested: 1. assisting the Turks "with money and officers and by troops"; 2. making use of Hungarian and Polish feeling to prevent Austrian interference on behalf of Russia; [24] 3. raising the Mo-

---

1877 (Received June 2, F. O., 363/2). Occasional references were made in the press to the desirability of occupying Gallipoli. See Lord Campbell, *The Policy of Great Britain* (London, 1877), pp. 9-10; *Edinburgh Rev.*, CXLVI (July 1877), 277-78; and *Blackwood's*, CXXII (Aug. 1877), 250-51.

[23] Layard, *Memoirs*, V, fos. 31-33.

[24] Layard explained in his *Memoirs*, V, fos. 79-80, that the Turks were trying to arouse Hungarian sympathies and had sent a mission of Softas to Pesth to present a book of Matthias Corvinus which had been found in the imperial library in Constantinople. Butler-Johnstone was understood to have paid the expense of this mission. General Klapka was also sent to Vienna and Pesth in July 1877 to stimulate feeling for the Porte.

hammedan states of Central Asia either occupied or threatened by Russia, and 4. informing Greece that she might not move against Turkey nor raise an insurrection. It was as the first step toward such a policy, which obviously implied close co-operation with Turkey if not open war against Russia, that Layard recommended the occupation of Gallipoli and the sending of the fleet to the Bosphorus.

In both communications he described the terms of peace proposed by Russia as inevitably leading to the dismemberment of Turkey in Europe, Asia, and Africa. He explained that the creation of Bulgaria as envisaged by Russia would lead to the extension of Greek territory and an increase in the pretensions of Serbia, Montenegro and Roumania. This weakening of the Sultan's power in Europe would in turn lead to the separation from Turkey of Egypt, Tunis, Tripoli, and Syria; and—worst of all—"the Pashalic of Baghdad, with the Vallies of the Euphrates and Tigris, would virtually belong to Russia, the mistress of Asia Minor." Furthermore, the dismemberment of Turkey in Europe would soon bring about the fall of Constantinople and the right of free navigation for the Russian fleet through the Straits which would give Russia the control of Suez unless England were prepared to annex Egypt and to keep at all times a very powerful fleet between the coast of Egypt and the entrance to the Dardanelles. Thus it was easy for Russia to agree to the points of British interest enumerated in the note of May 6 because Russian aims and intentions regarding all of them might be accomplished by indirect means.

If England were prepared to renounce her imperial position, Layard continued, let Russia have her way and perhaps make even greater demands at a later date. For he declared that it was vital to British imperial well-being to save Turkey from dissolution and that this policy was dictated not at all by Turkey's but by England's interest in maintaining the Ottoman Empire as a barrier to Russia and the Sultan as a valuable ally because of his leadership over the Moslem world.[25]

By the time these views had reached Beaconsfield and the government, it had become apparent that such a policy as Layard and the Prime Minister were advocating could not be adopted so long as Great Britain remained neutral, and the cabinet refused to take a step which might lead them into the conflict. Furthermore Simmons clearly pointed out that while an occupation of the Gallipoli Peninsula alone might enable England to keep open the navigation of the Dardanelles and give her a very favorable strategical position in case of war, it would not prevent Russia from taking Constantinople and should only be undertaken when England had secured her communications by sea and was assured of ample time and means to accomplish it.[26] Still the progress of Russian arms in July nearly brought the government to take all the measures which Beaconsfield was advocating.

At the end of June, the fleet instead of being sent to Constantinople was again ordered to Besika Bay which it had left in the previous December on the eve of the Conference of Constantinople. At the same time, secretly and unofficially, Layard persuaded the Porte to put the construction of Constantinople's lines of defense into the hands of English contractors.[27] When the news of General Gourko's cavalry dash through the Shipka Pass of the Balkans on July 14 reached London, the cabinet, which had steadily rejected the proposal of a vote of credit, agreed to a mild ultimatum to Russia. They declared that they regarded the occupation of Constan-

---

[25] Layard, *Memoirs*, V, fos. 34-40; Layard to Beaconsfield, Private, June 20, 1877 (Add. MS. 39,130, fos. 37-40. See appendix); and Layard Desp. No. 631, Therapia, June 19, 1877 (F. O., 78/2574 and printed in extract in C. 1952, "Turkey, No. 15 (1878)," No. 10). For another expression of Layard's opinion regarding the peace terms, cf. Desp. No. 612, June 13 (C. 1952, No. 8).

[26] Monypenny and Buckle, II, 1021; Simmons, Memorandum on "Advantages to be gained by Great Britain by occupation of Peninsula of Gallipoli," July 5, 1877 (F. O., 358/2).

[27] Thompson, II, 217-19; Layard to Tenterden, Private, May 23 (*loc. cit.*); and Hornby to Edwards, July 24, 1877 (F. O., 358/3). Cf. A. d'Avril, *Négociations Relatives au Traité de Berlin* (Paris, 1886), pp. 237-38.

tinople by Russian troops, "even though temporary in duration and dictated by military necessities, as most inexpedient,"
and, if it should appear likely to take place, they would hold
themselves "free to adopt any measure which in their judgment may be required for the protection of British interests." [28]

On July 21, since reports continued to arrive of Russia's
determination to march on the Turkish capital and since Russia still refused to give any pledge that she would not do so,
the cabinet decided to declare war if Russia took the city and
did not arrange to retire immediately. They also voted to
increase the garrison at Malta. Telegrams of July 27 from
Layard reporting that the Russians would soon be at Adrianople whence a few short marches would bring them to Gallipoli
and that the Sultan was preparing to flee to Broussa threw the
cabinet into such a panic that they at last decided to ask the
Sultan to invite the fleet to Constantinople, and laid plans for
removing or disabling the heavy guns on the European side of
the Dardanelles so that, if they fell into the hands of the
Russians, they could not be used against the fleet.[29]

By this time, however, the repulse of the Russians at Plevna
had turned the tide of war and prevented any further advances south of the Balkans. Fortunately there was no longer
any need for the hazardous and belated measures which
Beaconsfield had persuaded his colleagues to adopt. The
stubborn resistance of the Turks under Osman Pasha brought
to an end this dress-rehearsal of the 1878 crisis and allowed a
four months' respite to the British government from the night-

---

[28] Monypenny and Buckle, II, 1022-23; Cecil, II, 144; and Seton-Watson,
loc. cit., V, 431-32.

[29] Monypenny and Buckle, II, 1026-30; Gathorne-Hardy, II, 25-26; Buckle,
Victoria, II, 550-51, 554-55; Layard, Tel. No. 304, July 27 (F. O., 78/2598); Tel.
to Layard, July 28 (F. O., 78/2561); and Simmons, "Memorandum relative to
holding the position of Chanak on the Asiatic side of the Dardanelles," July 28
(F. O., 358/2). Captain Fraser was sent to the Dardanelles with several pounds
of gun cotton with which to blow up the forts if necessary to prevent them
from being of use to the Russians. His instructions and private letters describing the difficulties of traveling incognito with highly dangerous explosives from
England to Constantinople are to be found in F. O., 358/3. Cf. Hardinge, II,
362.

mare of Cossacks in Stamboul and Russian warships in the Straits.[30]

Nevertheless neither Beaconsfield nor Layard gave up their efforts to bring the cabinet and the foreign office to accept their views regarding the necessity for maintaining Turkey and adopting an energetic and active policy to this end. Moreover public opinion was slowly swinging to their side, and progress was being made toward the acquisition of a *place d'armes* in the Eastern Mediterranean and the realization of England's special interest in Asia Minor and Armenia.

Ever since the autumn of 1876, the need for some post nearer the scene of action than Malta had been brought forward for one of two reasons, either as a coaling and refitting station in case England should undertake military measures at Gallipoli or Constantinople or as compensation which would serve as a means of guarding the route to India if the Ottoman Empire were threatened with dismemberment. It was with something of both these contingencies in mind that General Simmons, on April 28, 1877, drew up a memorandum of instructions for Lieutenant-Colonel J. B. Edwards and Commander Egerton of the Navy in the search for a port "in which ships might coal and refit and even perform slight repairs in safety without the necessity of going back to Malta. . . ." The conditions which such a port should satisfy were that it be capable of defence by a small force in the absence of ships and that it be located on an inlet so that the establishment and ships within would be safe from the fire of enemy cruisers. It appeared to Simmons from an examination of the charts that neither Rhodes nor Cyprus, which had been considered by Home, contained such ports. He also rejected Crete on the grounds that while it contained suitable harbors, its size and the number of its inhabitants would compel the building of powerful works and the maintenance of a considerable land force in order to protect them. He suggested that Tristoma

---

[30] See Monypenny and Buckle, II, 1032-33; and Langer, *op. cit.*, 127-29.

on Karpathos, Syrmi and any other harbors proposed by the navy might be examined.[31]

On the basis of a joint report by Edwards and Egerton, Simmons on June 26 concluded that the port best adapted to the purposes in mind was Vathy on the Island of Stampalia (Astropalia). Its only defect was a bar at the mouth of the harbor, but it was an easily defensible site. The Admiralty, however, did not agree with Simmons and in a memorandum of August 2 stated their preference for Maltezana on the same island.[32] So far as the War Office and the Admiralty were concerned the matter was allowed to rest at this point until the following March when circumstances again compelled their attention to it.

Beaconsfield himself dropped the active interest in this question which he had retained so long as Russia seemed to threaten Constantinople and the Straits. When he returned to it at the end of November, Turkey's inevitable defeat and her weakened financial condition had become plain. Beaconsfield therefore discussed the subject of some territorial acquisition with Layard as a possible means of helping the Porte out of its financial difficulty and aiding it to withstand a second campaign with Russia. Anything in the Mediterranean, he explained in a letter of November 27, might excite general jealousy unless it were a coaling station which would not involve a sufficiently large sum. A port in the Black Sea such as Batoum if England were allowed the freedom of the Straits, or in the Persian Gulf, should Russia acquire Armenia, had occurred to him. He asked Layard to consider the matter and advise him, pointing out that if England could also send the fleet to the Bosphorus and occupy both Gallipoli and Derkos

---

[31] Simmons, Memorandum of April 28 (F. O., 358/1).

[32] *Idem,* Memorandum of June 26 (*loc. cit.*); and Confidential Print (0662) "Papers relative to a proposed coaling station for Her Majesty's fleet at the eastern end of the Mediterranean" (F. O., 358/3). Cf. Egerton, *op. cit.,* pp. 206-07; and Harold Temperley, "Further Evidence on Disraeli and Cyprus," *English Historical Review,* XLVI (July 1931), 457.

without a declaration of war, the Ottoman Empire might yet survive as an independent and vigorous power.[33]

In his reply of December 12, Layard reported that Server Pasha, the Turkish Foreign Minister, had declared that the Sultan could not cede territory for money because once a cession was made there was no telling what acquisition other powers might require. Although Server Pasha had attempted to find some means of guaranteeing a loan such as the administration of Crete or some other Ottoman territory by English delegates, Layard believed that he would not listen to any proposal for an outright cession of territory.[34] In regard to the best place for England to take in the East, Layard offered some very definite views. In the Black Sea, Batoum was the only port not in Russian hands which would be of any use to England. It commanded Armenia and therefore the Tigris and Euphrates valleys, but could only belong to a power commanding the Black Sea. The Persian Gulf might be a great object to England if Russia should occupy Armenia permanently and the position there which always appeared to him to be of the greatest importance was Mohammerah at the junction of the Karoon and Euphrates rivers. Layard went on to explain that when people scoffed at the importance to England of the Euphrates and Tigris as a means of direct communication with India they ignored the fact that a railway probably would in the course of time be carried through these regions eastward across Persia to Beluchistan and Scinde. Mohammerah would give England the command of these rivers, but it belonged to Persia. As to other points he doubted if the Porte were prepared to cede Crete, Cyprus or any other island in the Mediterranean to Great Britain. Egypt was a question of imperial policy on which he did not feel compe-

---

[33] Monypenny and Buckle, II, 1123-24.

[34] Layard, *Memoirs*, V, fos. 268-72 and copy in Add. MS. 39,030, fos. 195-99. Layard had written privately to Beaconsfield on Nov. 28, pleading for a decisive policy and pointing out that if he knew exactly what England were prepared to do, he would exercise much stronger language at the Porte and believed he would be listened to (Add. MS. 39,030, fos. 176-78).

tent to give an opinion and he doubted very much if Turkey would consent to part with it. On the other matters of British help to Turkey, mentioned by Beaconsfield, he agreed and added that now that Plevna had fallen he believed the road to Constantinople was open.[35]

Aside from the subject of a possible British acquisition in the Levant, this correspondence brings out strikingly the prominence which Armenia and Mesopotamia had assumed in the Eastern Question. To be sure, both Beaconsfield and Home had discussed it a year before and at the outbreak of the Russo-Turkish war Simmons had warned of the effect which a Russian occupation of Armenia would have upon Asiatic Turkey. "It would be felt that the Russian forces on the high plateau of Armenia, at the sources of the Euphrates, Tigris, and Kizil Irmat," he explained, "would have the command of the whole of Asia Minor with no obstacles to encounter in their onward march to the Mediterranean and Bosphorus but such as are presented by the difficulties of the country, its unsettled state, and the limited resources available for the support of their troops in the long and widespread marches they would have to make. . . . Being also at the head waters of the Euphrates and Tigris, their position would seriously menace the Persian Gulf.[36]

It was probably with such opinions as this in mind that the cabinet included the latter point in their note of May 6 to Russia.[37] But Layard was not satisfied that either the government or the country sufficiently appreciated the Russian menace in that region. In a lengthy despatch of May 30 which he later described as the "key to much which I did at Constantinople, and, to a great extent, to the policy which I advocated," he commented upon the immense advantages to

---

[35] Letter of Dec. 12, 1877 (*loc. cit.* See appendix).

[36] Simmons, Memorandum, April 17, 1877 (F. O., 358/2).

[37] Shuvalov reported on April 20 that Russian progress in the Caucasus preoccupied the English much more than the question of what might be done in Europe "en deçà des Balkans." See Seton-Watson, *loc. cit.*, V, 417; and Buckle, *Victoria*, II, 572.

Russia and the moral effect upon England's Mohammedan subjects in India of a Russian conquest of Armenia, and pointed out that whereas other powers were interested in the European side of the Russo-Turkish conflict, England was alone affected in Asia and hence had to act there without hope of aid. A few days later he wrote to Lord Cowley, urging him to use his authority and experience to enlighten public opinion upon the annexation of Armenia by Russia which would be the greatest blow ever struck at the British Empire.[38]

Whether or not Layard was directly or indirectly responsible for it, a greater and greater amount of attention began to be paid to the subject of Armenia and Asia Minor although Constantinople and the Straits were the points which mainly agitated the country.[39] But the two were not unconnected in the minds of those who, like Simmons, envisaged an overland attack upon the Bosphorus as well as upon the Persian Gulf or Syria in the other direction. Relying upon the writings of Kuhn von Kuhnenfeld, Moltke, and Baron Félix de Beaujour, the imagination of amateur strategists carried them to astonishing lengths until not even Cape Town, let alone India, was free from the aggression of Russia as she was pictured advancing in spite of mountain chains, deserts and rivers from conquest to conquest.[40] Nor was the military menace of Russia the only one considered. Layard's despatch of May 30,

---

[38] Layard, Desp. No. 546, Therapia, May 30, 1877, published with a few omissions in C. 1830 (Turkey No. 26, 1877), No. 60; *Memoirs*, IV, fo. 150; and private letter to Cowley, June 13, 1877 (Add. MS. 39,130, fo. 35). Layard's attention had been called to the situation in Asia Minor by a private letter from Major-General Sir Arnold Kemball, who was observing the war on the Caucasian front, and wrote that the "game is up in this quarter." Layard, Desp. No. 507, Therapia, May 24 (F. O., 78/2572).

[39] Lord Campbell declared that the point which "mainly agitates the country" is how far Constantinople is threatened; *Policy of Great Britain* (London, 1878), p. 5. Thompson in his book on public opinion only touches upon Armenia and Asia Minor occasionally. See *op. cit.*, II, 169, 214, 475 note, and 493. It was a clamorous but small group who talked much about it.

[40] Cecil, II, 151-56; M. E. Grant Duff, *Notes from a Diary, 1873-81* (London, 1898), I, 258; *Times*, June 12, 1877, p. 5; Stratford de Redcliffe, "Turkey, II," *Nineteenth Century*, I (July 1877), 751-52; É. de Laveleye, "British Interests in the Present Crisis," *Fortnightly Rev.*, XXVIII (July 1877), 31; "The

after its publication in the Blue Books, was often quoted to prove the political effect of Russian conquests upon the Moslem and Indian world, and other writers emphasized the blow to England's trade which would be dealt by the extension of Russia's protective tariffs over the route through Armenia to Persia and over the free trade area of Asia Minor.[41]

Naturally excitement reached its height after the fall of Kars in November which, as the *Daily News* remarked, "brought our English alarmists again to the front, if not with much force, certainly with great clamour." The *Daily Telegraph* characteristically declaimed: "Russia has now virtually conquered Armenia; Persia falls under her domination; the way to the East, West, and South are open; India will thrill with a suppressed excitement which no famine subscriptions will calm; the Czar is on the road to the Dardanelles, and the England of Nelson and of Pitt sits quietly watching the drama in a state of sentimental indecision." Another writer, in a rhetorical pamphlet which does credit to his literary ability if not to his cool judgment, called upon Lord Beaconsfield to prevent the ruin of England and upon the people to pay no attention to Gladstone.[42]

Russians in Asia Minor," *Edinburgh Rev.,* CXLVI (July 1877), 256-80; *Edin. Rev.,* CXLV (Jan. 1877), 45-46; Burnaby, II, 167-68; 321-22 and 333; *Revelations from the Seat of War* (London, 1877), pp. 10 and 92-93; and F. K. Wyman, *The War* (2nd Ed., Calcutta, 1877), pp. 70-71.

[41] For quotations from Layard, see A. Borthwick, *An Address on the Eastern Question* (London, 1878), pp. 38-39; Captain Fred Burnaby, *op. cit.,* II, 333; Captain Bedford Pim, *The Eastern Question, Addenda* (3rd Ed., London, 1878), pp. 18-19; and *Pall Mall Gazette,* Nov. 24, 1877, pp. 1-2. On trade, see Lucien Wolf, *The Russian Conspiracy* (London, 1877), pp. 6 and 12-19; Layard, *op. cit., Quarterly Review,* CXLIII, 304; "National Interests and National Morality," *ibid.,* CXLIV (July 1877), 306-07. A certain amount of interest was being aroused, especially among Liberals of whom James Bryce was most prominent, in autonomy or independence for the Armenians. See the pamphlet, *Armenians and the Eastern Question* (London, 1878), 72 pp., quoting letters to the *Times,* 1874-78, and speeches. The pamphlet was circulated by the Liberal organization, "The Eastern Question Association."

[42] *Daily News,* quoted in *Pall Mall Gazette,* Nov. 28, 1877, p. 2; *Daily Telegraph,* quoted in *ibid.,* Nov. 20, 1877, p. 2. Cf. *ibid.,* Nov. 19, p. 2; Nov. 24, pp. 1-2; Nov. 27, pp. 1-2; Alfred Austin, *England's Policy and Peril* (London,

Aside from the plea that England should meet this menace by supporting Turkey, two other suggestions were raised, the one as a substitute, the other as a complement to such a policy. The first of these was advanced by Émile de Laveleye and by Edward Dicey who argued that as compensation for Russia's advance in Armenia, England should occupy Egypt. Laveleye also included Cyprus and maintained that, "transformed into a Gibraltar," it would be an excellent position from which to guard the shores of Syria and the entrance to the Suez Canal.[43] Although both men argued with great force and clarity, and the idea of taking Egypt was occasionally voiced in the press as either a desirable or a necessary step, the suggestion was not a popular one with either the Liberals or the Conservatives. The former abhorred a policy of aggrandizement and the latter still hoped to preserve the Ottoman Empire. Furthermore, as in 1876, everyone, including the government, hesitated to arouse the jealousy of France.[44]

1877), 32 pp.; Borthwick, *op. cit., pp.* 31-32, 34-35; *Times,* Jan. 12, 1878, pp. 6 and 10; Crealock, *The Eastern Question* (London, 1878), p. 183; Edward Cazalet, *The Eastern Question* (London, 1878), pp. 30-32; *The Eastern Question; The Russian Policy in the East* (6th Ed., London, 1878), pp. 24-25 and 27-30; and Lord Stratford de Redcliffe's letter to the Editor, *Times,* Jan. 17, 1878, p. 8.

[43] É. de Laveleye, *loc. cit.,* pp. 25-34; *idem,* "England and the War," *Fortnightly Rev.,* XXIX (Feb. 1878), 163-64; and Edward Dicey, "Egypt and the Khedive," *Nineteenth Century,* II (Dec. 1877), 867. Cf. *Pall Mall Gazette,* Nov. 24, 1877, pp. 2-3; *Times,* Jan. 8, 1878, p. 9; Jan. 12, p. 7; and March 5, p. 5. Laveleye was a Belgian economist who wrote frequently for the *Fortnightly,* and Dicey was a journalist of considerable repute, having been connected with the *Daily Telegraph* and *Daily News,* and since 1870, editor of the *Observer.*

[44] "Home and Foreign Affairs," *Fortnightly Rev.,* XXVIII (July 1877), 142; *ibid.,* XXIX (Jan. 1878), 144; Goldwin Smith, "The Policy of Aggrandizement," *ibid.,* XXVIII (Sept. 1877), 303-24; W. E. Gladstone, "Aggression on Egypt and Freedom in the East," *Nineteenth Century,* II (Aug. 1877), 149-66; Edward Dicey, "Mr. Gladstone and Our Empire," *ibid.* (Sept. 1877), 292-308; "Russians in Asia Minor," *Edinburgh Rev.,* CXLVI (July 1877), 278-79; "The Fall of Plevna: Peace or War?" *Blackwood's Magazine,* CXXIII (Jan. 1878), 104; "The Meeting of Parliament," *Quarterly Rev.,* CXLV (Jan. 1878), 271-73; Borthwick, *op. cit.,* pp. 33-34; Campbell, *Policy of Great Britain* (1877), p. 22; Wyman, *op. cit.,* p. 72; and *Times,* March 8, p. 7, March 9, p. 8, and March 11, p. 10. Vivian wrote privately to Tenterden from Alexandria on July 1 to

The other suggestion was one to which Layard referred in his letter of December 12 and was the project of a Euphrates Valley railway. It was brought to public attention at the end of November 1877 when a delegation to the Foreign Office, led by Lord Campbell and Stratheden, mentioned it as one of the interests which Great Britain should protect in opposition to Russia's advance southward of the Caucasus.[45] This "alternate route to India" had been in the air since the Chesney Expedition down the Euphrates in 1836 and had last been thoroughly discussed by a Select Committee of the House of Commons in 1871 and 1872 under the chairmanship of Sir Stafford Northcote who was now Chancellor of the Exchequer in Beaconsfield's government. Though the plan of a railway from the Mediterranean to the Persian Gulf and even to India had been ardently promulgated by engineers, Anglo-Indians and British agents in Asiatic Turkey, every attempt to put it into operation had been thwarted through lack of support or the suspicions of the Turkish government.[46]

Except for occasional mention in the press, interest in the Euphrates Valley railway slumbered after 1872 until reawakened for a brief period in August 1875 when the Sultan announced that he was going to support the construction of railways from his own private purse. This aroused some com-

inquire if the Government had the idea which was being discussed of taking Egypt, and said that the French were telling the Khedive, "We told you so!" (F. O., 363/4). Derby in December 1877 again assured the French in the "strongest and plainest language" that England had no desire for the annexation, or the establishment of a protectorate or of exclusive influence in Egypt. Draft to Lyons, No. 726, F. O., December 29 (F. O., 27/2233); and 1 *Doc. Dip. Franç.,* II, 225. Cf. *ibid.,* II, 234-35 and 282-83.

[45] The *Times,* Nov. 29, 1877, pp. 6 and 9.

[46] For the most complete account of the Chesney Expedition and the discussions of a Euphrates Valley Railway, see H. L. Hoskins, *op. cit.,* Chs. 7, 13, and 17. Cf. "Report from the Select Committee on Euphrates Valley Railway . . . 27 July 1871," *Parliamentary Papers,* VII (1871), No. 386; "Report from the Select Committee on Euphrates Valley Railway . . . 22 July 1872," *ibid.,* IX (1872), No. 322; "Reports Respecting Communications with India through Turkey, by the Euphrates Valley Route," *ibid.,* XLV (1872), No. C. 534; and B. H. Sumner, "Ignatyev at Constantinople," *Slavonic Rev.,* XI (April, 1933), 565.

ment in England but was quickly lost to sight when the crisis in Bosnia and Herzegovina and the announcement of Turkish bankruptcy put an end to any hope of such undertakings.[47]

In 1877, however, the project was brought forward again for three reasons, aside from its natural association in the minds of men like Layard with the subject of Asia Minor. It appealed to some as a means by which, through the sale of the concession to be accompanied by a considerable tract of land, the Porte could be relieved from immediate financial embarrassment, thus enabling it to carry on the war and win back the affection of English bondholders.[48] A much larger group regarded the railway as a reforming agency which would open up "the richest provinces of the Turkish Empire" to commerce and trade, bring new revenue to the Ottoman treasury and the blessings of civilization to the Turkish people. All who had any faith in it emphasized its strategical value to England as an alternative and quick route to India which should not be allowed to fall into the hands of Russia and might even serve to counteract and stop Russian progress in

[47] W. P. Andrew, *The Euphrates Valley Route to India* (London, 1873), 62 pp., and *The Euphrates Valley Route to India in Connection with the Central Asian Question* (London, n.d.), 29 pp.; L. H. Griffin, *op. cit., Fortnightly Rev.,* XXI (Jan. 1874), 40-41. For the August proposal, see George Young, *Corps de Droit Ottoman* (Oxford, 1906), IV, 155; A. Du Velay, *Essai sur l'Histoire Financière de la Turquie* (Paris, 1903), 627-28; *Times,* Aug. 3, p. 5; Aug. 14, p. 9; Aug. 18, p. 7; Sept. 29, 1875, p. 4; *Pall Mall Gazette,* Nov. 26, p. 10, and Dec. 17, 1875, p. 10; Seton-Watson, *loc. cit.,* III, 426. English consuls reported an interest in the project: Skene to Elliot, Aleppo, Aug. 20, 1875 (F. O., 195/1067); and Gatheral Report, Angora, March 1, 1876 *(Parl. Papers, Consular Reports,* C. 1468, pp. 999 and 1001); and Malet, Memorandum on the Development of Trade in Bagdad, 1876 (F. O., 195/1208). A Professor Henry Tanner attempted unsuccessfully to get a concesson for a Syrian railway: Letters to Elliot, Therapia, Feb. 21, March 10, and March 13, 1876 (F. O., 195/1114).

[48] Captain Bedford Pim, *op. cit.,* pp. 36-37, 47-48; and *Addenda,* pp. 17-20. Pim declared (p. 37): "I have been assured, on excellent authority, that Turkey would gladly have paid her debts by the transfer of land on each side of the Euphrates Valley route, and conceding any amount of privileges to settlers, had it not been for Russia's unprovoked, not to say, brutal interference." See the suggestion of Salisbury after the Congress of Berlin, *post,* p. 142.

Armenia.[49]   Although Lord Derby ridiculed the idea that the Euphrates Valley could ever become a route to India and others were sceptical of a railway ever being built, the idea continued to play a part in the slowly emerging hopes and plans for a reformed and rejuvenated Ottoman Empire.[50]

By the end of 1877, in fact, all the elements of the policy which accompanied the acquisition of Cyprus had been introduced.   By far the most prominent among them was still the desire to establish a commanding position in the Eastern Mediterranean by means of a convenient naval base from which the mouth of the Dardanelles could be watched on the one hand and the Suez Canal could be guarded on the other. In addition there was in the background the idea advanced by Home and heartily advocated by Layard of England's attempting the reform of Turkey.   Finally there was the belief that Asia Minor was of great importance in connection with the route to India and that here England could not rely on the help of others as might be the case in dealing with Turkey-in-Europe.

Although public opinion in England at the beginning of 1878 was supporting Beaconsfield or at least demanding the protection of British interests, divisions in the cabinet and the equivocal attitude of European Powers upon whose cooperation Beaconsfield had hoped to rely in checking Russia, prevented him from adopting the energetic policy which he wished and for which Layard was begging.   The Russo-Turkish armistice was signed on January 31, but the advance of the Russian armies by arrangement with the Turks to a position within the lines of Buyuk Chekmedje and close to Constantinople so aroused British fears that Beaconsfield was able

---

[49] Borthwick, *op. cit.,* pp. 5-6, 17-18; *Pall Mall Gazette,* Nov. 26, pp. 2-3; Nov. 27, p. 1; Dec. 1, p. 3 (summarizing *Saturday Review* and *Economist*); Dec. 3, p. 5 (quoting the *Economist*); and Dec. 4, 1877, p. 5; Layard, *op. cit., Quarterly Rev.,* CXLIII, 302-03; "The Meeting of Parliament," *ibid.,* CXLV (Jan. 1878), 267; "Travels in the Caucasus," *Edinburgh Rev.,* CXLV (Jan. 1877), 46; "The Khedive's Egypt," *Blackwood's Magazine,* CXXII, 487.

[50] *Times,* Nov. 29, 1877, p. 6; and Jan. 5, 1878, p. 11.

to secure a vote of extraordinary credit and after much hesitation and one resignation in the cabinet to send the fleet to Constantinople early in February. The Russians now insisted, however, that the action of England gave them a right to occupy Constantinople and were finally satisfied only by the withdrawal of the fleet to Mudania and an agreement that neither power would occupy the Asiatic side of the Dardanelles, and that England would not land troops on the European side of the Straits if Russia refrained from occupying Gallipoli. In this situation the Russians had the advantage, for now England was excluded from occupying that Peninsula and the fleet was powerless to prevent an attack on Constantinople.[51]

To make matters worse, the Turks showed a disposition during the negotiation of peace terms to ally with Russia; and Austria, who had seemed on the point of making a definite agreement with England to oppose Russia, failed to come to final terms. The spectre of the League of the Three Emperors again haunted the English statesmen and Bismarck returned to his favorite theme of partition. Under the circumstances there seemed little to be gained from the European conference for which Andrassy was pressing. Beaconsfield took a discouraged view of the situation in early March but at the same time made what proved to be another abortive attempt at an alliance, this time a Mediterranean League, and also began preparations for the defense of British interests by force if necessary.[52]

---

[51] See Thompson, II, 329-59; Langer, *op. cit.*, pp. 130-36; and Dwight E. Lee, "The Proposed Mediterranean League of 1878," *Journal of Modern History*, III (March 1931), 33-35.

[52] Langer, *op. cit.*, pp. 137-38; Lee, *op. cit., J. M. H.*, III, pp. 35-45. Public opinion in England became most thoroughly aroused against the *Dreikaiserbund* in the months of December 1877 to April 1878. See "Historica," *The Imperial Triumvirate. A Warning and Exposure of Ambitious and Unscrupulous Designs* (London, 1877), 7 pp. (Appeared early in Dec. and might well have been inspired by Beaconsfield); Borthwick, *op. cit.*, p. 20; Campbell, *op. cit.* (1878), pp. 8-9; *Pall Mall Gazette*, Dec. 5, p. 4; Dec. 15, 1877, p. 2; April 29, 1878, p. 1; *Times*, Feb. 4, pp. 5-6; Feb. 5, p. 5; Feb. 16, p. 5; March 1, p. 5; March 8, 1878, p. 9; John Lemoinne, "The Situation," *Nineteenth Century*,

Layard, too, despaired of repairing the damage done to Turkey-in-Europe by the apparent triumph of Russia, as his private letter of March 6 to Beaconsfield indicated. In it he reported a long interview with the Sultan at a private dinner on the previous evening in which plans for aiding Turkey against Russia were discussed. The Sultan thought that with English officers and money he could drive the Russians back across the Balkans and despite the treaty of peace, signed at San Stefano on March 3, he would feel justified in doing so, since he had been forced to accept humiliating terms. Layard wrote:

. . . "I endeavored to make him understand that there was very little, if any, hope of his being able, under any circumstances, to recover his former authority over the Christian population of Turkey in Europe, and I pointed out that they had always been an element of danger and disturbance to his Empire, and the cause of its most disastrous wars. I showed him that with a good and enlightened administration and by pursuing a wise and liberal policy, he might out of his great Asiatic and African possessions form a powerful and compact Empire and one which might especially command the sympathy and support of England. I dwelt upon the importance of connecting Constantinople with the Persian Gulf by a railway, which could be united with the Mediterranean by a branch line carried to Alexandretta or some other port. I showed him how the resources of Asia Minor and of the magnificent valleys of the Euphrates and Tigris might be developed and how by opening a wide field for the extension of British Commerce and by affording us a rapid and safe alternative route to India he would be promoting the interests of England and laying the foundation of a real and permanent alliance, far more valuable to him and his country than any we could have with him as an European Power. We had no special interests, I said, in Bulgaria or Servia, but we had in Asia Minor and Mesopotamia. By promoting them to the utmost he would secure the support and sympathy of England and would best be able to hold his own against Russia.

"These views appeared to be acceptable to him and he entered with his usual good sense into the matter. He told me, and Said Pasha confirmed what he said, that the idea of connecting Constantinople with Baghdad and the Persian Gulf had occurred to him when he came to the throne, and that he was fully alive to the great importance of the

III (March 1878), 567-70; Edward Dicey, England's Policy at the Congress," *ibid.*, III (April 1878), 779-81; 3 Hans. CCXXXIX, 792; Newton, II, 139; Sir H. Drummond-Wolff, *Rambling Recollections* (London, 1908), II, 152; and Layard to Lytton, Dec. 5, 1877 (Add. MS. 38,971, fos. 90-91); and *Mem.*, V, fos. 286-87 and 302.

undertaking which he said, he would like to see in the hands of an English Company. Did I think that England would help him in carrying it out? I replied that when the time came for it, I should be glad to do what I could for him in the matter, and that it was more probable that he would receive assistance from England in a direction in which her commercial and other interests were deeply affected than in any attempt to maintain his rule in the European Provinces of Turkey. . . ."

In conclusion Layard summarized what he thought English policy concerning Turkey should be:

". . . to make Turkey a strong Asiatic Power, to assist her in developing the wonderful resources of Asia Minor, and of the Euphrates and Tigris valleys, and to secure for ourselves the route through them to India, remembering that the time will come, and may perhaps be not even far distant, when a continuous line of railway may unite Baghdad and the mouth of the Euphrates with the Indus. I believe the Sultan to be really convinced that an alliance with England is the one most conducive to his own welfare and to that of his Country. There cannot be a doubt as to his present anti-Russian feelings. How far he will be able to resist the pressure and intrigues that may and will be brought against him is another question. For the present he certainly does look to England and to me, both as her Representative and, I would fain believe, from personal feelings. It is the fashion to say that my influence is gone, but without unreasonable boasting I may venture to say that an English Ambassador has perhaps rarely before been able to name a Prime Minister and to turn out a Minister for F.A. within a few days. If we pursue a firm and truly English policy, our influence here ought always to be predominate. . . ."[53]

Here, in concise form, was Layard's conclusion regarding England's policy in Turkey as he had worked it out under the impression that there was no longer any hope of preserving the Sultan's dominions intact in Europe. His later comments on the peace terms signed by Russia and Turkey at San Stefano and his letters to Salisbury pursued the same theme enlarging on the possibilities of strengthening the Ottoman Empire. Two ideas remained prominent: the Sultan was to be made strong in Asia by the co-operation of English officers and money and Turkey, thus reinforced, was to become England's ally and guardian of the alternative route to India.

Layard found a ready listener in Lord Salisbury who became Secretary of State for Foreign Affairs on March 28 when

[53] *Layard Papers,* Add. MS. 39,131, fo. 43.

Derby resigned over the measures advocated by Beaconsfield to meet the crisis caused by the failure of proposals for a European congress.[54] It will be remembered that while at the Conference of Constantinople, Salisbury had discussed means of safeguarding British interests in the East along lines very similar to those which Beaconsfield and Layard were now developing. Also during the month of March, as part of the Prime Minister's plans for the defense of British interests, definite steps had been taken toward the acquisition of some post in the East. Discussions carried on by Simmons, Gathorne-Hardy, Lord Napier and the Duke of Cambridge showed that several places were under consideration; and the circumstances under which Lord Derby resigned indicate that Beaconsfield had suggested the acquisition of Cyprus on March 27th although that particular place had not, apparently, been definitely decided upon. Salisbury had likewise consulted Home and made arrangements for further investigations in the East by competent officers,[55] and it was the new Foreign Minister upon whom fell the task of bringing the three objectives together: that of Beaconsfield who was seeking primarily a naval base, that of Home and himself who wanted a share in the partition of Turkey, and that of Layard who was contemplating the reform of Asiatic Turkey and the development of its natural resources under English guidance.

In his first private letter to Layard on April 4, Salisbury remarked that the Ambassador's task had been "to prevent Russian preponderance by sustaining the Turkish breakwater," but he feared that the breakwater was now shattered beyond repair and the flood pouring over it. He then hinted that the substitute for it might have to take the form of an acquisition of territory at the expense of the Porte, however repellent that might be to England and difficult to accomplish as a friendly act toward Turkey. He concluded his letter by

---

[54] See Monypenny and Buckle, II, 1125-40; Cecil, II, 211-24.

[55] *Ibid.* Cf. Langer, *op. cit.*, pp. 141-43; Temperley, *loc. cit.*, pp. 276, and 458-59; and Sir James Headlam-Morley, "The Acquisition of Cyprus," *Studies in Diplomatic History* (London, 1930), Ch. VII, especially, pp. 194-95.

saying that he only intended to direct Layard's thoughts into a channel in which they might have to run and thus gently began to prepare the Ambassador for a policy of compensation.[56]

In his reply on April 17, Layard emphasized as he had done before in his letters to Beaconsfield that Turkey could still offer a stronger bulwark against Russia than any other state or combination of states created out of Turkey-in-Europe. He admitted that the whole administration was corrupt and rotten and would have to be altered even if England had to take the government into her own hands. In his opinion it would be better to make the attempt to reform Turkey than to allow a general break-up of the Ottoman Empire and a scramble for the fragments which would be the inevitable result of the ratification of the San Stefano peace.[57]

In a long despatch on April 24, which was accompanied by a private letter to Salisbury of much the same tenor, Layard again developed his views on England's policy in Turkey at full length. In his belief that only England could properly undertake the reform of Turkey he was in full agreement with the views of Home, but he went farther and in accord with the majority of Englishmen in the East, maintained that the people themselves would welcome English control. This arose, he said, from the conviction that the reform which the Sultan's subjects desired "can be best brought about by England, that she would effect it disinterestedly and in the interests of Turkey and of the Mussulmans as well as of the Christians, . . . that she is prepared to obtain just, impartial and equal Government for all. They consequently believe that if England

---

[56] Cecil, II, 264-65. Layard had already written privately to Salisbury on April 3, offering to correspond with him and saying that he had "never given the Turks any encouragement to hope for assistance from England, although I might have told them that if they desired to obtain our sympathy and help they could only do so by showing that they are willing and able to govern their Christian as well as all other subjects justly and well and to develop the resources of this magnificent country over which they rule." *Memoirs*, VI (Add. MS. 38,936), fos. 291-92.

[57] Add. MS. 39,131, fos. 64-66.

is averse to annexing any portion of the Turkish Empire, the
next best thing for her to do would be to make use of her influence to reform and direct the administration, and virtually
to take the Government into her own hands."[58] Continuing
this argument, Layard proposed a policy for England as
follows:

"I venture to think that if England were to avail herself of this state
of feeling amongst the Mussulman population of the Turkish Empire, and
to adopt, if I may be permitted to so express myself, a broad, liberal and
statesmanlike policy as distinguished from one which has for its object
the interests and welfare of any particular race or religion, she might
do a vast amount of real good, further to an incalculable extent the
cause of humanity, and, at the same time, promote the true interests of
the British Empire. But in order to effect these results, the fanciful and
sentimental theories of nationalities and the narrow sympathies for
particular creeds that have unfortunately misled public opinion, must
be put aside. We must not look to the development of a Hellenism without
Hellenes, or of a Slavism without Slaves [*sic!*], persuading ourselves that
the modern Greek deserves our special support because he traces a fantastic descent from Miltiades and Alexander the Great, or that Bulgarians
are Slavs and consequently should be united to them, because they speak
a corrupt Slavonian dialect and profess the Russian faith. We must look
to the general well-being, prosperity and good government of all the
various populations, whatever may be their origin and creed that com-
pose the Turkish Empire. Of these populations, certainly the one which
has the highest qualities are the Turks, and one or two other Mohammedan
races. . . . Under a well-organized Government, Turkey could still furnish
a splendid army and a formidable navy. Her vast resources could enable
her to restore her finances, and to attain to prosperity and wealth. But
in order that she may be able to accomplish these things she should be
freed from the incessant attempts of Russia to destroy the authority of
the Sultan, and to impede the real progress of the country by her constant provocation of the Christian populations to discontent and
insurrection."

Repudiating the idea that separate Christian states would
contribute to the welfare of the Christians or to the peace of
Europe, Layard prophesied with noteworthy acumen that on
the contrary such an arrangement would be a constant source
of agitation and disturbance which in the end would compel

---

[58] Quotation from Desp. No. 525, April 24, 1878 (F. O., 78/2786). Cf. private
letter to Salisbury, April 24, 1878 (*ibid.*, fos. 76-78). For opinion that Turks
would welcome English administration, see *Times*, April 8, 1878, p. 8; and
post, p. 145-46.

some strong neighboring power to step in and put a stop to it by annexation. Reiterating his belief that Turkey could still be made a bulwark to Russia and a support to the true interests of the British Empire, he declared that if Her Majesty's Government were prepared to adopt such a policy it must be upon a distinct guarantee that the Sultan and governing class would accept the conditions of a radical reform of administration, perfect equality of treatment of all creeds, the admission of Christians as well as Mohammedans to a full share in the government of the country, the development of its resources and the setting in order of its finances. He closed his despatch by saying:

> "The influence of England is, I am persuaded, paramount at the present moment in the East. We might yet avail ourselves of it to promote the happiness and welfare of a large portion of the human race, and our own interests at the same time." [59]

As if anticipating Layard's views, Lord Salisbury had written on April 18:

> "The point to which your attention should be most distinctly drawn is that this country, which is popularly governed, and cannot, therefore, be counted on to act in any uniform or consistent system of policy, would probably abandon the task of resisting any further Russian advance to the Southward in Asia, if nothing but speculative arguments can be advanced in favour of action. But it will cling to any military post occupied by England as tenaciously as it has clung by Gibraltar; and if any movement were made which would threaten it, while assailing the Ottoman dominions, its action might be counted on."

He accordingly cautioned Layard to strengthen his influence with the Sultan and suggested that England must establish herself at some strong place on the Persian Gulf or the Aegean coast.[60]

Little now remained to be done in the development of a British policy except to choose the place to be occupied and to put the aims and methods to be pursued in Turkey into more precise form. Salisbury and Layard quickly agreed that

---

[59] Layard, Desp. No. 525 (*loc. cit.*).

[60] Layard, *Memoirs,* VI, fo. 294; and the original in Add. MS. 39,037, fos. 60-62.

an alliance with Turkey was necessary and that one indispensable condition should be the Turkish promise to reform. They also agreed that the problem of Asiatic Turkey was different from that of European Turkey, and that in the former region England had to protect her interests in the face of Russian encroachment without the help of other powers. While Salisbury did not seem to concern himself in his letters with the question of commerce and trade in the Mesopotamian region, Layard still emphasized very strongly the need for securing this future alternative route to India.[61]

The formal negotiations for the acquisition of Cyprus and the alliance with Turkey did not mention nor hint at such things as railway building or the means by which England was to aid in reforming the administration of Asia Minor. Thanks to Layard's insistence and interest, however, the question of an English built railway was inextricably bound up with the policy of a *place d'armes* and the reinvigoration of Turkish rule under British auspices.   In his last letter to Salisbury before receiving Salisbury's own final conclusions about the Cyprus policy, Layard pointed out, as he had previously done in letters to Beaconsfield, that the route to India through northern Syria was necessary and would become the great highway sooner or later.   Since the Turks were quite ready to build a railroad to Bagdad if they had the money, England must preserve control of the countries through which it would pass.   He suggested that in seeking a port some point on the north coast of Syria would be advantageous as commanding the terminus of the railway through Mesopotamia.[62] In fact, Layard's correspondence in April and May inevitably leaves the impression that British control of a Euphrates Valley railway and the lands through which it would pass constituted in his opinion the best compensation England could

---

[61] Layard to Salisbury, private letters, May 1, 8, and 15, 1878 (Add. MS. 39,131, fos. 83-94); Salisbury to Layard, private letters, May 2, 9, and 10, 1878 (Add. MS. 39,137, fos. 74-97). Cf. Cecil, II, 266-69; Monypenny and Buckle, II, 1162-63; and Newton, II, 137.

[62] Layard to Salisbury, May 15, 1878 (*loc. cit.*).

find for the weakening and partial dismemberment of Turkey embodied in the treaty of San Stefano.

Undoubtedly such an idea played some part in the choice of Cyprus as the point which England should occupy. The decision to take Cyprus was made some time between April 18 and May 10, largely upon the responsibility of Colonel Home.[63] In a memorandum reflecting his idealistic enthusiasm, he summarized the reasons for a British acquisition in the Near East. They embraced political, military, naval and commercial considerations. Under the first, he explained in terms reminiscent of his reasons for recommending the acquisition of Gallipoli that England required territory "sufficiently large, possessed of sufficient material resources and inhabited by such races of people as shall allow the experiment of what good government will do being fairly tried. The political effect produced by observing the rapid development of a country under English rule—the peace and prosperity that would reign in it and the satisfaction of the inhabitants at the change from Turkish to British government—would be incalculable and would do more to maintain English prestige than half a dozen Campaigns."

From a military standpoint the place should give Great Britain "potentially the Keys of Asia Minor" and furnish a base from which an army could check any hostile advance from the Caucasus or "the head waters of the Tigris and Euphrates" on either the Persian Gulf or the Suez Canal. It should also be capable of defense by a small garrison. For naval requirements, it should provide a good and easily defensible harbor and a place in which to coal near the lines of communication with India.

Finally, the commercial motive for seeking a place in the

[63] See Temperley, *loc. cit.*, pp. 276-77 and 459-60; and Dwight E. Lee, "A Memorandum Concerning Cyprus, 1878," *Journal of Modern History*, III (June 1931), 235-41. Both Mr. Temperley and the present author worked and published independently of one another and neither saw the other's article until his was published. This accounts for the lack of reference to the work of the other in the above publications.

East demanded a depot from which English manufacturers could make their way into the Levant and to which the carrying trades of the region could be attracted. What he had in mind was further brought out in his discussion of Alexandretta which he explained was considered to be the gate of Asia and the probable terminus of the Euphrates Valley railway if it were ever constructed.[64] These ideas were not only being mooted by Layard whose despatches and letters Home probably had seen or talked over with Salisbury and Beaconsfield, but were also being discussed at both the War Office and the Foreign Office. On April 8, Captain Grover, who had been one of the men at work with Home at Constantinople in 1876-77, printed a fourteen page confidential report on "Iskanderun" in which he paid much attention to the commercial aspects of that port and of the hinterland as far as Aleppo. His notes were based upon the writings of Euphrates Valley railway promoters like Colonel Chesney, Ainsworth, W. P. Andrew, and the Report in 1872 of the Parliamentary Select Committee in addition to general economic and descriptive studies of Turkey and military and naval reports.[65] The India Office forwarded to Lord Tenterden on May 7 translations of articles in the *Oesterreichische Monatsschrift für den Orient* among which two discussed the construction by England of a railway through Mesopotamia; and about the same time Lord Salisbury himself was discussing Arabia and railways with W. S. Blunt.[66] Thus commercial and financial schemes along with strategical and political aims were fully permeating the atmosphere in which Home was working.

Upon the premises he had summarized, he quickly eliminated one after another of the places under consideration during the previous two years. Gallipoli was too far from the

[64] Lee, "Memorandum," *J. M. H.*, III, pp. 237-38 and 240.

[65] Captain G. E. Grover, "Notes on Iskanderun, Compiled in the Intelligence Branch of the Quarter-Master-General's Department, London, 8th April 1878" (F. O., 358/5). Cf. Gathorne-Hardy, II, 74; and *Edinburgh Rev.*, CXLVII (April 1878), 569.

[66] Stanhope to Under-Secretary of State for Foreign Affairs, India Office, May 7, 1878 (F. O., 78/2831) ; and Blunt, *op. cit.*, pp. 28-29.

line of Indian trade, too menacing to other powers who were interested in the Black Sea and the Straits, and did not "command the very country Syria and Mesopotamia that it is so requisite to retain control over." Much the same reasoning applied to Lemnos and Mitylene which were "rather points of observation for watching the mouth of the Dardanelles" than what was needed. Stampalia was near enough to the Indian trade route but was nothing more than a coaling and naval station. Crete was too large. "Scanderoon" or Alexandretta had many advantages especially in relation to trade but was on the mainland and might cause difficulty because of the lack of a good natural boundary.[67] Acre and Haifa did not have good harbors and were limited in their influence by the desert east of the Jordan. Alexandria, though it also offered many advantages, was left out of consideration because its occupation meant the occupation of Egypt.

Cyprus, then, was the only place which combined all the requisite characteristics of location, size, population, defensibility, and commercial prospects because "Whoever holds Cyprus potentially holds Scanderoon, in short . . . holding Cyprus gives Scanderoon." Home admitted, however, that the harbors were deficient but believed that there were many facilities for making one. He also failed to point out just how the occupation of Cyprus was to prevent an attack upon the Persian Gulf from the highlands of Armenia but perhaps relied upon future railway construction from Alexandretta, as others later did, to accomplish that purpose.[68] All things considered his choice of Cyprus was the most logical and the best solution to all the problems which he set out to solve.

Moreover, his conclusions were in keeping with a traditional

[67] It is interesting to note that Home does not mention French feeling as one of the reasons for not recommending Alexandretta and yet it was regard for French feeling which probably prevented England from considering it, if the debates in Parliament and the communications with France are to be taken at their face value. See *post*, p. 113, and 1 *Doc. Dip. Franç.*, II, 352 ff.

[68] Lee, "Memorandum," *J. M. H.*, III, pp. 240-41.

view of Cyprus which was European as well as English.   In 1818 an Indian officer, J. M. Kinneir, wrote:

"The possession of Cyprus would give England a preponderating influence in the Mediterranean, and place at her disposal the future destinies of the Levant. Egypt and Syria would soon become her tributaries, and she would acquire an overawing position in respect to Asia Minor, by which the Porte might at all times be kept in check, and the encroachments of Russia, in this quarter, retarded, if not prevented. It would increase her commerce in a very considerable degree; . . . It is of easy defence; and under a liberal government would, in a very short space of time, amply repay the charge of its own establishment, and afford the most abundant supplies to our fleets at a trifling expense." [69]

Disraeli, thirty years later, was reflecting the same current of thought and the newer ideas which had arisen with the Eastern crisis of 1838-40 when he adverted in *Tancred* to the English desire for markets in Syria and declared that the English would not do the business of the Turks again for nothing but would demand Cyprus as compensation.[70]   After another thirty years, French, Belgian, and German writers joined with English to affirm that Cyprus commanded Asia Minor and Egypt and would guard the terminus at Alexandretta of a Euphrates Valley railway.[71]   It is clear therefore that the choice of Cyprus and the policy which accompanied it was not the result merely of one man's vision, but the by-product of many minds in search of imperial well-being and many years of thought which exigencies similar to those of 1878 had stimulated.

In May of that year, the situation in the Near East was somewhat different from that of the previous December when Beaconsfield and Layard began to explore the possibility of an English acquisition in the Levant.   Most of their worst

[69] John MacDonald Kinneir, *Journey through Asia Minor, Armenia, and Koordistan, in the years of 1813 and 1814* (London, 1818), pp. 185-86.

[70] *Tancred*, Book IV, Ch. I; Monypenny and Buckle, II, 1171-72; and Headlam-Morley, *loc. cit.*, pp. 203-07.

[71] See E. Paridant van der Cammen, *Étude sur l'Ile de Chypre Considerée au Point de Vue d'une Colonisation Européenne* (Aerschot and Bruxelles, 1874), p. 49; Chéon, *L'Ile de Chypre* (Paris, 1878), pp. 5-9; Victor Graf Folliot de Crenneville, *Die Insel Cypern* (Wien, 1879), p. 49; L. de Mas Latrie, *L'Ile de Chypre* (Paris, 1879), pp. 74-79; and Burnaby, *op. cit.*, II, 385.

fears were in the process of realization, including the Russian possession of Kars and Ardahan and the promise to her in the San Stefano treaty of Batoum. To be sure, the question of the Straits was not to be settled by Russia alone, but, in Layard's opinion, the great Bulgaria which she had demanded would be under Russian domination and thus available for the next move on the Bosphorus, and in any case with a sea-board on both the Black and the Aegean waters it would constitute a means of bringing Russia indirectly into the Mediterranean. The application of autonomy to European Turkey might also produce grave results in other parts of the Ottoman Empire and the huge indemnity which was beyond Turkey's strength to pay might furnish Russia with an additional means of wresting Constantinople and the Straits from Turkish hands.[72] Moreover, Austria throughout April was pressing the Sultan for Bosnia and Herzegovina and applying to England for support. This fact might be turned to account by an agreement whereby Austria would support England in revising the terms of the Russian treaty as they touched Europe, but would not be of avail in connection with Asia Minor where France, too, might have to be considered but could not be relied upon for help.

Meanwhile Beaconsfield and his government had not been idle. Great Britain's military forces had been increased in the Mediterranean by contingents from home and from India, and popular opinion had been successfully awakened once more to the necessity of opposing Russia in the interests of England if not of Turkey.[73] Lord Salisbury in one month of

---

[72] The most detailed and complete criticism of the San Stefano treaty is that of Layard, Desp. No. 343, Constantinople, March 13, 1878 (F. O., 78/2781); and the official, published view of it is to be found in Lord Salisbury's Circular of April 1, 1878 (*Parl. Papers*, C. 1989). Cf. "The Aggression of Russia and the Duty of Great Britain," *Quarterly Rev.*, CXLV (April 1878), 534-70; Cecil, II, 227-29; and Langer, *op. cit.*, pp. 138-40.

[73] The occupation of Cyprus had apparently first been definitely considered in connection with the decision to bring troops to the Mediterranean from India. See Headlam-Morley, *loc. cit.*, p. 195; and Monypenny and Buckle, II, 1134.

office had explored the diplomatic terrain and decided that the best hope of gluing the shattered Turkey into a semblance of the bulwark so ardently desired lay in direct negotiations with Russia, reinforced as regards the European side by an agreement with Austria and, if necessary, by a Turkish alliance with reference to the Asiatic portions of the Ottoman Empire. Accordingly on May 1 with Beaconsfield's assent, he told Count Shuvalov that he was ready to initiate negotiations with St. Petersburg looking to the modification of the San Stefano treaty and on May 3 summarized the views which Shuvalov was to carry to his government for discussion. On May 4 he despatched a plea to Austria for support in pushing the future Bulgaria back from the Aegean Sea.[74]   It was not until May 10, however, that he finally laid down the general terms upon which an alliance with Turkey might be made, and even then his plans were entirely tentative and dependent upon Russia's answer to his memorandum of the 3rd. In that communication he had plainly indicated that England objected to the extension of Russian boundaries in Armenia and hoped for concessions in this region to British feeling.[75]

Salisbury therefore wrote his letter of May 10 to Layard while there was still a chance that Russia might herself remove the need of British action in regard to Asia Minor. After summarizing the possible effect upon Mesopotamia and even Syria of a Russian retention of Kars in much the same vein as Layard himself had done, Salisbury outlined the project of a defensive alliance with Turkey as the only feasible compromise between letting Russia have her way entirely or England's taking the territory for herself, both of which alternatives he considered to be "formidable." The conditions upon which the agreement might be based were specific assurances

[74] Salisbury Memorandum, May 3 (F. O., 181/567); Draft to Elliot, No. 293, F. O., May 4, 1878 (F. O., 7/924); and Cecil, II, 255. For excellent short discussions of these negotiations, see Langer, *op. cit.*, pp. 143-46; and Headlam-Morley, *loc. cit.*, pp. 195-98.

[75] Salisbury Memorandum (*loc. cit.*); and Draft to Loftus, No. 305, F. O., May 7, 1878 (F. O., 65/994).

from the Porte of good government in Asiatic Turkey, and the concession to England of the occupation of Cyprus. The whole arrangement, however, was to be dependent upon the Russian retention of her conquests in Armenia, and he advised Layard that it was "possible, though not probable," that Layard would not have to proceed at all to negotiate with the Porte along the lines laid down.[76]

Hardly had Layard answered this letter in an obviously noncommittal tone with a reiteration of the idea that Turkey was not yet helpless and the suggestion that her need of money might furnish the opportunity for broaching the subject of a territorial cession to England,[77] when he was informed by telegraph on the night of May 24-25 that he was to propose Salisbury's scheme for an alliance to the Sultan.[78] The occasion for this step was the return of Shuvalov from St. Petersburg on May 22 with proof that Russia was unwilling to give up her conquests in Armenia. Discussions with him, however, enabled Salisbury to report that he was about to complete an arrangement by which the Russian army would be withdrawn from the vicinity of Constantinople and the autonomous Bulgarian principality would be limited to the north of the Balkans. Layard was to warn the Sultan that if he did not consent to the terms of the alliance which England offered him, "it will not be in the power of England to pursue negotiations any further, the capture of Constantinople and the partition of the Empire will be the immediate result." England alone had saved the Sultan but would desist in the future unless he made a written engagement by Sunday (May 26).[79]

Layard's task was a very difficult one, for the Sultan whom he interviewed on the 25th was in such a state of nervous col-

[76] Cecil, II, 269; and Temperley, *loc. cit.*, 277-78.

[77] Layard, Private, May 22, 1878 (Add. MS. 39,131, fos. 99-101).

[78] Layard, *Memoirs*, VII (Add. MS. 39,937), fos. 83-85; and Headlam-Morley, *loc. cit.*, pp. 198-99.

[79] Salisbury Tel., received by Layard, May 25, 1878, Layard, *Memoirs*, VII, fo. 86. This was the third telegram received by Layard concerning the Cyprus Convention. The first was dated, May 24. See Temperley, *loc. cit.*, 278, and Buckle, *Victoria*, II, 623-24.

lapse as a result of the discovery of a plot a few days before to depose him that he thought Layard had come to assassinate him, or have him carried off to an English warship. The interview took place in the presence of the British dragoman and a Turkish general with an armed guard of Circassians in the background ready to intervene if need be. Hardly had Layard launched upon his introduction when the Sultan, increasingly alarmed by the low tone of voice which Layard was using in order to preserve secrecy from possible eavesdroppers, arose and declared that he was too ill to hear any more. Layard insisted that there was more to follow and that he had come to propose a defensive alliance with Turkey which would secure the Sultan's Asiatic possessions from Russian aggression in the future. Nevertheless the Sultan retired, but after consultation with his Prime Minister sent Layard word that he approved the proposal made to him and empowered his ministers to carry on negotiations.[80] Under the circumstances there was no opportunity to employ the threatening language suggested by Lord Salisbury and indeed every reason against it, considering the Sultan's nervous excitement.

Nor did Layard use it in talking with the Prime Minister, Sadyk Pasha, and the Foreign Minister, Safvet Pasha. Rather did he stress the importance to Turkey of the agreement which would secure to the Sultan his most valuable dominions. "English capital would flow into them," he argued, "and would develop their great natural resources, which ought to be a source of immense wealth to the Empire." All this and more would be secured by an English occupation and administration of Cyprus. Whether or not he came to specific points such as railroad building, Layard does not state either in his correspondence or his memoirs, but he probably did not, for, he asserts, both Sadyk Pasha and Safvet Pasha were statesmen who saw at once the advantages to Turkey and the reasonableness of the price. The negotiations proceeded smoothly

---

[80] Layard, *Memoirs*, VII, fos. 87-89; and Desp. No. 692, Therapia, May 27, 1878 (F. O., 78/2789).

and rapidly so that, after a consultation with some other ministers, and the approval of the Sultan, Safvet Pasha and Sadyk Pasha by eight o'clock Sunday evening signed documents which fixed the principal conditions of the Convention.[81]

A formally drafted convention was sent out from the Foreign Office on May 30, but Layard preferred not to wait for it in view of the uncertain political state of affairs at Constantinople when the Sultan's suspicious frame of mind might lead to a change of ministers at any moment. The Convention and the Annex, guaranteeing certain religious and legal rights to the Moslems and the Sultan, upon which Safvet insisted in order to make a good impression on the population of Cyprus, were therefore drafted under Layard's personal direction at Constantinople and signed on June 4 and July 1 respectively.[82] This haste accounts for ambiguities and one or two mistakes in form which appear in the Convention but do not seriously affect its validity.[83]

Thus the policy which had been slowly formulated by Beaconsfield, Home, Layard, and Salisbury was put into effect almost overnight in an effort to check Russia's further advance toward the Mediterranean and the Persian Gulf. As the Convention of June 4th stood, however, only one of the methods by which Great Britain was to accomplish her purpose of bolstering up Turkey and safe-guarding her route

---

[81] Layard, Desp. No. 692, May 27, 1878 (*loc. cit.*).

[82] Layard, Desp. Nos. 693 and 694, Therapia, May 31, 1878 (F. O., 78/2789) and despatch of June 5 (*Parl. Papers*, C. 2057 (1878), No. 2) ; Layard, *Memoirs*, VII, fos. 94-95. The convention followed Salisbury's instructions of May 10 and declared that if Batoum, Ardahan, Kars, or any of them were retained by Russia, and if Russia should take further territories of the Sultan in Asia, England would join the Sultan in defending them by force of arms. In return, the Sultan promised England to introduce reforms, to be agreed upon between them, and consented to assign the Island of Cyprus to be occupied and administered by England.

[83] Lord Hammond called Layard's attention to the fact that the French and English texts were not quite identical, that the engagements should have been made in the name of the Queen, not England, and that there were ambiguities of expression in the matter of Cyprus. Hammond, Private, July 10, 1878 (Add. MS. 38,956, fos. 130-31).

to India was explicitly included. That was the occupation of Cyprus which by itself fulfilled only the desire for a *place d'armes* in the East. There remained to be fixed the means by which British co-operation in the government of Asiatic Turkey was to be effected and by which the hopes of British participation in the opening up of Turkey's resources and the building of a Bagdad railway could be realized.

There was scarcely time for such considerations, however, for while Layard was struggling to get the Cyprus Convention adopted by the Porte, Salisbury and the cabinet were devoting all their attention to the negotiations with Russia and Austria. As a result of the discussions with Russia, two memoranda were signed on May 30 which registered the points upon which they could agree and those upon which they were free to raise further discussion at a European congress. So far as Turkey in Asia was directly concerned, Russia agreed to give up Bayazid and the valley of Alashkert but refused to yield Kars and Batoum. In a third memorandum signed on May 31, however, Shuvalov pledged the Tsar's word that Russia would not attempt to extend her boundaries in Asia Minor beyond those fixed by the Treaty of San Stefano and rectified by the agreement with England. Beaconsfield objected to conceding as much as the three memoranda did, and only agreed to them, apparently, because of the Cyprus Convention which supplemented the arrangement with Russia on the Asiatic side.[84]

As regards Europe, another supplementary agreement was concluded with Austria on June 6. According to the understanding finally reached with Andrassy, Austria and England were to support each other in their respective views concerning Bosnia and Bulgaria, although Andrassy intimated that he

---

[84] The Memoranda excepting that of May 31, were printed in the *Globe*, June 14, 1878 in substantially correct form, and may be referred to in *Staatsarchiv*, XXXIV (Leipzig, 1878), No. 6749; and Thompson, II, 456-59. The originals are to be found in F. O., 65/1022. For the negotiations, see Monypenny and Buckle, II, 1165-70; Cecil, II, 258-60; Buckle, *Victoria*, II, 621-26; Newton, II, 142-43; and Langer, *op. cit.*, 147-48.

considered the pledges to be only a gentlemen's agreement and subject to modification.[85]

Thus the secret agreements negotiated with Russia, Turkey, and Austria cleared the way for the acceptance on June 3 of Bismarck's invitation to a congress at Berlin. Taken together they represented a policy which, though not what Beaconsfield and his supporters had wanted a year before, nevertheless was definite and once more elevated England to a central place in the settlement of the Eastern Question.

[85] William A. Gauld, "The Anglo-Austrian Agreement of 1878," *English Hist. Rev.*, XLI (Jan. 1926), 108-12; Elliot, Desp. No. 455 and Tel. No. 162, Vienna, June 6, 1878 (F. O., 7/932).

CHAPTER III

THE CYPRUS POLICY AND THE CONGRESS OF BERLIN

BEACONSFIELD and Salisbury, who had finally shaped England's policy, and Lord Odo Russell, the able and amiable Ambassador to Germany, were chosen to represent Great Britain at the Congress of Berlin which was formally opened on June 13, 1878. Despite the secret agreements by which the ground had been prepared, there proved to be many difficulties in the path of the British plenipotentiaries. The boundaries of the Bulgarian province to be erected south of the Balkans and the character and extent of the Sultan's control over it proved to be so difficult of settlement that nearly two weeks of strenuous labor were required to bring about agreement.[1] While these questions were regarded as separate from the problems of Asia Minor both geographically and as to the method of approach, they nevertheless were considered by Beaconsfield and Salisbury to have a bearing upon British interests because of their relation to the balance of power in the Mediterranean. The principal problems involved were the removal of Russian influence as far as possible from the shores of the Aegean and the assurance of Turkish control over the regions north of it at least up to the crest of the Balkans.[2]

The other difficulties encountered by England at the Congress concerned her interests even more directly and arose in connection with the disposition of Batoum, Turkey's Asiatic

---

[1] See Monypenny and Buckle, II, 1189-1204; Cecil, II, 279-88; 1 *Doc. Dip. Franç.*, II, 328-36, 355-59; and, for an excellent brief discussion of these negotiations and those of the Congress together with a critical bibliography, Langer, *op. cit.*, pp. 150-69.

[2] Monypenny and Buckle, II, 1187 and 1197; and Salisbury to H. M.'s Principal Secretary of State, Berlin, July 13, 1878 (*Parl. Papers*, C. 2081, pp. 1-3).

boundaries, the Straits, and arrangements for the actual occupation of Cyprus. The negotiations over these points were
complicated for the English plenipotentiaries by the unfortunate revelation in *The Globe* on June 14, the day after the
Congress opened, of the first and second memoranda signed
by Salisbury and Shuvalov on May 30.[3] So embarrassing was
the effect of this publication on public opinion, particularly in
Austria and Turkey and among the supporters of the government at home, that many suspected a Russian plot behind the
disclosures.[4] While Andrassy did not, despite the feeling in
Vienna, waver in his promised support of England at Berlin,
the reaction in Turkey greatly endangered the good relations
established between England and the Porte where the disclosure was being represented, said Layard, "as a secret arrangement for the partition of Turkey, and as proving that the

[3] A summary of the memoranda had been published in the *Globe* on May
31, but was declared by Lord Salisbury to be "wholly unauthentic." Upon the
publication of the text, the government declared that "as an explanation of the
policy of the Government, it is incomplete, and, consequently inaccurate." Such
a statement was justified by the fact that neither the third memorandum nor the
agreements with Austria and Turkey were revealed. See Thompson, II, 455-61;
and 3 Hans. CCXL, 1061, 1569-70 and 1614.

[4] Neutral observers, like Radowitz at the Congress and Montgelas at the
Austrian Embassy in London, tended to exonerate Russia of blame, but the
English plenipotentiaries and diplomats almost all believed that the Russians
had arranged the disclosure. This was also the opinion of Sir Charles Dilke
after he had examined the papers in the Foreign Office. It seems to be supported
by circumstantial evidence, especially in view of the fact that the third memorandum which Russia refused to permit England to publish was not revealed in
the *Globe*. Marvin, whose trial disclosed some unpleasant facts about remunera-
tion in the Foreign Office, stoutly maintained that he had committed the
memoranda to memory. Radowitz, II, 41; Montgelas to Andrassy, Tel. No.
163, London, June 15, 1878 (Austrian Arch.); L. Raschdau, *loc. cit.*, pp.
373-74; Gwynn and Tuckwell, I, 254; Cecil, II, 282; Layard, *Memoirs*, VII
(Add. MS. 38,937), fo. 143; Anderson Memorandum, June 21; Tenterden Memorandum, June 17; and Currie to Tenterden, Private, Berlin, June 17, 1878
(F. O., 363/5); Loftus, Tel. No. 135, St. Petersburg, July 20, 1878 (F. O.,
65/1010); Elliot, Desp. No. 471, Vienna, June 24, 1878 (F. O., 7/932);
Thompson, II, 459-60; and Charles Marvin, *Our Public Affairs; Embodying an
Account of the Disclosure of the Anglo-Russian Agreement* (London, 1879), pp.
267-85.

British Government had been from the first in league with Russia and Austria for the division of the spoils."[5]

Something of a storm was raised in England although little was said in Parliament, perhaps because of the government's denials of the authenticity and accuracy of the revelations and a desire not to compromise the negotiations at Berlin. Both Liberals and Conservatives regarded the documents as genuine and considered them to be a betrayal of the "lofty moral position" taken in the Salisbury Circular of April 1 where the government had based its plea for the submission of the San Stefano treaty to a congress on the grounds that no European treaty could be modified without Europe's consent.[6] A few Russophils seized with exultation upon the concessions to Russia as evidence that Beaconsfield "agrees to everything and carries out Mr. Gladstone's policy."[7] The ultra supporters of the government, however, quickly called attention to the clauses by which England promised not to contest the acquisition by Russia of Batoum, although real concern over the fate of Batoum was confined to a rather small circle at this time as it had been in the previous months.[8]

The British government had evidently decided that Batoum was not worth fighting for and had been content so far as the Asiatic boundaries were concerned to get the restoration to Turkey of Bayazid which controlled the trade route from

---

[5] Cecil, II, 282; Salisbury, Tel., Berlin, June 18, 1878 (F. O., 78/2901); Elliot, Desp. No. 471, Vienna, June 24, 1878 (F. O., 7/932); and Layard, *Memoirs,* VII, fos. 141-45 and 151-52. Cf. Bertrand Bareilles, *Le Rapport Secret sur le Congrès de Berlin* (Paris, 1919), p. 104; and *Pall Mall Gazette,* June 3, p. 1, and June 26, 1878, p. 6.

[6] Cecil, II, 285-86; Gwynn and Tuckwell, I, 254; 3 Hans. CCXL, 1570-71; *Pall Mall Gazette,* June 15, 17, 18 and 19, 1878, leading articles; and Thompson, II, 461-65.

[7] W. T. Stead, *The M. P. for Russia* (London, 1909), I, 506. Cf. Argyll, *op. cit.,* II, 136.

[8] *Pall Mall Gazette,* June 15, p. 1; June 27, p. 3; June 29, pp. 1-2; July 3, p. 1; and July 4, pp. 1-2; *Times,* June 15, pp. 10-11; June 17, p. 10; June 18, p. 10; June 21, p. 4; June 29, p. 12; July 3, p. 9; July 5, p. 9. No doubt as a result of inspiration some papers such as the *Times* (June 17) pointed out that Russia had recognized that England had a right to a guardianship over Asia Minor. Cf. Hohenlohe, II, 225; Egerton, *op. cit.,* pp. 273 and 280-81.

Trebizond to Persia.[9]   Russia had never captured Batoum,
however, and the Lazes who inhabited the district around it
had raised a vigorous protest against annexation by Russia.
The Porte had included the retention of Batoum among the
main points of its instructions to the Turkish plenipotentiaries
at the Congress and the Sultan and his ministers begged Layard for British support.[10]   In view of this situation and the
jingo outbreak at home which frightened both Northcote and
Beaconsfield, Salisbury decided to make capital of the *Globe*
revelation either to get a Russian renunciation of Batoum or
to gain the freedom of the Straits for the British fleet.[11]   His
first move was to telegraph Layard on June 15 asking him to
secure, if possible, the Porte's consent to the following agreement:

"In case Russia should seek to acquire or having acquired to retain
Batoum, and England should be of opinion that the presence of a naval
force in the Black Sea is expedient with a view to protecting the Sultan's
interests in regard to H.M.'s territories as defined in the preliminary
Treaty of San Stefano, or in any definitive treaty of Peace, which shall
supersede it; His Majesty will not offer forcible opposition to the passage
at any time of the English fleet through the Straits of the Dardanelles
and Bosphorus for that purpose."[12]

[9] This decision may have been based on the view expressed by Consul
Biliotti that British commercial interests were not affected at Batoum whereas
they were at Bayazid; Desp. No. 1, Political, Trebizond, April 13, 1878 (F. O.,
195/1187). Although Bismarck was astonished that England should allow
Russia to retain Batoum and Kars, and Beaconsfield claimed that he intended to
urge that Russia give them up, Salisbury's action at the Congress clearly indicates that he did not share his chief's views very strongly. See Hanotaux, IV,
339-40; Monypenny and Buckle, II, 1180; and Hohenlohe, II, 219.

[10] *Parl. Papers*, C. 2009, pp. 58-69; Bareilles, *op. cit.*, pp. 83 and 104; Layard,
Tels. No. 586, June 17, and No. 609, June 23, 1878 (F. O., 78/2811); and
Mem., VII, fos. 155-56.

[11] Cecil, II, 288-90; Hanotaux, IV, 353-54; and Currie to Tenterden, Private,
June 17 (*loc. cit.*). Currie, one of Salisbury's secretaries, wrote that the
plenipotentiaries "fear the effect on the ultra supporters of the Gover[nmen]t
who are crying that it is a surrender. It will have the effect of making our
P. P. stiffer and the proposal for a general permission to enter the Straits
(which I own rather makes my hair stand on end) was the first result." Salisbury had reserved the right in paragraph (e) of the Second Memorandum of
May 30 to discuss the Straits at the Congress. See appendix.

[12] Salisbury to Layard, Personal and Secret Tel., Berlin, June 15 (F. O.,
363/4) and Tenterden Memorandum, June 24 (F. O., 363/5). Cf. Cecil, II,
291, footnote.

This was indeed a bold step which Salisbury in his telegram to Layard justified by the explanation that such an agreement would probably prevent Batoum from being taken, or if it was taken, would enable England "to provide for the security of the Porte without putting upon them the burden and the danger of summoning us under the Treaty of 1871."[13]   To Cross, left in charge of the Foreign Office at London, he pointed out that since England was much the stronger naval power, her exclusion from the Black Sea was a greater loss to her than the gain of Russia's exclusion from the Mediterranean.[14]

Layard brought the proposal to the attention of the Grand Vizier but left out the reference to Batoum because he claimed that he could not make the Grand Vizier understand it. The latter felt obliged to consult the Grand Council on such an important matter but was disposed to consent to the agreement provided it was kept very secret. He suggested some understanding to satisfy Russia such as that the Porte should protest at the passage of English ships or fire some blank cartridges while intending no opposition.[15]

Meanwhile, Salisbury had begun discussions at the Congress on the subject of Batoum. To the Russians he intimated that, while it was not the intention of England to go to war over the recovery of Batoum if other matters were settled satisfactorily, she had extreme misgivings on the subject. He pointed out that Russia would have great difficulty in subduing the district around Batoum because the Lazes who inhabited it were hostile to her and loyal to the Sultan. He professed to fear that Russia would attempt to effect her conquest by an attack on Constantinople or by a further advance into Asia Minor, and either of these courses might result in the gravest complications. He made the same statements to Bismarck and also warned him that if Russia took Batoum and estab-

---

[13] Salisbury to Layard, Tel., June 15 and Tenterden Memorandum, June 24.
[14] Cecil, II, 291.
[15] Layard, Tel. No. 606, June 22, 1878 (F. O., 78/2811).

lished a naval station and arsenal there her acts would constitute a menace to Turkey and the Bosphorus and would compel England to stand on the defensive. Briefly summarizing his views already expressed to Layard, he declared that England would reserve her freedom in regard to the Straits and urged Bismarck to induce the Russians to modify their plans concerning Batoum.[16]

So far as Batoum was concerned, Salisbury was obviously bluffing without very great personal conviction of the dangers to Turkey and England upon which he had enlarged, for he wrote privately to Layard on June 25:

> "Against the danger resulting from the capture of Kars and Batoum the Convention [of June 4] you have signed is a sufficient guarantee. . . . On both sides Batoum is little more than a flag—a sentiment. It will bring little real advantage to Russia: and without a very large expenditure of money, it will not enable her to threaten or injure Turkey. To Turkey the port is of the smallest possible value, and can only have the sentimental value mentioned to you by Safvet Pasha.
>
> "As, however, the resistance of the Lazi promises to be very obdurate, we think we may possibly prevent Russia from attacking it by threatening her with a change in our treaty relation to the Straits, slight in itself, but involving important consequences. . . . I suspect that the Russians will very particularly dislike this prospect; and it may have an effect upon them." [17]

On the same day, the cabinet met to consider Salisbury's proposal regarding the Straits. The members must have been greatly surprised by it in view of the attitude publicly proclaimed since the outbreak of the Russo-Turkish war. To be sure, English public opinion had been somewhat divided on the issue of *status quo* or freedom of the Straits, and both Salisbury and Beaconsfield had at one time played with the idea of opening them, but Conservative and even some Liberal opinion still inclined toward the maintenance of the existing treaty provisions.[18] It is not surprising therefore that,

---

[16] Salisbury, Desp. No. 10, Berlin, June 19, 1878 (F. O., 78/2899).

[17] Add. MS. 39,137, fos. 256-58.

[18] For arguments in favor of the freedom of the Straits to all nations, or for neutralization, see *Edinburgh Rev.*, CXLVI (July 1877), 262; *Pall Mall Gazette*, Dec. 6, 1877, p. 3; *Times*, Jan. 3, 1878, p. 11; Jan. 5, p. 11; Jan. 7, p. 10; Jan. 12, p. 10 (all these *Times* references are reports of meetings at which

although the cabinet consented to the use in negotiations of the threat to open the Straits in order to preserve Batoum for Turkey or have it made a free port, they looked upon any private or secret agreement with Turkey as inconsistent with a public agreement of all the powers on the subject of the Straits. They also believed that a change in the law of the Straits that would open them to all powers would be "dangerous and unpalatable to Turkey." Furthermore, they pointed out that the Convention of June 4 gave England a leverage with which to force Turkey to permit the use of the Straits to England even if the Treaty of 1871 were maintained.[19]

Salisbury immediately adopted this view and assured his colleagues at home that any idea of a special agreement with Turkey could be put aside. It was not necessary and he had abandoned it. The Porte had, in fact, informed Layard that the Grand Council would not consent to it.[20] But Salisbury insisted that the language of the Treaty of 1841, repeated in

the freedom of the Straits was recommended); *ibid.*, Feb. 7, p. 9; March 7, p. 4; and W. Robinson, *The Straits of the Dardanelles and the Bosphorus* (London, 1878), pp. 54-55 (arguments very similar to those of Salisbury in his despatches of June). On the other side of the question, see *Pall Mall Gazette*, Nov. 27, 1877, pp. 1-2; *Quarterly Rev.*, CXLV (Jan. 1878), 268-69 (This view of the Straits met Hammond's approval. Add. MS. 38,956, fo. 14); S. Laing (Liberal M. P.), "Plain View of British Interests," *Fortnightly Rev.*, XXIX (March 1878), 344-45; *Blackwood's Magazine*, CXXIII (April 1878), 515; (May 1878), 646-47; and CXXIV (July 1878), 124; and *Quarterly Rev.*, CXLV (April 1878), 536. For Salisbury and Beaconsfield, see Cecil, II, 214, and Monypenny and Buckle, II, 1066, 1124. The army and navy men were opposed to the opening of the Straits. See Egerton, *op. cit.*, 212; Fraser, Memorandum on "British transport of troops in Egypt," December 1877 (F. O., 358/3); and Simmons, Memorandum of Jan. 9, 1878 (F. O., 358/2).

[19] Cross to Salisbury, Secret and Personal Tel., June 25, 1878 (F. O., 363/4). Lord John Manners was the only member of the Cabinet who was willing to agree to Salisbury's proposal. See Cecil, II, 291.

[20] Layard, Tel., June 24, 1878 (Add. MS. 39,137, fo. 251) and Salisbury to Tenterden, Personal and Secret Tel., June 25, 1878 (F. O., 363/4). Layard asked if the arrangement made in April would be sufficient. He was referring to a pledge made by the Sultan and the Prime Minister that in case the fleet were withdrawn in agreement with Russia to retire her army, the Porte would not resist the re-entry, if necessary, of the British fleet into the Dardanelles. Layard, Desp. No. 543, Therapia, April 28, 1878 (F. O., 78/2786).

1856 and 1871, was ambiguous and he proposed to put into the protocols a statement that England felt she must guard against the menace to the Bosphorus which the Russian acquisition of Batoum would constitute in fact if not in intention, and must look upon her obligations to European powers not to enter the Straits as undue restraint upon a freedom of action which these novel circumstances might render necessary; Great Britain in accepting a renewal of the previous stipulations would therefore regard herself as entering upon an engagement with the Sultan only and not with any other power and would reserve to herself the right of assisting him with her fleet whenever in her judgment his independence was threatened.[21]

The advantages of such a method of procedure were many, said Lord Salisbury. It would clear up the ambiguous language of former treaties. The threat of making such a declaration might induce Russia to come to terms respecting Batoum. Even if she did not yield, it would be the wisest course to pursue, for it would supplement existing arrangements exactly where they had been found wanting and would make the control of the Straits a real control by the Turkish government and not by another government standing behind it. The irony of this remark when viewed in connection with the previous admission that the Cyprus Convention gave England a leverage over the Porte was still further brought out by Salisbury's elaboration of this point. Under existing conditions, he wrote, the Sultan had to summon his allies formally in case of a threat from Russia and thus commit an act of defiance. Under the proposed plan, the Sultan need only say that he was too weak to resist England and the English government instead of being taunted in Parliament with having entered forbidden waters and committed an act of war against Europe would be in a position to dispense with the formal summons of a friend who was under duress.

[21] "Draft Statement for Congress with Respect to the Straits," enclosed in Salisbury, Desp. No. 39, Berlin, June 26, 1878 (F. O., 78/2899. See appendix).

Salisbury's final argument, however, which was calculated to win over colleagues frightened by the reaction among their supporters to the agreement of May 30 with Russia, was that the contemplated declaration regarding the Straits would make good the only weak place in British policy. As matters stood, he expected to cover every ground of objection to the Treaty of San Stefano stated in his circular of April 1st with one exception. It could scarcely be said, he admitted, that much had been done to restore the balance of power upset in the Black Sea by the alienation from Turkey of Varna, Bessarabia, and Batoum. "If we reserve to ourselves the practical power of entering the Straits whenever the independence of Turkey is threatened, we shall have done enough even if we are not able to recover Batoum." [22]

The cabinet in reply approved the memorandum which Salisbury proposed to read to the Congress and took the occasion to impress upon their plenipotentiaries at Berlin "their sense of the public feeling daily increasing and likely to swell into violent indignation against Batoum passing into the hands of Russia." Also they insisted that if Russia were to "undertake a fresh warlike operation in order to obtain Batoum the Cabinet would think that the great object of the Congress, namely peace, would be frustrated and that a state of things would arise not contemplated in the memorandum of May 30th, and which would make it extremely difficult for this country to avoid interference." [23]

Lord Salisbury's hopes that Russia might be persuaded to give up Batoum by threats of opening the Straits were doomed to disappointment. On June 28, he discussed the question with Shuvalov at great length, using all the arguments he could find, including the threat to redefine England's treaty relations with respect to the Straits. He again admitted, however, that England would not go to war over the question and suggested an independent Khanate of Lazistan hinting that if

[22] Memorandum, enclosure No. 2, in Desp. No. 39 (*loc. cit.*).
[23] Cross to Salisbury, Personal Tel., June 29, 1878 (F. O., 363/4).

there was to be no fort at Batoum, England would not object to a military road from it to the Russian frontier with the right of passage for troops. In such an arrangement Turkey was to evacuate the town. Shuvalov, in answer, merely stated that he was unable to deal with such a proposal without consulting his government.[24]

England's position at the Congress at this moment was not a happy one. The suspicion of her policy which was created in Turkey by the *Globe* revelation was now still further increased by England's motion at the Congress on June 28, in compliance with the Andrassy agreement, that Austria occupy Bosnia. The Greek claims to an extension of frontiers were being brought to the fore, the granting of the firman for the occupation of Cyprus was being postponed from day to day at the Porte, and still the problem of Batoum was as far from settlement as ever. Layard warned Salisbury that the Porte suspected a secret agreement among the powers to partition the Ottoman Empire, and if it saw Thessaly, Epirus and Crete taken away from Turkey in addition to Bosnia, in the "temporary" occupation of which it did not believe, there was a danger that it might prefer San Stefano and unite with Russia. "Our position here," he concluded, "may be seriously compromised if it is not already." [25]

The Sultan or Turkish ministers were almost daily reiterating the hope that Batoum could be kept from Russia, and the English press was reporting fully the distrust of England

[24] Salisbury, Desp. No. 55, Berlin, June 28, 1878 (F. O., 78/2899).

[25] Layard, Tel. No. 631, Therapia, June 29, 1878 (F. O., 78/2907). Salisbury had hoped that Turkey would acquiesce in the Austrian occupation of Bosnia before the subject was brought up in the Congress and telegraphed that the refusal of the Sultan to do so would "place Austria materially and England morally against him" and might cause all the negotiations to fall through. At the same time he reported that the English were doing all they could to create an independent Lazistan with Batoum a free port. Salisbury to Layard, Tel. No. 12 Congress Special, June 27, 1878 (F. O., 78/2901). For the sitting of June 28, see the 8th Protocol, *British and Foreign State Papers*, LXIX (1885), 946-67.

which was being aroused in Turkey.[26] Striking proof of
Turkish feeling arrived at Berlin on July 4th when Layard
telegraphed that the Turkish Grand Council had been sitting
all day and, while it had decided to ratify the Convention with
England, had deemed it inexpedient to issue the firman authorizing the transfer of Cyprus until the Congress was over. The
Council put its refusal on the grounds that the English occupation might make Russia refuse to give up any of the Asiatic territories assigned to her in the Treaty of San Stefano; it might
lead other Powers to demand similar territorial concessions;
and it might have a bad effect upon public opinion in Turkey.[27]
But the further implication that the Turks were anxious to
guarantee England's loyal support of their wishes is obvious.

Both Layard and Salisbury protested vigorously against this
decision, the latter describing it as a flagrant breach of faith
and "an act of gross ingratitude for the efforts Her Majesty's
Government have made to save Turkey." In order to put
pressure upon the Porte, he telegraphed Layard that Prince
Bismarck, who had proposed to give Thessaly, Epirus and
Crete to Greece, had dropped the proposition at England's
refusal, but "if the firman is not issued at once, England will
offer no further opposition. Inform Sultan and spare no efforts or threats to get firman at once."[28] As it turned out,
Layard was shortly afterward able to get the firman by means
of almost constant attendance upon the Turkish officials. The
episode illustrates, however, the temper of the Turks whose
procrastination over the firman for the transfer of Cyprus
scarcely contributed to relieve the tension under which the
English plenipotentiaries were working at the Congress, worried as they were by the state of public feeling at home

---

[26] Layard, Tel. No. 639, July 1, 1878 (F. O., 78/2907); *Times,* June 27, p. 5;
June 28, p. 5; June 29, p. 7; July 1, pp. 4, 5; and July 4, 1878, p. 9 (leading
article); and Egerton, *op. cit.,* p. 282.

[27] Layard, Tel. No. 643, July 3, 1878 (F. O., 363/2); and Layard, *Memoirs,*
VII, fo. 152.

[28] Salisbury to Layard, Personal and Secret Tel., Berlin, July 4, 1878
(F. O., 363/2).

and the details of the Asiatic settlement on which they felt that little support could be had from the other powers.

In regard to Batoum progress had been slow, although on July 5th the Russians agreed to make Batoum a free and unfortified port and gave Salisbury some reason to think that they might permit the frontiers to be drawn in such a way that about 100,000 Mussulmans including all the Lazes would remain in Turkey.[29] In the meeting of the Congress on the next day, Gorchakov and Shuvalov announced that Batoum would be a free and "commercial" port and on the insistence of Beaconsfield agreed that the subject of the Lazes should be reserved for a further meeting between the Russian and English plenipotentiaries. Lord Salisbury apparently felt satisfied with the Russian concessions, for he announced his acceptance of the *status quo ante* in regard to the Straits.[30] At the same time he was compelled by fear of an unofficial and disastrous exposure to set the stage for the announcement of the Cyprus Convention.

It is obvious that from the first Salisbury intended to announce the grand *coup* only after the settlement of Turkey's Asiatic boundaries, and that after the *Globe* revelation it was the more necessary to keep the secret until the utmost concession had been wrung from Russia in order to appease the wrath of friends both at home and at Constantinople.[31] He had also to consider what effect the announcement might have on the powers and their support of England at the Congress. Andrassy, who learned of the Convention from Zichy

[29] Salisbury, Tel. No. 17, Berlin, July 5, 1878 (F. O., 78/2901); Cecil, II, 291-93; and Monypenny and Buckle, II, 1204.

[30] Salisbury, Tel. No. 20, Berlin, July 6, 1878 (F. O., 78/2901); Protocol No. 14, *loc. cit.*, 1021-28; and Raschdau, *loc. cit.*, p. 377. The *Times* reported (July 8, p. 10) that Russia agreed to make Batoum a commercial port only after Beaconsfield had threatened that England would send her ironclads through the Straits when ever she pleased.

[31] Cecil, II, 276-77; Salisbury to Layard, Private, May 30, 1878 (Add. MS. 39,137, fos. 138-41); Salisbury to Layard, Tel., Berlin, June 27, and to Cross, Tel., Berlin, July 1, 1878 (F. O., 363/4). In this last telegram, Salisbury said of the Cyprus Convention: "Every day's delay in bringing it out is a diplomatic advantage here just now."

as early as June 9, and Bismarck who was informed of it by Lord Beaconsfield himself made no difficulties; indeed Bismarck expressed much pleasure over the news.[32] But France was another matter and the desire to square Waddington played as large a part in Salisbury's plans as did the Asiatic settlement.[33]

July 9, the day on which it was hoped to settle the remaining questions concerning Batoum, was set for the announcement. Late on July 6 word came that the firman authorizing the transfer of the island to British rule was being prepared and on July 7, that it had been granted. On the same day, Mr. Baring and a Turkish Pasha carrying the firman left Constantinople for Cyprus and orders were issued to Sir John Hay to proceed with some warships under his command to the island, although Lord Salisbury asked that troops be held back for a few days in order to avoid any appearance of a menace to other powers.[34] On the night of July 6 Lord Salisbury wrote a long personal letter to Waddington explaining the Convention and the circumstances that had made it necessary, and sent a much shorter one to Bismarck to whom the English policy had already been explained.[35]

---

[32] Zichy to Andrassy, Tel. No. 328, Pera, June 9, 1878 (Austrian Archives); and Monypenny and Buckle, II, 1204. Salisbury, in a telegram of June 22 (F. O., 363/2), warned Layard that Andrassy knew of the Convention. For the rumor reported by the French Ambassador at Constantinople on June 24, see Michel Lhéritier, "Le Sens de l'Occupation de Chypre, d'après des Documents Nouveaux," *Mélanges Offerts à S. Lambros* (Athènes, 1933), p. 237.

[33] Salisbury to Layard, Private, May 30, 1878 (*loc. cit.*); Cecil, II, 270 and 294; and Newton, II, 144.

[34] Salisbury to Tenterden, Tel., July 6; *idem,* to F. O., Tels. Nos. 18 and 19, July 6; Tels. at 2 P. M. and No. 25, July 8, 1878 (F. O., 78/2901); Layard to Salisbury, Tel. No. 649, July 7, 1878 (F. O., 78/2907). The difficulties which Layard encountered in obtaining the firman and arranging for the transfer of the island are graphically described in two despatches and a private letter to Salisbury: Desp. No. 869, July 4, and No. 879, July 8 (F. O., 78/2793); private letter, July 6, 1878 (Add. MS. 39,138, fos. 30-33). In all three documents he emphasized the ill effect upon the Turks of the Salisbury-Shuvalov agreement.

[35] The copy of the letter to Bismarck is dated July 7, 1878 (F. O., 363/5). The published copy of the letter to Waddington is dated July 7 and Lady

His plans were slightly upset, however, when the news of the Convention appeared in *The Daily Telegraph* on the morning of July 8 and the government was compelled to make a full announcement in answer to questions in both Houses of Parliament on the same evening.[36] Mr. Cross telegraphed that the announcement was very well received but warned that "all still very anxious to know about Batoum final arrangement." [37]

At this point the negotiations over Batoum were taken entirely out of the hands of Salisbury and Shuvalov, who had conducted the burden of the discussions up to July 6, and were continued between Beaconsfield and Gorchakov. Both men were no doubt a little dissatisfied with the way Batoum had been handled by their subordinates. Gorchakov had sulked during the settling of Bulgarian affairs in a way to show his disapproval of his colleague's policy, and now he hoped, no doubt, to win some laurels at Shuvalov's expense.[38] Lord Beaconsfield was anxious to counteract the bad impression made in England by the publication of the Salisbury-Shuvalov agreements and perhaps did not altogether approve of them, for he wrote to Tenterden that "something must be done about Batoum, and after that unfortunate Schou: Sal Memorandum,

Gwendolen Cecil accepts that date, but the copy in F. O., 363/4 is dated July 6 and it appears from other sources to be the correct one. See Cecil, II, 294; Newton, II, 148; and Waddington to Dufaure, Berlin, July 8, 1878, 1 *Doc. Dip. Franç.*, II, 352.

[36] 3 Hans. CCXLI, 952-53 and 965-66. The secret had been remarkably well kept from the public considering the number of people at the Porte who knew of it. The Greek minister learned of it, probably from one of the Sultan's physicians, on June 21 and the Russians apparently knew about it at least by July 3. Layard, Tels., Personal and Secret, June 21 and No. 643, July 3, 1878 (F. O., 363/2); and *Mem.*, VII, fos. 99-101. See mention of Cyprus in *John Bull*, June 29, 1878, p. 412; and *Times*, July 4, 1878, p. 5.

[37] Cross to Salisbury, Tel. at 6.25 P. M., July 8, 1878 (F. O., 78/2901). Cf. Cecil, II, 294; and Monypenny and Buckle, II, 1215. The Congress was quite excited over the news of the Convention. See Hohenlohe, II, 230; and Radowitz, II, 57.

[38] Cf. Bareilles, *op. cit.*, p. 119; Raschdau, *loc. cit.*, p. 373; and *Grosse Politik*, III, 3-4.

it is difficult to say what." [39] The two elderly men began their discussions on July 7 and concluded them on the 9th when Beaconsfield believed that he had obtained the desired rectification of frontiers and the promise that Batoum would be an "exclusively" commercial port. [40]

At the meeting of the Congress on that day, however, it appeared that Gorchakov had persuaded Beaconsfield to accept "essentiellement" in place of "exclusivement" as an adjective describing the character of the port of Batoum. Furthermore, a misunderstanding arose in regard to the boundaries agreed upon, for Beaconsfield and Gorchakov each produced maps upon which the frontier line differed and swore that the other had agreed to it. Lord Salisbury believed that Gorchakov had taken advantage of Beaconsfield who was ignorant of detail and nearly exhausted by an attack of asthma and even Shuvalov admitted that the English had been done, although he professed himself unable to help. [41] At Bismarck's suggestion the matter was referred to a committee in which the neutral members, disgruntled by the Cyprus Convention, voted for a compromise between the two lines presented by the English and the Russian plenipotentiaries. [42] Thus, in part because of

[39] Beaconsfield to Tenterden, Private, Berlin, July 2, 1878 (F. O., 363/1). The Germans at the Congress noted that Beaconsfield and Salisbury did not always agree and the latter told Münster that he wanted the Prime Minister to go to the Congress in order to help bear the responsibility for the concessions which would have to be made to Russia. Raschdau, *op. cit.*, pp. 371 and 373-74; Hohenlohe, II, 217; and *Grosse Politik*, II, 334.

[40] Monypenny and Buckle, II, 1210. Public opinion in England had been as much aroused over the frontier question which was regarded as important for the safety of the route to India, as over Batoum, and the fate of the Armenians had also been discussed. See *Times,* June 6, p. 4; June 11, p. 9; June 13, p. 6; July 1, p. 9; July 2, pp. 5 and 8; July 4, p. 9; July 5, p. 8; July 6, p. 13; July 8, p. 10; and July 11, 1878, p. 10. Cf. 3 Hans. CCXL, 1243-46; and Monypenny and Buckle, II, 1207-09.

[41] Bertie to Tenterden, Private, [Berlin], July 9, 1878 (F. O., 363/1); Monypenny and Buckle, II, 1209-10; and Cecil, II, 291-93.

[42] Salisbury to F. O., Tel. No. 30, July 10, 1878 (F. O., 78/2901); Hanotaux, IV, 356-58; Hohenlohe, II, 228-31. Bismarck's story of his intervention on the Batoum question, when he declared that he had compelled the English to allow Russia to retain it, is a little difficult to place in the chronology of the

the Cyprus Convention and in part because of Gorchakov's determination to outdo Beaconsfield, the English lost the two points for which they had been contending since the beginning of discussion, the exclusively commercial character of the port of Batoum and the retention of the Mohammedan Lazes by Turkey.

This outcome of the Asiatic boundary question undoubtedly confirmed Salisbury in his desire to make the declaration regarding the Straits which the cabinet had earlier approved and which he had apparently rejected on July 5 when it appeared that Russia would concede what England wanted. Explaining that Russia's decision to keep Batoum brought about a new state of affairs in the Black Sea and that any fortification of Batoum could only be regarded as a menace in fact if not in intention to the Bosphorus, he declared in Congress on July 11, that England must be free from any engagement which might prevent her in case of need from taking necessary measures of precaution. Summarizing the arguments which he had drawn up for the cabinet regarding the defects of the existing Treaties, he gave notice that England would henceforth consider herself bound only toward the Sultan in accepting the renewal of the stipulations of the Treaty of 1841, confirmed in 1856 and 1871, and would not take any obligation toward another power which would prevent her, if it seemed necessary, to order her fleet through the Straits in case

negotiations but his reference to Beaconsfield's illness makes it fit the period of the 9th and 10th rather than the earlier days. See Bismarck, *Die Gesammelten Werke*, VIII, 323, and IX, 21. Simmons tells a different story regarding the maps from the current one. He says that Shuvalov declared that at London he had misunderstood the telegraphic instructions sent to him and drew the wrong line for the agreement with Salisbury, but since he had agreed to it, he would stick to it. Simmons to Odo Russell, Berlin, July 11, 1878 (F. O., 78/2893). The exact wording of the Treaty article regarding the Asiatic boundary was finally settled on July 12 between Salisbury, Shuvalov and Mehemet Ali and the protocol of July 10 was changed to fit the wording of that of July 12. Simmons to Sir Julian Pauncefote, Sept. 10, 1879, and to Tenterden, May 10, 1880 (F. O., 363/2). Cf. Hohenlohe, II, 232-33.

the independence of the Sultan was menaced.[43] This declaration, together with Shuvalov's announcement on the next day that Russia considered the closure of the Straits to be a European concern and an obligation taken not only toward the Sultan but toward the European powers as well, thus found its way into the protocols and proved to be the basis for mistrust and alarm in the future.

The only other matters dealt with in the latter days of the Congress in which England took a special interest were those of Turkey's Persian boundaries and Armenian reforms. It was agreed that Khotour and its territory should be ceded by the Porte to Persia with exact boundaries to be determined by an Anglo-Russian commission. Turkey's obligation by the 16th Article of San Stefano to institute reforms in Armenia was changed to an engagement with all the powers and a promise to report to them from time to time on the measures taken.[44] After the reaction in Turkey to the *Globe* publication and the part taken by the English plenipotentiaries in the transfer of Bosnia and Herzegovina to Austrian rule, it could scarcely be expected that Beaconsfield and Salisbury would take the further risk of actively championing the claims of Greece to a great extension of territory and they accordingly left the leading role in this matter to France.[45]

In fact the publication of the Salisbury-Shuvalov agreements and the fear of an inopportune revelation of the Cyprus Convention had hung like dark clouds over the English plenipotentiaries. Up to the 28th of June they were on the whole fairly successful in all that they had undertaken to do. After that the attitude of the Turks, taken as a result of the agree-

---

[43] Protocol No. 18, *loc. cit.*, p. 1070; and "Batoum, declaration as to passage of the Straits" (F. O., 78/2911). This document is the final French version of the memorandum which Salisbury submitted to the cabinet on June 26. While there is nothing on this copy to indicate that it was read to the Congress, there is every reason to believe from the short summary in the protocol and the position of the document in the papers that it was.

[44] Articles LX and LXI, Treaty of Berlin, *British and Foreign State Papers*, LXIX, 766.

[45] Monypenny and Buckle, II, 1207; and 1 *Doc. Dip. Franç.*, II, 350-52.

ments with Russia and Austria, and the attitude of the Russians and the neutral powers after the announcement of the agreement with Turkey, hampered the fulfillment of England's desires in connection with Asia. Except for the Straits declaration which was of dubious value, England obtained a little less than Beaconsfield and Salisbury had hoped to secure. Moreover, the occupation of Cyprus on July 12 and the signature of the Treaty of Berlin on July 13 meant not the end, but the beginning of increased anxiety and responsibility for Lord Beaconsfield and Lord Salisbury. They had to face irritation among the friendly powers, disgruntled supporters and a critical opposition at home, and the vexatious problems involved in the application of a policy which meant a virtual protectorate over Asiatic provinces that were at the same time possessions of a recalcitrant Turkey, and borderlands of a bad-humored Russia ready to use whatever weapons she could find against the chief author of her disappointments.

Aside from Russia the European nations which most resented the Cyprus Convention were Italy and France.[46] Lord Salisbury had not forewarned the Italian plenipotentiary, Count Corti, of England's policy as he had Waddington, and the unfortunate Count feared that he would be turned out of office on his return home if he did not anticipate such action by resignation. The Italians at the Congress resented the fact that they had obtained nothing, even more than that England had taken Cyprus.[47] Popular feeling in Italy also turned against Beaconsfield because he took such pains in his address in Parliament to speak of France in most friendly terms while he did not even mention Italy. Since the real disappointment

---

[46] Cf. Cecil, II, 294-95; Monypenny and Buckle, II, 1216-17; Buckle, *Victoria*, II, 628-29; Ponsonby, *op. cit.*, p. 165; É. Bourgeois and G. Pagès, *Les Origines et les Résponsibilités de la Grande Guerre* (Paris, 1921), p. 191; and *Times*, July 9, p. 10; July 10, p. 5; and July 11, 1878, p. 5.

[47] Salisbury to Lyons, Tel. No. 3 C. S., Berlin, July 10, 1878 (F. O., 363/2); and Bertie to Tenterden, Private, Berlin, July 14, 1878 (F. O., 363/1). It is interesting to note that Salisbury definitely warned the Italians that England would not countenance any attempt on their part to secure the Trentino. Salisbury to Paget, Tel. No. 2 C. S., Berlin, June 21, 1878 (F. O., 78/2908).

for them, however, was Austria's occupation of Bosnia, resentment toward England was quickly swallowed up in the agitation over *Italia Irredenta*.[48]

The French were not so easily placated. Waddington admitted that he was very much affected by the news of the Convention despite Salisbury's explanations of the limitations by which the arrangement was surrounded.[49] His excitement was nothing compared to the outburst of the radical press of Paris. Gambetta's organ, the *République Française*, declared that England had fired a diplomatic pistol shot which would reverberate around the world but would not enhance her renown in view of the way she had gone back on principles enunciated in the April 1st circular. It was already sufficient for England to control Gibraltar and Malta and perhaps too much that she should direct the destinies of Asia Minor from Cyprus. The French plenipotentiaries should not sanction the Convention and if it were not submitted to Congress, they should consider whether or not they could sign the final acts of the Congress with safety. Though other papers such as the *Journal des Débats,* perhaps as a result of official inspiration, argued that it was better to have Russia confronted in Asia Minor by a politically and commercially liberal power such as England than to be left unrestricted, Lyons was so alarmed by the tone of the press that he telegraphed Salisbury on July 10 to hurry the signature of the final act lest Waddington be instructed to come home without signing the Treaty. In answer to a question from Salisbury, Lyons reported that such a proposal was likely to come from Gambetta but that Marshal MacMahon and the ministers were disposed to let Waddington act on his own initiative.[50]

---

[48] MacDonald, Tel. No. 2, Rome, July 10, 1878 (F. O., 78/2908) ; 1 *Doc. Dip. Franç.,* II, 369; and C. Grove Haines, *The Irredentist Movement and Italian Foreign Policy, 1866-82* (MS. Thesis, Clark University Library), fos. 191-208.

[49] 1 *Doc. Dip. Franç.,* II, 352-53. Cf. Hanotaux, IV, 386; and Charles de Moüy, *Souvenirs et Causerie d'un Diplomate* (Paris, 1909), 85-86.

[50] Lyons to Salisbury, Desp. No. 549 and Tel., Paris, July 10; Desp. No. 556 and Tel., Paris, July 11, 1878 (F. O., 78/2908). Cf. Newton, II, 151-52 ; *Gazette*

In view of the excitement in France it was fortunate that the English had a man of Waddington's stolid "bourgeois" temperament to deal with.[51] His only immediate move was to ask Salisbury to put his private letter of July 6 into the form of a despatch which could be published. This was done with slight alterations of wording and the changing of the date to the 7th, after Waddington's approval had been secured on July 20th. But at the same time he had discussed with Salisbury the compensation which France might seek and had been assured that England would have no objection if France should take Tunis.[52] After his return to Paris, Waddington, impressed perhaps as he had not been while at the Congress, by public opinion, desired to secure confirmation of these views from Lord Salisbury in a form which might be made public. He told Lyons that if the French Chambers had been in session when the news of the Cyprus Convention first reached Paris, he thought it would have led to war or something very like war between France and England. Happily they would not meet for three more months and if the proper steps were taken before that time the bad feeling might pass away and indeed a close and cordial understanding between the two countries might be established. One of the steps which he proposed was the placing of Salisbury's assurances in regard to Tunis, Egypt and Syria, in a written, official, and binding form, so that they could be produced if necessary. He was about to

---

de France, quoted in *Annual Register,* 1878, pp. 78-79; and *Times,* July 10, p. 5 and July 11, 1878, p. 5. Cf. Egerton, *op. cit.,* p. 282.

[51] Bertie wrote privately to Tenterden on June 23 (F. O., 363/1): "The Berliners like Waddington; he is, they say, 'so burgerlich', and that he is." Cf. Newton, II, 145-48; Cecil, II, 280; Monypenny and Buckle, II, 1199; and E. Hippeau, *Histoire Diplomatique de la Troisième Republique* (Paris, 1889), pp. 165-67.

[52] Salisbury to Lyons, Tel. No. 4 C. S., July 10, 1878 (F. O., 78/2908); and Lyons, Tel. No. 24, Paris, July 20, 1878 (F. O., 27/2311). For the letter to Waddington, see *Parl. Papers,* C. 2138, pp. 1-2, and extract in Newton, II, 149-50. For the discussions at Berlin, see Cecil, II, 332-35; Newton, II, 154-59; 1 *Doc. Dip. Franç.,* II, 361-67 and W. L. Langer, "The European Powers and the French Occupation of Tunis, 1878-1881," *American Historical Review,* XXXI (October 1925), 55-78.

write a despatch to London for this purpose and hoped that Salisbury would answer it cordially and without delay in order to enable him to contend with the anger which was rife in Paris.

Waddington went beyond this, however, and emphasized to Lyons the necessity for Anglo-French co-operation not only in Egypt and the East, but also in Western Europe. If things were properly managed he hoped to put an end to the existing irritation and also "to proceed to the establishment of a close union, and indeed a virtual alliance, between the two countries." The time was coming, he explained, when a close union between England and France would be essential to the vital interests of both. While he did not believe that either Holland or Belgium were in any danger from Germany at the moment, because Bismarck was anxious to preserve peace in order to devote his whole attention to internal affairs, this situation would not last forever and the time might not be far off when the safety of Holland and Belgium might depend upon the conviction in other countries that France and England were united in defending them. On the other hand, the success of England's task in the East would be immensely promoted by the support of France whose ill-will would of itself create great difficulties for her. His final argument for a close understanding was that public opinion, if not brought round to England, would "eagerly call for an alliance with Russia," and, Waddington pointed out, there was no reason to suppose that Russia would be insensible of the advantages to her from such an alliance.[53]

On July 21, Waddington sent two despatches to London in one of which he recorded the assurances of Beaconsfield and Salisbury that England had no intention of changing the existing state of affairs in Egypt and Syria and would respect French traditions and interests in both regions, and in the other he reported their suggestions that France take Tunis as com-

[53] Lyons, Desp. No. 572, Paris, July 19, 1878 (F. O., 27/2311).

pensation for England's acquisition of Cyprus.[54] Although Salisbury took no exception to the first of the despatches, he was not eager to have his conversations about Tunis made public nor have it made to appear, as Waddington did, that the English government had offered Tunis to France.[55] The French Foreign Minister accordingly modified the wording of this despatch and promised not to publish it, but left it with the English government as a *procès verbal* in order to establish an engagement with them.[56]

Meanwhile the Prince of Wales helped to sooth Gambetta's feelings and the tone of the French press became calmer. Nevertheless Lyons continued to worry over the bitterness still in evidence and professed to fear that a real danger might exist in the desire of many to spring "a surprise on England" by seizing some island in the Mediterranean such as Chios, Rhodes or Crete. On the other hand, many Frenchmen, he believed, hoped that the influence which the Cyprus Convention would give England in Turkey would tend to secure the interests of bondholders and that the reforms in Asia Minor would create new and important outlets for French trade and enterprise. Also, following the same line of reasoning as Waddington, many regarded the East as a secondary matter compared to the problems of the West, where it was hoped that England would also exercise some influence. Lord Lyons was obviously attempting to support Waddington's plea for some assurances which could be published if necessary in order to quiet opposition to the government.[57]

Salisbury complied with the wishes of the French government by confirming Waddington's despatch concerning Egypt and Syria and publishing these notes, together with his letter of July 6, on August 15, although he avoided an official pro-

---

[54] 1 *Doc. Dip. Franç.*, II, 363-67.

[55] *Ibid.*, pp. 369-70; Newton, II, 157-59; and Buckle, *Victoria*, II, 634-35.

[56] 1 *Doc. Dip. Franç.*, II, 370-73.

[57] Lyons, Desp. No. 617, Paris, August 6, 1878 (F. O., 27/2312). For the Prince of Wales and Gambetta, see Newton, II, 156-57; and Sir Sidney Lee, *King Edward VII* (New York, 1925), I, 366-68.

nouncement regarding Tunis. He further set Waddington's mind at rest, however, in private conversations with him early in September when the latter declared that France made no claims on Asiatic Turkey and would entirely support any policy which England might pursue there. French jealousy of England in the Near East was thus declared to be ended, but the fundamental elements of friction caused by the Cyprus Convention and the policy which it represented were by no means removed.[58]

While these negotiations were in progress with Waddington, Lord Salisbury and Lord Beaconsfield returned home to jubilant and well-staged party receptions and the measured and sometimes bitter criticism of the opposition. In Parliament and banquet halls they defended the Treaty of Berlin and the Convention with Turkey by means of the arguments coined in the weeks of diplomatic conflict with Russia over the San Stefano treaty. As to their future policy in Asiatic Turkey and their plans concerning Cyprus, they and their colleagues in Parliament contented themselves with generalizations and hopes, for indeed no details had as yet been agreed upon.

In regard to the Treaty of Berlin, the government took the attitude that the objections to the Treaty of San Stefano which were enumerated in Salisbury's circular of April 1 had been satisfactorily removed and that peace had been preserved without the cost of further bloodshed.[59] Lord Hammond correctly gauged the debates when he wrote that the Treaty of Berlin was "generally accepted as, with all its shortcomings, the best that could be done under the circumstances." [60] The

[58] *Parl. Papers*, C. 2138 (Turkey No. 48, 1878); Salisbury to Layard, Private, October 29, 1878 (Add. MS. 39,138, fos. 166-69; and published in extract in Cecil, II, 332). Cf. 1 *Doc. Dip. Franç.*, II, 383-86 and 388-90.

[59] Salisbury to H. M.'s Principal Secretary of State, Berlin, July 13, 1878 (*Parl. Papers*, C. 2081); Beaconsfield in the Lords, 3 Hans. CCXLI, 1753-74. Cf. Monypenny and Buckle, II, 1221-26; Cecil, II, 297-301; Henry W. Lucy, *Diary of Two Parliaments* (London, 2nd Ed., 1885), pp. 440-45; and Thompson, II, 478-81.

[60] Hammond to Layard, Private, July 20, 1878 (Add. MS. 38,956, fo. 138). Cf. Dilke, 3 Hans. CCXLII, 560; and *Edinburgh Rev.*, CXLVIII (Oct. 1878), 564.

principal points brought out in discussion were that the result constituted a partition of Turkey disguised very thinly by Beaconsfield's phrase "redistribution of territory"; that the Greeks had not been properly supported by England at the Congress; and that the government's method of achieving its ends was a secret and unconstitutional one and therefore discreditable to England's past professions and her honor.[61]

The first of these was made by both Conservatives and Liberals, the former still harboring regretful memories of a Turkey once in possession of such provinces as Bosnia, Bulgaria, and Bessarabia, and such ports as Batoum and Varna, and the latter rejoicing that so much territory had been taken from the Sultan. As Sir William Harcourt declared: "I will not quarrel about words, nor use the term 'partition'; but no one can say that the breaking up of the Turkish Empire has not been effected by the Treaty of Berlin." He went on to explain that this result was what the Liberals had been fighting for since 1876.[62] The trump cards of the Liberals were, however, that England had abandoned Greece and that the government had negotiated secret agreements behind the backs of Parliament and friendly powers. These criticisms were answered ably if not always conclusively by reference to England's actual commitments to Greece and the history of her diplomacy in connection with the East since 1829.[63] The opposition also frequently attempted to make political capital of

[61] See 3 Hans. CCXLI, 1774 ff., and CCXLII, 344 ff., 527 ff., 644 ff., 871 ff., and 998 ff. Among the best of the discussions of Berlin in either House was that of Lord Derby, *idem*, CCXLI, 1787-92. Cf. Thompson, II, 481-89.

[62] 3 Hans. CCXLII, 1071-76; and Monypenny and Buckle, II, 1220-23. Cf. 3 Hans. CCXLI, 1830-31; Clayden, *op. cit.*, pp. 426-28; Thompson, II, 486; M. E. Grant Duff, "Echoes of the Late Debate," *Nineteenth Century*, IV (Sept. 1878), 480-82; and H. L. Walters, *An Open Letter Addressed to the English Nation* (London, 1878), 25 pp.

[63] For Greece, see 3 Hans. CCXLI, 1775 (Granville), 1973 (Hartington resolution); CCXLII, 531-34 (Hartington), 562-66 (Dilke), 357-59 (Salisbury), 553-55 (Plunkett), and *passim*. Grant Duff thought the government held its own on this question, *op. cit.*, *Nineteenth Century*, IV, 482. On the issue of secrecy, see 3 Hans. CCXLII, 345-51 (Roseberry), 352-57 (Salisbury), 359-66 (Carnarvon), 536-37 (Hartington), 668-69 (Sandon), 687-89 (Gladstone).

the government's claims to successful peacemaking by asserting that whatever was good in the Treaty of Berlin was the result of Russia's activities and the Treaty of San Stefano, and that the same results could have been achieved a year earlier when the Tsar communicated his proposed peace terms. Supporters of the government met these charges with the claim that the Liberals had carried on subversive propaganda which weakened the unity of British policy and belittled the great destiny of the British Empire.[64]

The heaviest guns were brought into operation on both sides over the issues raised by the Cyprus Convention although here too, despite the obligations of party loyalty and the personal triumphs of Beaconsfield and Salisbury, the arrangement was looked upon "with the same suspicion, distrust and apprehension in the Conservative as well as the Liberal ranks."[65] The vagueness of the government in regard to the nature of the obligations entered into, the geographical characteristics of the new acquisition and the policy to be pursued in Cyprus and Asia Minor was partly responsible for this feeling.[66] In general the issues in the parliamentary and press debates resolved themselves into three main divisions: Was England's promise to protect Turkey against Russia a necessary and a wise policy? Was Cyprus valuable because of its position and its fitness for a military and naval station? Was Turkey's promise to reform worth anything and was England justified in assuming the burden of responsibility for the carrying out of reforms in Asiatic Turkey?

The government based its defense of the Cyprus Convention on the premises that for the sake of the Indian Empire, Russia

[64] 3 Hans. CCXLI, 1778 (Granville); CCXLII, 587 (Grant Duff), 873-75 (Lowe), 717; Salisbury at Knightsbridge, July 27, quoted by Thompson, II, 482. Cf. Argyll, II, 201-02; *idem, Our Responsibilities for Turkey* (London, 1896), pp. 65-67; and Chéon, *op. cit.*, p. 14.

[65] Hammond to Layard, Private, July 20, 1878 (Add. MS. 38,956, fo. 138). Much of the exuberation over the "peace with honor" was no doubt due to party manipulation. See Cecil, II, 296; and Thompson, II, 478-80.

[66] Cf. Cecil, II, 301; Thompson, II, 492-96; 3 Hans. CCXLII, 912-13 and 1076-79; and *Edinburgh Rev.*, CXLVIII (Oct. 1878), 563.

must be prevented from further encroachments upon Asiatic Turkey and that the Ottoman Porte was too weak to perform that task alone. England's task was therefore to take a position which would enable her better to defend Turkey and to influence the improvement of economic and political conditions in the Asiatic portions of the Sultan's dominions. England was not only to take the responsibility of defending Turkey, which was thrust upon her by her imperial interests and not by the caprice of the government, but also to perform a civilizing influence in a backward region where trade and commerce were to be developed for the benefit of its inhabitants, the Ottoman Empire and the world in general. For both these purposes, Cyprus was excellently situated and admirably adapted, although it was admitted that there were other locations equally good or better which had been avoided out of consideration for the feelings of France.[67] Lord Beaconsfield touched upon all these aspects when he addressed the House of Lords on July 18 and declared: "We do not, my Lords, wish to enter into any unnecessary responsibility; but there is one responsibility from which we certainly shrink; we shrink from the responsibility of handing to our successors a diminished or weakened Empire. . . . In taking Cyprus the movement is not Mediterranean; it is Indian. We have taken a step there which we think necessary for the maintenance of our Empire and for its preservation in peace. If that be our first consideration, our next is the development of the country." [68]

These arguments were repeated and amplified in the press by government supporters among whom the most ardent was the *Times* which had begun to foreshadow a British protectorate over Asiatic Turkey as early as May 27 when, as a result of inspiration no doubt, it declared that England should

[67] Beaconsfield, 3 Hans. CCXLI, 1769-74; Salisbury, *ibid.*, 1804-14; Cranbrook, *ibid.*, 1826-30; Lord Napier and Ettrick, *ibid.*, 1839-43; Salisbury, *idem,* CCXLII, 508-10; Bourke, *ibid.*, 599-603; Sandon, *ibid.*, 664-72; and Northcote, *ibid.*, 1106-14. Cf. Cecil, II, 301-04.

[68] 3 Hans. CCXLI, 1772-73. Cf. Monypenny and Buckle, II, 1224-28.

exert a regulative authority over Turkey's administration of
her remaining territories and thus place a bar to her further
disintegration.[69] While recognizing the grave responsibilities
assumed by the country in the Cyprus Convention, the *Times*
nevertheless insisted that they were necessary and explained in
commenting upon the Prime Minister's pledge of "peace with
honor" and revived prosperity, that "the boldness which has
designed our new policy must be supplemented by sustained
patience, energy, and carefulness; but, with a due exercise
of these qualities, there is every reason to hope that the aspirations expressed in Lord Beaconsfield's brief speech of yes-
terday will be realized."[70] The *Times* had less to say, however, about the fitness of Cyprus for the purposes which the
government had in mind than many other writers, although a
lively correspondence was carried on in its columns regarding
the harbors, climate and strategic value of the island, and the
editors remarked that Cyprus would be "an admirable naval
station, whether for the purpose of protecting the Suez Canal,
securing a second road to India, or giving this country the
requisite authority in its relations with the Porte."[71]

Other journals which accepted the policy adopted by the
government because they felt it to be inevitable, did so with
obvious regret. The *Pall Mall Gazette's* comment on the Anglo-
Turkish Convention was: "It is no triumph, and only a gain
in one sense: without it, the prestige and power of England
in the East would have gone down to nought offhand." The
same paper interpreted Beaconsfield's speech of July 18 in a
pessimistic vein and concluded: "The substance of it is that
French and Italian jealousies on the one hand, and the sovereign dignity of the Sultan on the other, paralyze the hope that

---

[69] *Times,* May 27, 1878, p. 9. Cf. 3 Hans. CCXL, 767; and *Pall Mall Gazette,* June 1, 1878, p. 3.

[70] *Times,* July 17, 1878, p. 9. Cf. *ibid.,* July 9, p. 9; July 11, p. 9; July 12, p. 9; July 18, p. 9; July 19, p. 10; and August 3, pp. 9-10.

[71] *Times,* July 10, 1878, p. 9. For correspondence, see *Times,* July 13, p. 12; July 15, p. 6; July 16, p. 11; July 18, p. 6; July 20, p. 8; July 22, p. 8; July 24, p. 5; July 26, p. 8; Aug. 1, p. 4; Aug. 2, p. 11; Aug. 30, p. 3; and Sept. 5, p. 11.

the convention will be anything better than what it must be without large rights of control in Asiatic Turkey—an unguarded and uncompensated peril." [72] *Blackwood's Magazine* also emphasized the magnitude of Great Britain's Near Eastern task which overwhelmed for a time the satisfaction felt at the conclusion of "a peace so honourable to this country that it amounts to a bloodless yet decisive victory." They admitted along with all other good party men that the policy of the government was a necessary one and that "the protectorate which we have assumed over Asia Minor, with the serious efforts which it may entail on the next generation, and the liability to military warfare which it may involve, represents the price at which war has been averted." [73]

The majority of the pamphleteers who rushed into the market with their historical sketches of Cyprus or their interpretations of the government's policy followed the glowing accounts and fulsome praise of the *Times* rather than the doubtful comments of the more independent Conservative editors. Edward Cazalet who was nominally a Liberal, declared that the Cyprus Convention was "an indispensable complement of the changes sanctioned by the Congress of Berlin, . . . the keystone of the arch, without which that work must forthwith have tumbled to pieces." [74] An anonymous writer who may well have been inspired by Colonel Home, if he was not that gentleman himself, asserted that Great Britain would gain "strategically and commercially, as well as from a political, a moral and a naval point of view," by holding Cyprus. [75] The

---

[72] *Pall Mall Gazette,* July 9, 1878, pp. 1-2; and July 19, pp. 1-2.

[73] "The Treaties of Peace," *Blackwood's Magazine,* CXXIV (Aug. 1878), 238. Cf. *ibid.,* pp. 157 and 258.

[74] Edward Cazalet, *The Berlin Congress and the Anglo-Turkish Convention* (London, 1878), p. 24. Cf. *idem,* pp. 7-12 and 29-31; "England in the Levant," *Edinburgh Rev.,* CXLVIII (Oct. 1878), 578.

[75] *Cyprus: its Value and Importance to England* (Manchester, n.d.), pp. 3-4. On the strategic value of Cyprus, cf. "Treaties of Peace," *loc. cit.,* p. 245; B. Harris Cowper, *Cyprus: its Past, Present and Future* (London, 1878), pp. 24-25; R. Hamilton Lang, *Cyprus* (London, 1878), pp. 197-98; Sir S. W. Baker, *Cyprus as I Saw it in 1879* (London, 1879), p. xiv; F. T. Gammon, *Cyprus*

same author in harmony with the majority of those who up-
held the government likewise declared: "With Constantinople
now easily accessible to us, we shall be able to take the place
of Russia, and possess over the Councils of the Porte a preponderating authority. It will thus be in our power to see those
reforms carried out in Asiatic Turkey, which it is desirable
should be accomplished if we are to undertake the guardianship of the Ottoman Empire in that part of its possessions."[76]

On the other hand, the opposition in Parliament attacked
the Cyprus Convention on the grounds that it was unnecessary
to assume the obligation of protecting Asiatic Turkey from
Russian encroachment in order to protect India or the route
to it, and that such a policy was unwise because England would
assume a responsibility both difficult and costly to fulfill and
expose herself to attack from Russia on the new frontier of
Asiatic Turkey where Russia would have all the advantages
both of geographical proximity and the choice of the time of
attack.[77] Cyprus, they believed, was badly situated and un-
suitable for aiding England to defend Turkey. Granville even
made the startling assertion that he did not know a single
naval officer who had not pronounced against it as a naval

(London, 1878), pp. 8-9; Cazalet, *op. cit.*, p. 22; E. B. Eastwick, letter to the
Editor, *Times,* July 17, 1878, p. 8; Ex-Consul General, *The Occupation of
Cyprus* (London, 1878), pp. 3-4.

[76] *Cyprus: its Value and Importance to England*, pp. 4-5. There was a good
deal of talk of England's commercial and "civilizing" mission in the East. See
É. de Laveleye, "Two Foreign Opinions on the Treaty of Berlin," *Fortnightly
Rev.*, XXX (Nov. 1878), 624-25; Lang, *op. cit.*, pp. 198-99; *Cyprus, Syria, and
Palestine* (London, 1878), pp. 39-40; Rev. Richard M. A. Glover, *Cyprus*
(London, 1878), pp. 19-20; Theta, *The Secret of Cyprus and our Eastern
Protectorate* (London, n.d.), 8 pp.; J. J. Lake, *Ceded Cyprus* (London, 1878),
p. 4; *Cyprus and Asiatic Turkey* (London, 1878), p. vi; and R. S. Poole,
"Cyprus: its Present and Future," *Contemporary Rev.*, XXXIII (Aug. 1878),
137-54.

[77] Granville, 3 Hans. CCXLI, 1784-86; Derby, *ibid.*, 1795-1802; Hammond,
idem, CCXLII, 25-26; Carnarvon, *ibid.*, 364-66; Dilke, *ibid.*, 568-69; Hartington, *ibid.*, 543-47. Some members of Parliament emphasized especially the
great expense which the obligation to protect Turkey would entail. Cf. *ibid.*,
883-84, 907-08, 918, 920, 928, 938, 957-58, 974-75, 1025 and 1555-64.

station.[78] Furthermore, England's policy would arouse the jealousy and opposition of Russia and the Mediterranean powers who would inevitably resent her assumption of a virtual protectorate over the Asiatic possessions of the Sultan, which England would be compelled to assume if she really intended to make the Sultan carry out the reforms he had promised to introduce.[79]

Questions and issues raised by the government's critics regarding the geographical characteristics of Cyprus, the method of reform in Turkey and of military plans for protecting her brought little light from ministers and helped to produce the impression that the government had entered somewhat blindly into a policy whose outcome they had not squarely faced and which was likely to lead either to a tremendous expenditure of effort and money or to a complete sham. Lord Kimberley anticipated Gladstone's judgment that the Convention was an "insane covenant" when he declared "I cannot help thinking that this country has been embarked upon a policy more rash, more dangerous, and less well considered and more likely to lead to disaster than any I remember in our past history." [80] Finally, as in the case of the negotiations leading to the Treaty of Berlin, the government was attacked for straining the prerogative rights of the crown in entering into such an engagement without the sanction of Parliament and for dis-

---

[78] 3 Hans. CCXLII, 24. Cf. *idem*, CCXLI, 1794-95, 1817-20, 1822; and CCXLII, 538-39, 588-89, 881-85, 928 and 1373. Cf. J. C. McCoan, *Our New Protectorate* (London, 1879), I, 31.

[79] 3 Hans. CCXLI, 1783-84, 1823-26, 1834-37; and CCXLII, 569, 578, 730-31, 742, 881, 1022, 1054 and 1060. Cf. J. L. Farley, *Egypt, Cyprus and Asiatic Turkey* (London, 1878), Ch. 18; and Samuel Laing, "The Convention with Turkey," *Fortnightly Rev.*, XXX (Aug. 1878), 159-74.

[80] Gladstone, quoted in Thompson, II, 489-90; and Kimberley, 3 Hans. CCXLI, 1839. Cf. Forster, *idem*, CCXLII, 1025; Harcourt, *ibid.*, 1079-81; Hartington, *ibid.*, 1121; and Jenkins, *ibid.*, 2088-89. For questions and answers regarding Cyprus, see 3 Hans. CCXLI, 1225-26, 1242-43, 1433-36, 1469-70, 1572-75, 1578-79. Members of the government later admitted that they had been misled as to Cyprus and its condition. See Sir F. Maurice and Sir G. Arthur, *Life of Lord Wolseley* (London, 1924), p. 106.

regarding the public law of Europe by not submitting it to the other powers.[81]

Liberal writers supported the opposition in Parliament as ardently as the *Times* and pamphleteers defended the government. The *Daily News* declared upon the announcement of the Cyprus Convention that it thrust upon Great Britain "a task involving limitless cost, unceasing stress, strain, and danger, a sort of task which, we may fairly say, has never in history been satisfactorily performed, or ended in anything but failure, and that this has been put upon England without her consent, without her knowledge, and in disregard of the settled practices of her constitutional system. . . . We have accepted a tremendous responsibility, without adequate means of fulfilling it, on quite insufficient grounds of policy, and under no urgency of duty."[82] A commentator on the parliamentary debates thought that they constituted "the most destructive body of criticism that ever fell upon any diplomatic arrangement" and thus summarized the result of what he considered to be the territorial hunger aroused by Beaconsfield: "An island, two hundred miles long, ravaged by famine, a nest of malaria, with a fatal fever of which it enjoys a monopoly, without harbours, and possessed of a growing population of lepers, is held by Englishmen adequate consideration for an obligation to spend scores or hundreds of millions in defending an empire which either cannot or will not defend itself."[83]

The parliamentary opposition and Liberal journalists were not the only ones who were dubious of the value of Cyprus

---

[81] 3 Hans. CCXLII, 370-79, 505-06, 559-68, 590-92, 711-19, 936-40 and 1026-28. Cf. H. D. Traill, "The Democracy and Foreign Policy," *Nineteenth Century*, IV (Nov. 1878), 910-24.

[82] July 9 and 11, 1878, quoted in Thompson, II, 477-78.

[83] "A Political Epilogue," *Fortnightly Rev.*, XXX (Sept. 1878), 311-12 and 317. Cf. S. W. Baker, *op. cit.*, pp. xviii-xx, and 436-53; *op. cit., Edinburgh Rev.*, CXLVIII, 583-89; Sir Julian Goldsmid, B. Samuelson, and A. Otway, *Times*, Oct. 24, 1878, p. 10; and Mr. Childers, *ibid.*, Nov. 28, 1878, p. 10. For an excellent summary of the objections raised to the Cyprus Convention, see Cazalet, *op. cit.*, pp. 19-20; and devastating criticisms: W. E. Gladstone, "England's Mission," *Nineteenth Century*, IV (Sept. 1878), 560-84; and Archibald Forbes, "The 'Fiasco' of Cyprus," *ibid.*, IV (Oct. 1878), 609-26.

and the policy which its acquisition represented. Curiously enough, the question of the Straits and Salisbury's declaration attracted very little attention in public discussions; [84] but, in a carefully reasoned memorandum, General Sir Lintorn Simmons showed that the Straits were the important point which Great Britain had to guard in case of difficulties with Russia in Asia and that Cyprus was not well fitted for that purpose. Since England could not take possession of the Dardanelles herself, nor entrust them to another power except Greece, who should be groomed for that office at some future time, she should occupy Stampalia or some other equally well situated Aegean island as a coaling and refitting station from which the Aegean Sea could be blockaded in case of need. The government, moreover, was sufficiently impressed by his arguments to send the fleet on an inspection tour of Aegean islands, but did nothing more. [85]

Other naval and military authorities were divided over the value of Cyprus. General Wolseley who took possession of the island and governed it until replaced by a civilian administrator was reported to believe that the government had been deceived about the value of Cyprus by their advisers, and Admiral Sir William F. Martin wrote a devastatingly critical pamphlet condemning the taking of Cyprus from political and economic as well as strategical points of view. [86] On the other

[84] It was mentioned directly only once in the Parliamentary debates, 3 Hans. CCXLII, 378-79.

[85] Simmons, Memorandum, April 10, 1879, returned to him by Beaconsfield, June 6, 1879 (F. O., 358/1). For the activity of the fleet and the inspection in the summer of 1879 of Milo and Stampalia, see Egerton, *op. cit.*, pp. 318-20.

[86] Wolseley was disappointed with the conditions he found in Cyprus and apparently talked freely about it, but made amends by publishing a letter which he closed by saying: "Laugh at anyone who tells you Cyprus is not going to be a complete success." "Letter from Cyprus," *Macmillan's Magazine*, XXXIX (Nov. 1878), 96; Maurice and Arthur, *op. cit.*, p. 94; Blunt, *op. cit.*, p. 50; and Admiral William F. Martin, *Cyprus as a Naval Station and a Place of Arms* (London, 1879), 12 pp. Cf. the condemnation of Cyprus as a naval and military station, but approval of England's taking it, by the wife of an official under Wolseley, Esme Scott-Stevenson, *Our Home in Cyprus* (London, 1880), pp. 65-66 and 72-73.

hand, Admiral Hornby professed to be "agreeably disappointed" with Cyprus on a visit which he made in the autumn. He found the people satisfied and what was more important as regards Great Britain's political interests, he believed that an excellent harbor could be made at Famagousta at a small expense.[87]

Sir Austen Henry Layard, whose ability and success in obtaining the consent of the Porte to the Cyprus Convention had been immediately rewarded by the G.C.B., was one of the severest critics of the Berlin Treaty and like Simmons was unconvinced of the value of Cyprus although he could scarcely protest against the "protectorate" over Asiatic Turkey which he had done so much to promote. His was the position of those supporters of Beaconsfield who believed that too much had been granted to Russia and that as a result of Berlin, Turkey was dangerously weakened. He laid most of the blame for this state of affairs on the "slovenly and hasty manner" in which all questions which did not involve peace and war were settled because of Bismarck's resolution to "finish in time to let him go to the baths." It was not that England had gone back on her promises to the Sultan, for she had obtained most important modifications of the Treaty of San Stefano "which had placed him, bound hand and foot, at the mercy of Russia" and had done enough at the risk of war to deserve his gratitude; but that the English plenipotentiaries could have obtained more in the interest of England as well as Turkey had they followed a decided course. He believed that they could have retained Batoum and Sofia for Turkey. They made a serious mistake in leaving the war indemnity to be settled between Russia and Turkey and in giving Russia

---

[87] Hornby to the Secretary of the Admiralty, Jan. 20, 1879 (*Parl. Papers,* C. 2224) ; and Egerton, *op. cit.,* pp. 297-300. Cf. Mrs. Annie Brassey, *Sunshine and Storm in the East* (New York, 1880), p. 324; and Thomas Brassey, *Recent Letters and Speeches* (London, 1879), pp. 1-2 and 29. Hornby did not like the idea of taking Cyprus when he first heard of it because he thought it looked "so much like a sharing of spoil with the other robbers." Egerton, *op. cit.,* p. 281.

some right of interference in Armenia by Article LXI. These were but a few of the many instances which, in Layard's opinion, contained the elements of "endless future disturbance and of war." [88] His own position had, moreover, been endangered by the Salisbury-Shuvalov Memorandum and his task rendered much more difficult by the suspicion which it and England's action at the Congress had created.[89]

As regards Cyprus, Layard blew both hot and cold. He believed that the absence of a harbor or port appeared to render it almost useless as a naval station, but fully recognized its importance as commanding the Eastern end of the Mediterranean and being near Egypt and the Suez Canal. He also believed, as did Colonel Home, that its possession might have a considerable moral and material effect upon the Asiatic dominions of the Sultan by helping to develop trade and agriculture in Asia Minor and Syria and affording an example of good government. Yet, it seemed to him that if England's main objects were to advance her political influence and her commerce in the East and at the same time to have a position which would enable her to assist Turkey in checking further advances of Russia in Asia Minor and in carrying out reforms, a port or station on the Persian Gulf would have been of the greatest value and importance.

He still believed that Mohammerah or a position on the right bank of the Shatt-el-Arab, should the former place be impossible to obtain because of Persia's claim to it, would have been the proper places to consider. They would give England control of the Tigris and Euphrates rivers which reached into the heart of the country England wanted to protect and develop, and would furnish easy means of transport for English troops, whereas forces from Cyprus would be compelled

---

[88] Layard, *Memoirs,* VII, fos. 209-14; private letter to Tenterden, July 16, 1878 (F. O., 363/2); and Newton, II, 160. Layard especially deprecated the surrender of Batoum to Russia and enlarged upon its significance in *Memoirs,* VIII, fo. 3.

[89] Layard to Salisbury, Private, July 26, 1878 (Add. MS. 39,131, fos. 128-31); and Layard to Elliot, private, July 26, 1878 (*loc. cit.,* fos. 131-32).

to traverse a long distance over difficult and mountainous country to reach the scene of a possible Russian advance southward. The commercial advantages, he argued, were obvious, considering not only the rich provinces through which the Tigris and Euphrates flowed, but those of Persia reached by the Karoon River which also emptied into the Shatt-el-Arab. The presence of English steamers on these rivers would increase trade and pacify the Arab tribes, and a British position at their outlet would enable England also to command the inevitable Mesopotamian railway which would form one of the alternative routes to India. Finally, whilst the acquisition of Cyprus, "even allowing for the unscrupulous and unpatriotic attempts of the opposition to discredit it," was not altogether understood or acquiesced in by English opinion, "the political and commercial advantages offered by the command of the Tigris and Euphrates would have received the willing and unanimous approval and support of the British nation." [90]

While the "philosophical historian," to whose judgment in the future Gladstone appealed, must admit that such critics as Gladstone, Derby and Layard were more nearly right than Beaconsfield, Salisbury, and their ardent supporters as regards the outcome of the Cyprus policy,[91] he must also point out that they overlooked the chief triumph of the government viewed from the wider angle of European politics. It was from the standpoint of rivalry with Gorchakov and Bismarck that Beaconsfield had most consistently studied the question of the Near East. He had from the first attempted to put England into a commanding position and in this he was more successful

[90] Layard, *Memoirs,* VII, fos. 103-13. Cf. Temperley, *loc. cit.,* pp. 279 and 459-60. Layard shared the belief of many Conservatives that while the acquisition of Cyprus was an experiment and a great responsibility, the policy had been forced upon the government. Letter to G. T. Clark, July 29, 1878 (Add. MS. 38,946, fos. 174-75).

[91] Gladstone in the House of Commons on July 30, 1878, declared: "In my own opinion, the philosophical historian, . . . will say that it is from the councils of statesmen, or councils that are called such, that, upon this occasion, there has proceeded the most extraordinary crop of wild and speculative ideas which were ever grown in the hottest of all the hot-houses of politics." 3 Hans., CCXLII, 700.

than he had been in maintaining the integrity of the Ottoman Empire or in guaranteeing order and tranquillity in her Asiatic provinces, which he declared to be the chief objects of the Cyprus Convention.

Every energetic step from the sending of the fleet through the Dardanelles in January to the calling out of the reserves and the resolution to take some *place d'armes* in the East had been taken when the situation was such that it seemed as if Great Britain would be compelled to yield to a pre-arranged settlement between Russia, Austria, and Germany. It is true that much in the end had been conceded to Russia and to Austria, but the latter had been won over to England's side in the final settlement and with her, Germany. The result was the break-up of the *Dreikaiserbund* and the establishment of Great Britain in a position at the end of the Congress of Berlin which, contrasted with that after the Berlin Memorandum, or at the out-break of the Russo-Turkish War, was indeed a commanding one.[92] While this situation did not directly aid England in the ambitious Asiatic policy to which the Cyprus Convention had committed her, it did indirectly give her a freer hand to work out her policies there than she would otherwise have gained, had she not isolated Russia and won the friendship of Bismarck and Andrassy.

Furthermore the critics of the Cyprus Convention failed to take into account sufficiently the significance which the mere occupation of Cyprus had not only for the conflicts between Russia and England in the Near East, but also for the trend in world politics. As Lord Salisbury declared in the following year, "Men are much more readily persuaded by acts than by words, and therefore we occupied the Island of Cyprus to

---

[92] See an interesting interpretation of the situation by a contemporary, Chéon *(op. cit.,* p. 19) who believed that England prevented the alliance of the three emperors from settling the terms of peace between them and that "Lord Beaconsfield par sa politique belliqueuse, avait forcé les trois empereurs à négocier avec lui," but to the exclusion of France and Italy. Cf. "The Congress," *Blackwood's Magazine,* CXXIV (July 1878), 122; and Monypenny and Buckle, II, 1200. For Beaconsfield's boast that his aim had been to break up the *Dreikaiserbund* and that he had succeeded in it, see Sir Henry Drummond-Wolff, II, 264-65.

show our intention of maintaining our hold in those parts. . . . When the interest of Europe was centered in the conflicts that were waged in Spain, England occupied Gibraltar. When the interest of Europe was centered in the conflicts that were being waged in Italy, England occupied Malta; and now that there is a chance that the interest of Europe will be centered in Asia Minor or in Egypt, England has occupied Cyprus."[93] But such imponderable values as these were not likely to carry much weight with practical men who were all too conscious of the great obstacles to the fulfillment of the Cyprus policy.

No one was more fully aware of the immense difficulties still to be overcome than Salisbury who had borne the major part of the work of salvaging England's interests, so long jeopardized by hesitation and indecision. In reply to Layard's gloomy prognostications regarding the battle which any English Ambassador would now have to wage at Constantinople in consequence of the Berlin Treaty, Salisbury admitted that there would be a constant struggle. "But had we any other choice?" he asked. "Battle there must be—for there are rival interests to satisfy; and we had to choose between an immediate appeal to arms, or postponing, with the chance of avoiding, that arbitrament by substituting for it a protracted diplomatic struggle." The chief difficulty which he foresaw was the problem of Asiatic reform.[94]

In this he was right, although other matters also occupied for a time a prominent place on the stage; and important among them were the Euphrates Valley railway proposals which were connected indirectly with questions of reform and the defense of Turkey and India, as well as directly with that desire to develop trade and commerce upon which much emphasis had been laid in Parliament and the press.

[93] "Lord Salisbury at Manchester," *Times,* Oct. 18, 1879. Cf. H. T. F. Duckworth, *Some Pages of Levantine History* (London, 1906), pp. 12-13; and Sir Charles Dilke, *The Present Position of European Politics* (London, 1887), pp. 327-30.

[94] Salisbury to Layard, Private, July 24, 1878 (Add. MS. 39,138, fo. 55).

CHAPTER IV

THE POLICY APPLIED, 1878–80

IF the explanations of Her Majesty's Ministers as to how they hoped to protect, reform, and develop Asiatic Turkey left something to be desired, journalists, engineers, promoters and members of Parliament supplied the deficiency by pointing out that the building of a Euphrates Valley railway constituted one of the proper methods. The thin and barely trickling stream of opinion, fed between 1872 and the spring of 1878 by such fountain heads of enthusiasm as William P. Andrew, suddenly, upon the announcement of the Cyprus Convention, broadened out into a wide and swift current in favor of railway promotion in Asiatic Turkey.

In the parliamentary debates of July and August there were many speakers who touched upon the subject, either directly or indirectly. While Beaconsfield on July 18 refused to go into the details of how the development of Turkey, which he declared to be the second object in making the Cyprus Convention, was to be accomplished, Granville in his reply asked ". . . what is the course Her Majesty's Government is prepared to take in regard to the Euphrates Valley Railway?" Lord Derby was even more explicit and declared: "Now, my Lords, I come to consider what I am given to understand is the principal object in selecting Cyprus—namely, because it is a station which commands the line of the Euphrates Valley Railway." In the Commons, Hartington spoke of a possible future Euphrates Valley railway in connection with his discussion of British interests in Asia Minor and recalled the conclusions of the committee over which Northcote had presided that while such a railway might be of importance to the Indian government, it was not a paramount necessity.[1]

[1] Beaconsfield, 3 Hans. CCXLI, 1773 and 1769-70; Granville, *ibid.*, 1783; Derby, *ibid.*, 1794; and Hartington, *idem*, CCXLII, 540.

Thus far, no one had done more than give the project notice or utter a few words in deprecation of it. Curiously enough, the strongest advocacy of a railway came from a Liberal. Sir Charles Dilke on July 29 reminded his hearers that he had advocated a line from Constantinople to the Persian Gulf as an alternative route to India when it appeared that English influence in Egypt would not be dominant. Now the situation was somewhat changed, but, he declared "I am favourable to the construction of the Bagdad line, and to that amount of intervention in Asiatic Turkey which is necessary to secure it; and I should contemplate a military occupation of Cyprus and Scanderoon in time of war, in order to provide for the security of our line." A fellow Liberal, Grant Duff, also believed that the building of railways in Asia Minor and Syria was a most desirable thing to encourage, but thought that it "should never be allowed to take off our thoughts from the infinitely more important Egyptian transit." [2]

Government spokesmen, however, remained vague and indefinite whenever they touched upon the question of a railway. Bourke, parliamentary Under-Secretary for Foreign Affairs, would not say whether a railway would or would not be built through the Euphrates Valley, but said that "there were plenty of districts in Asia Minor where railways, if made, would be of great value and importance in opening up the country." The Home Secretary, Cross, emphasized the necessity for assuring peace and security in Asia Minor in order that English and European capital should flow into the country. But the opposition continued to believe that the government was interested in railways and Mr. Lowe declared: "I think it extremely probable that there may be found gentlemen who will induce the Government to make a railway for some 900 miles across that howling desert, with a suitable guarantee from the Government to its friends in the City who agree with the Marquess of Salisbury that trade never flour-

[2] Dilke, 3 Hans. CCXLII, 567-68; and Grant Duff, *ibid.*, 588.

ishes so much as under the influence of an Imperial despotism." [3]

Likewise, in many pamphlets and articles which attempted to describe Cyprus or to explain the policy connected with it, the project of a Euphrates Valley railway received attention either as an explanation and justification of the choice of Cyprus or a step to be taken in defending and developing the new Asiatic protectorate. The *Times* and the *Mail* on July 10 both called attention to the possibility of the government's taking up the scheme for a railway and suggested that Cyprus would command the starting point for it. Cazalet, in a pamphlet written early in August, declared: "England has assumed the protectorate not only of Syria, but of the whole of Turkey in Asia; and that one of the principal reasons which led our Government to adopt this policy was the importance of the Euphrates route to this country, is shown by their choice of Cyprus as a military depot." [4] An anonymous writer talked in much the same strain and declared that Cyprus holds the key of the Gulf of Scanderoon, "which we may look forward to as becoming in a few years a grand and flourishing emporium of the commerce of the Levant." [5] Others echoed the same ideas both in 1878 and for many years later. Such interpretations, moreover, were not confined to England, for a German commentator on the British acquisition of Cyprus declared: "Die kommerzielle Wichtigkeit der Insel wird sich noch mehr heben, wenn von Syriens Küste nach dem Euphrat und Tigris und weiter nach Persien die längst projektirte grosse Bahn führt, die nun ernstlich in Angriff genommen wird." [6]

---

[3] Bourke, *ibid.*, 599; Cross, *ibid.*, 753-54; and Lowe, *ibid.*, 884. Cf. *ibid.*, 921 and 927; and *Times,* July 29, 1878, p. 10.

[4] *Times,* July 10, 1878, p. 9; *Mail,* July 10, p. 4; and Cazalet, *The Berlin Congress and the Anglo-Turkish Convention* (London, 1878), pp. 3-4.

[5] *Cyprus: its Value and Importance to England,* p. 4.

[6] A. Rauchhaupt, "Cypern," *Grenzboten*, II, 1 (1878), 192. For other references to the government's choice of Cyprus because of its connection with a possible Euphrates railway, see Paris Correspondent, *Times,* July 10, 1878, p. 5; *Edinburgh Rev.*, CXLVIII (Oct. 1878), 584; E. C. Blount, *Memoirs,* edited by S. J. Reid (New York, 1902), pp. 108-09; S. S. Cox, *Diversions of a*

It was undoubtedly the recollection of former dreams and the natural drift of British speculation, set in motion by the prospect of peace in the Near East, which caused the Cyprus Convention to be connected in the public mind with railway enterprises in Asiatic Turkey. As Mrs. Joyner remarked: "Again must Cyprus bear a prominent position in the eyes of the World. For many years eminent statesmen, soldiers, and engineers have been proclaiming the advisability of making Cyprus the point through which that grand scheme, the Euphrates Valley Railway, soon we hope to be a reality, would receive its principal source of traffic, and forming it into the terminal station of a line of railway and steamers destined to chain us more firmly to our Indian possessions, and to open again the long deserted or neglected land that lies between it and the Persian Gulf." [7]

More than three weeks before the Cyprus Convention was announced, Sir Frederick J. Goldsmid, who had seen service in the Crimea, India and China and had directed the building of the telegraph line across Persia in 1864, addressed the United Service Club on the subject of "Communications with British India." After discussing the history of Russian and British projects for railways to the East, he proposed that Great Britain inaugurate "operations for urgent overland communications with India by establishing a depot, for men and materials both, at the Island of Cyprus." This done, work should commence at once on a railroad from some point on the Mediterranean to Koweit on the Persian Gulf and thence to Kurachi in India. He thought that such a line would not only furnish a more rapid means of communication with India, but also would help to develop the country. On this last point, objections were raised at the meeting and in the *Times,* and the discussion showed that there was little unanimity of opinion in regard to the value of a Euphrates Valley railway,

Diplomat in Turkey (New York, 1887), p. 627; Franz von Löher and Mrs. A. B. Joyner, *Cyprus, Historical and Descriptive* (London, 1878), pp. 269-71; and B. Haughton, *A Railway to India* (Privately printed, 1879), p. 4.

[7] Löher and Joyner, *op. cit.,* p. 269.

its practicability, and the route it should follow.[8] Sir Frederick Goldsmid's address, however, helped to prepare the way for the lively discussion of railway building which followed the publication of the Anglo-Turkish agreement.

All the old arguments, familiar since the days of the Chesney Expedition, were then advanced in favor of a railway connecting the Mediterranean and the Persian Gulf. It would open up the "rich resources" of Syria, Mesopotamia, and Asia Minor and thus contribute to the development of trade and to the establishment of order and tranquillity in those backward regions, while it would furnish a short route to India. A writer who signed himself "Ex-Consul General" declared: "Should Colonel Chesney's project of a railway from Tripoli-in-Syria to Bagdad be carried out, a new overland route to India will be opened to England, and the lawless tribes of Central Asia Minor and Syria will be brought under civilized rule. A British protectorate over the Asiatic provinces of the Ottoman Empire must mean good government for the races inhabiting it if it means anything, and must bring in its train great commercial and industrial revival in those distant lands." [9] Another enthusiast believed "that good communications mean good civilization." [10]

It was also argued that the people of the region were most anxious for the construction of roads and railways and would support them.[11] More stress was laid by the advocates of the Euphrates Valley railway upon its usefulness in defending

[8] *Times*, June 17, 1878, p. 6 and (leading article) p. 11. Cf. W. P. Andrew to the Editor, *ibid.*, June 20, p. 10; Kemball to the Editor, *ibid.*, June 21, p. 7; Goldsmid to the Editor, *ibid.*, June 25, p. 11; Blantyre to the Editor, *ibid.*, June 25, p. 11; and Löher and Joyner, *op. cit.*, pp. 269-70.

[9] Ex-Consul General, *Occupation of Cyprus*, p. 4. Cf. *idem*, pp. 5-6.

[10] V. Lovett Cameron, *Our Future Highway* (London, 1880), II, p. 332. See also, "Treaties of Peace," *Blackwood's Magazine*, CXXIV (Aug. 1878), 239-41; "New Routes to India," *ibid.* (Oct. 1878), 490, 494-95; "The Road to India," *Edinburgh Review*, CXLIX (Jan. 1879), 136-38; Grattan Geary to the Editor, *Times*, July 25, 1878, p. 4; J. E. Severne and Sir Baldwin Leighton, *ibid.*, Sept. 26, 1878, p. 4; Theta, *op. cit.*, p. 7; and Consul-General Nixon, Report on Bagdad, 1877-78 (*Parl. Papers*, C. 2088, p. 1353).

[11] Cameron, *op. cit.*, I, 64, and II, 322-23.

both Asiatic Turkey and India from Russia and its necessity as an imperial link and an alternative route between England and her Eastern Empire. Indeed, without this connecting link a protectorate over Asia Minor and Syria, Cazalet asserted, would be a senseless undertaking.[12]

This point of view suggests that many disappointed supporters of the government saw in the proposed railways a means of defending those British interests which they believed the government had failed to safeguard either by the Berlin settlement or the mere acquisition of Cyprus. "But if Cyprus is the first step in a great policy;" to quote Cazalet again, "if it is to form an outpost in connection with a new road to India and the East; if it is to be a basis to enable us to carry out the obligations we have incurred by assuming a protectorate over Asia Minor and Syria, then it may prove the foundation-stone upon which the peace and prosperity of the East may be built up."[13]

To offset the enthusiasm of promoters and imperialists, men of cool judgment like Lord Derby and Admiral Sir William Martin ridiculed the idea of a railway and the value of Cyprus in forming a commercial depot at the Mediterranean terminus. The former declared in the House of Lords: "Now, opinions have differed very much as to the Euphrates Valley Railway.

---

[12] Cazalet, *Berlin Congress,* p. 29. For expositions of the strategic value of a Euphrates Valley railway, see *idem,* pp. 21-22; Löher and Joyner, *op. cit.,* p. 272; *Cyprus, its Value and Importance to England,* pp. 10-13; Grattan Geary, *Through Asiatic Turkey* (London, 1878), II, 288-89; W. P. Andrew, *India and Her Neighbors* (London, 1878), pp. v-viii; "New Routes to India," *loc. cit.,* pp. 485-489 and 493-98; "Treaties of Peace," *loc. cit.,* p. 246; "The Road to India," *loc. cit.,* pp. 126-28 and 138-39; V. L. Cameron, "The Indo-Mediterranean Railway, II, Its Political Aspect," *Macmillan's Magazine,* XLI (Nov. 1879), 33-35; and "Peter the Great and Syria," *Blackwood's Magazine,* CXXVII (May 1880), 565-74. Cf. sixteen "general features" of a Euphrates Valley railway, summarized in W. P. Andrew, *The Euphrates Valley Routes to India* (London, 1882), pp. 52-54.

[13] Cazalet, *England's Policy in the East* (London, 1879), pp. 19-20. Cf. *ibid.,* pp. 18 and 30. Cazalet was primarily interested in developing Syria into a flourishing settlement for Jews. On the possible connections between Zionism and Beaconsfield's interest in this region and Cyprus, see Headlam-Morley, *op. cit.,* pp. 205-07.

I have looked into the question, and, certainly, I have satisfied my mind that a more hopelessly unremunerative undertaking never was set on foot, even by British speculators at the expense of British capitalists." Admiral Martin pointed out that even if "this dreamed-of railway" should ever be built, passengers and goods passing over it would not affect Cyprus which offered no advantage as a stopping place between Europe and Asia.[14] Other critics agreed with Lord Derby concerning the poorness of the investment and also believed that the Suez Canal was a sufficient link with India. The *Fortnightly Review* referred to it as "a possible line of railway to British India, which cannot be constructed except at the most enormous cost, and when constructed will have neither goods nor passengers to carry." [15]

Even among those who favored building the alternative route to India, great differences of opinion existed over the path it should follow. The Select Committee of 1872 had considered five, of which they seemed to favor that running from Alexandretta by way of Aleppo to the Euphrates River and thence down the right bank to Koweit. At the time the report was being presented a civil engineer named Pressel was making preliminary surveys for the Sultan and in his conclusions recommended that the Porte should allow only those railways to be constructed which served the best interests of the Ottoman Empire. The elaborate network of roads and railways which he suggested probably influenced many British and other promoters to consider how their own interests might be made to coincide with those of the Sultan.[16]

[14] 3 Hans. CCXLI, 1794; and Martin, *op. cit.*, p. 10.

[15] "Home and Foreign Affairs," *Fortnightly Rev.*, XXX (Aug. 1878), 310. Cf. 3 Hans. CCXLII, 927; Samuel Laing, "A Plain View of British Interests," *Fortnightly Review*, XXIX (March 1878), 342; and W. S. Blunt, "An Indo-Mediterranean Railway: Fiction and Fact," *ibid.*, XXXII (Nov. 1879), 702-15, especially 704-05.

[16] See Hermann Schmidt, *Das Eisenbahnwesen in der Asiatischen Türkei* (Berlin, 1914), p. 4; and J. L. Haddan to the Editor, *Times,* Aug. 19, 1878, p. 6. A map was published in August, 1878 by Chapman and Hall showing the railway network approved by the Ottoman government. It is published with additional data by J. C. McCoan, *Our New Protectorate: Turkey in Asia* (London, 1879), I. Cf. *idem*, II, 25-27.

In any case, by 1878, five routes in addition to those of 1872 were being suggested for railways in Asiatic Turkey. While most of them ended at some place on or near the Persian Gulf, they differed from one another mainly by their points of departure. Ports all the way from Scutari, opposite Constantinople, to St. Jean d'Acre, including Smyrna, Alexandretta, Tyre, and Sidon were advocated, depending upon what consideration was uppermost in the mind of the promoter or writer, whether ease of construction, natural resources of the region traversed, defense against Russia, or the shortest route to India.[17] Since the Euphrates Valley route could be easily joined with that from Constantinople through Anatolia to Bagdad, the greatest attention was given to these two routes which would at the same time meet the interests of Turkey as shown by the Pressel network and those of England represented by the triangle of Alexandretta, Diarbekir or Mardin in the direction of the Armenian highlands, and the Persian Gulf.

While the discussion of Turkish railways was primarily aroused and carried on by engineers, speculators and imperialists outside the government, many of its agents and advisers were in close touch with the various proposals and brought them to the attention of Her Majesty's Ministers. In addition to Layard, whose championship of railway building in Turkey has already been noted,[18] other men in the diplomatic and consular service urged upon the government the advantages of promoting one or the other of the numerous

---

[17] Löher and Joyner, *op. cit.*, pp. 271-72; Cameron, II, 290-93; C. E. Austin, *The Undeveloped Resources of Turkey in Asia* (London, 1878), pp. 61-68 and 115-23; George E. Dalrymple, *The Syrian Great Eastern Railway to India* (London, 1878), 26 pp.; J. L. Farley, *Egypt, Cyprus and Asiatic Turkey* (London, 1878), Ch. XIII; Grattan Geary, *op. cit.*, II, 275-95; "New Routes to India," *loc. cit.*, pp. 488-92; "The Road to India," *loc. cit.*, pp. 108-24; letters to the *Times*, June 21, 1878, p. 7; June 25, p. 11; July 11, p. 6; July 12, p. 10; July 13, p. 12; July 25, p. 4; Aug. 12, p. 10; Aug. 19, p. 6; Sept. 17, p. 4; and Sept. 19, p. 3; and letters to the *Pall Mall Gazette*, July 9, 1878, p. 5, and July 11, p. 5.

[18] See *ante*, p. Layard again talked to the Sultan about railway building in June, Desp. No. 768, June 12, 1878 (F. O., 78/2791).

projects. Sir Richard Temple, head of the Bombay Government, advocated the Euphrates Valley railway as did Consul-General Nixon at Bagdad.[19] Consuls Gatheral at Angora and Reade at Smyrna emphasized the need for railways connecting the interior of Asia Minor with the capital and with seaports, the latter favoring the idea of making Smyrna the terminus for a line through Persia to India.[20] While there is no direct evidence that General Sir Arnold Kemball who was actively associated with the formation of a railway company in July ever pressed his views upon the government, he was sufficiently close to Beaconsfield to be considered for the post of principal military adviser to the Prime Minister at the Congress of Berlin, and publicly championed a line from the Persian Gulf to Constantinople.[21]

In fact, throughout June and July railway projects were being mooted on all sides, and proposals were at length inevitably made by promoters to the British government. The first to make a definite move were Mr. W. P. Andrew and Sir John Macneill who, on June 23, decided that the time had come to strike once more for the project in the interests of which they had been working since 1857. The latter and also his son, Captain Robert Macneill, accordingly wrote to General Sir J. L. A. Simmons at Berlin suggesting that "steps should be taken to secure for England, from the Porte, the privilege of constructing a railway from some port on the Mediterranean to the head of the Persian Gulf by the Euphrates or Tigris as

[19] Sir R. Temple to Salisbury, Bombay, May 14, 1878 (F. O., 78/2791). Nixon, Report on Bagdad, 1877-78 *(loc. cit.)*, and Commercial Report No. 2, Bagdad, June 21, 1878 (F. O., 195/1188). Cf. *Times*, Oct. 23, 1878, p. 6. Nixon's report No. 2 contains a very long description of the state of trade at Bagdad, its legal aspects, and the advantages to England of a railway from Alexandretta to Bagdad.

[20] Gatheral to Layard, Angora, June 22 and August 3, 1878 (F. O., 195/1161); and Reade to Salisbury, Political, No. 10, Smyrna, July 27, 1878 enclosing a Memorandum by Mr. Robert Wilkin *(ibid.)*. Reade called attention to the firman just granted for the extension of the Smyrna-Aidin railway. Cf. *Pall Mall Gazette*, July 23, 1878, p. 8, and Young, *op. cit.*, IV, 202.

[21] *Dictionary of National Biography*, 2nd Supplement, II, 387-88; and *Times*, June 21, 1878, p. 7.

recommended by the Committee of the House of Commons." The report of 1872 was forwarded with some other papers to Simmons and it was suggested that Robert Macneill might go to Berlin as the representative of Sir John and Mr. Andrew if that would facilitate matters.[22] Simmons was far from encouraging in his reply to these letters, and merely suggested that Andrew and Macneill present a memorial to Prince Bismarck in order that the members of the Congress might have an opportunity to see it. He thought that the Congress had so much to do that it would not take up the Euphrates Valley railway which was not directly concerned with the San Stefano treaty or the war.[23] But any further steps by these men alone were rendered unnecessary by the formation on the same day that the Cyprus Convention was announced of a railway association under the presidency of the Duke of Sutherland in the organization of which both Andrew and Macneill participated.

The Duke of Sutherland—sportsman, traveller, and "amateur" speculator—was in a position to gain the ear both of the British and the Turkish governments for any scheme which he might wish to promote in the Ottoman Empire. He had represented England at the coronation of Alexander II in 1856 and at the opening of the Suez Canal in 1869, and had accompanied the Prince of Wales on his trip to India in 1876. During the Russo-Turkish War, he had organized the Stafford House Committee which rendered invaluable service to Turkey by maintaining hospitals and performing other humanitarian work. Among his personal friends or acquaintances could be counted Midhat Pasha who was enjoying the hospitality of Dunrobin Castle when summoned from exile by the Sultan in August 1878; Musurus Pasha, the Turkish Ambassador in London; General Sir Arnold Kemball, who had made himself *persona grata* to the Porte in the course of his official duties in the East as British political agent in the Persian Gulf,

[22] John Macneill to Simmons, Private, "Orkney House, Cromwell Road, 23rd June, 1878," and R. Macneill to Simmons, Private, "Army and Navy Club," June 23, July 2, and July 8, 1878 (F. O., 358/2).

[23] Simmons to Sir John Macneill, Berlin, July 5, 1878 (*ibid.*).

Consul-General at Bagdad, and member of the British military mission with the Turkish army at first on the Serbian and later on the Armenian front; Hobart Pasha, Admiral of the Turkish fleet; and many others of similar connections.[24]

Whether or not Sutherland was tipped off by Kemball regarding the government's policy, it is interesting to note that he began steps to secure a concession for the working of the coal mines at Heraclea (Eregli) on the 11th of May, two days after the cabinet had decided to acquire Cyprus. In this enterprise he enlisted the aid of Layard who sent two military attachés to examine the mines and the condition of the abandoned road-bed which was begun in the days of Sultan Abdul Aziz for a railway to them from Ismid. Their favorable report was sent to the Duke on June 17; but nothing came of this venture.[25] Some time in June, however, Sutherland turned his attention to the more ambitious prospect of a railway from Constantinople through Asia Minor to the Persian Gulf.

Sutherland and his friends and Andrew and Macneill came into touch with one another, and on July 8 met at Stafford House and formed "An Association for Promoting the Construction of a Railway from the Persian Gulf to Constantinople and the Mediterranean Affording Alternative Routes to British India and for Developing the Resources of Asia Minor," to be known briefly as "Asia Minor and Euphrates Railway." The officers were the Duke of Sutherland, President; Mr. W. P. Andrew, Chairman; and Sir Arnold Kemball, Vice Chairman.

[24] See Cecil, II, 306; *Dictionary of National Biography*, XXXIII, 147-48; and the *Times*, Aug. 31, 1878, p. 9.

[25] Sutherland to Layard, Private, Stafford House, May 9, 1878 (Add. MS. 39,020, fo. 68); Kemball to Layard, Private, May 10, 1878 (*ibid.*, fo. 73); Layard to Sutherland, Private, May 22, 1878 (Add. MS. 39,131, fo. 103); Chermside to Hornby, Therapia, May 22, 1878 (F. O., 78/2892); De Winton to Layard, No. 8, Therapia, May 25, 1878 (F. O., 195/1207); Draft to Sutherland, F. O., July 17, 1878 (F. O., 78/2892); Kemball to Layard, July 1, 1878 (Add. MS. 39,021, fos. 3-4); and Layard to Sutherland, July 12, 1878 (Add. MS. 39,131, fo. 120). Major de Winton and Lieutenant Chermside were sent to examine the mines. Over a year later, French interests were attempting to obtain a concession to work them; Dickson to Layard, No. 148, July 29, 1879 (F. O., 358/4). Cf. Austin, *op. cit.*, pp. 103-05.

The Executive Committee was to consist of the officers named and Lord Blantyre, Sir H. Drummond-Wolff, H. Chaplin who was known as the "great squire" of the House of Commons and was an ardent Conservative, Telford Macneill,[26] Frederick Greenwood of the *Pall Mall Gazette*, J. Staniforth, Baron G. de Worms, A. Borthwick of the *Morning Post*, Sir Henry Green who had been associated with Sutherland on the Stafford House Committee and Mr. Wright who had been secretary of that organization. On the General Committee there were, among others, Hobart Pasha; John Fowler, a civil engineer who had been consulted on railway matters by the Khedive Ismail Pasha in 1869; Sir John and Robert Macneill; Sir Frederick Goldsmid who has already been noted for his speech in June advocating railways and the taking of Cyprus; Lord Kinnaird, Sir H. W. Tyler, and Mr. Edward Thornton, all three of them members of the Corporation of Foreign Bondholders and the last a director of the P. & O. Steamship Company; and Lord Shaftesbury who had apparently retained an interest in the Euphrates Valley railway since 1857 when he played the unfamiliar role of leading the deputation which asked Lord Palmerston to back the project at that time.[27] Almost every member of the organization had been connected in some way with the Near East or with India, although a very few were business men and members of Parliament who had no direct interest in the project other than as a speculation.

The Duke of Sutherland who had already begun to sound out the Porte gave his friends to understand that he had also

---

[26] Telford Macneill was the son of a second Sir John Macneill, a civil engineer who was interested in railway building. The Sir John Macneill who wrote to Simmons was a surgeon who had spent many years in India and the middle East, and had been British envoy to Persia. See *Dictionary of National Biography*, XXXV, 249, and 251-52.

[27] Sir John Macneill to Simmons, Private, July 9, 1878 (F. O., 358/3); and "Memorandum, Proposed Asia Minor and Euphrates Railway" (F. O., 78/2893). Cf. Andrew, *Euphrates Valley Routes* (1882), p. 95, where the complete list of members is given, and pp. 64-65 and 74, giving the deputation to Palmerston of 1857 and those connected with the Select Committee of 1872. The similarity in the lists is striking.

communicated with Lord Beaconsfield, and Macneill turned over to the association his letter from Simmons.[28] With the ground thus prepared no time was lost in communicating further with Layard and the Foreign Office.[29] Already others outside this company had begun to put forward proposals for railways and Layard informed Sutherland that General Klapka, a former Hungarian refugee of pronounced Turkophil views, had commenced negotiations with the Grand Vizier for one such group, but he believed that the Grand Vizier and the Sultan would most favor Sutherland's project and preferred that the railway be built with English capital and by Englishmen.[30] In reply the Duke of Sutherland explained at length to Layard that he was very anxious that the Porte should support his proposals with sincerity and liberality because his chances of getting the financial backing which he was seeking from the British government very much depended upon what terms in the way of grants of land and similar solid support from the Porte he could obtain.[31]

Apparently the Duke of Sutherland and his association were not quite clear regarding the exact terms to be asked of the Porte. At any rate the memorandum presented to the British government on July 17 did not specify them, but expanded upon the advantages of the proposed railways in "strengthening the Sultan in his Asiatic dominions" and securing the route to India. It was asserted that the safety and security of the Sultan's Asiatic territories, "rich in agricultural and mineral products," would be promoted by the construction of a railway "from *Constantinople* to *Ismidt, Angora, Sivas, Diabikir* [*sic!*], *Mosul* and *Bagdad* to the head of the *Persian*

---

[28] Macneill to Simmons, July 9, 1878.

[29] The Memorandum was communicated to the Foreign Office by one of Lord Beaconsfield's secretaries on July 17, but Sutherland apparently telegraphed Layard very shortly after the meeting of July 8. See Layard to Sutherland, Private, July 12, 1878 (*loc. cit.*).

[30] Layard to Sutherland, Private, July 12 and 24, 1878 (Add. MS. 39,131, fos. 120 and 127-28). Cf. *Times*, July 16, 1878, p. 5; July 17, p. 5; July 23, p. 5; and July 26, p. 5. The last reference mentions the Duke of Sutherland's scheme.

[31] Sutherland to Layard, Private, July 25, 1878 (Add. MS. 39,021, fo. 115).

Gulf, the through line *being in railway connection with Alex-andretta or some other Port on the Mediterranean;* thus having its three termini resting on the sea as a basis of operations." After describing in glowing terms the commercial possibilities of the region to be traversed, the memorandum declared that this "design would give England with the recent addition of Cyprus the first strategic position in the world enabling her Army in India to co-operate with that in England with the rapidity and force of an irresistible power in defence of a Country in whose progress and consolidation England is vi-tally concerned, securing at the same time in the most ef-fective manner our communications with our Indian Empire."

It was estimated that the completion of about 2500 miles of railway would cost from twenty to twenty-five million pounds, but suggested that a section connecting some commer-cial center with a port might be built and then extended if the result were "sufficiently encouraging." What was essen-tial in order to give public confidence was to know whether Her Majesty's Government would look with favor upon the scheme and would co-operate "with such moderate pecuniary support as might be necessary to enable the capital to be raised for the construction of a carefuly selected section of the undertaking." [32]   Put more flatly, what the association wanted to know, wrote Lord Beaconsfield's secretary, was "will the Gov't guarantee their loan?" [33]

Until the presentation of this memorandum and even after-ward, it is difficult to determine what part in the promotion of the "Asia Minor and Euphrates Railway" project ministers may have played. Sir Stafford Northcote, who was chairman of the Select Committee of 1872, at least encouraged Suther-land to believe that he would support the latter's scheme.[34]

---

[32] "Memorandum. Proposed Asia Minor and Euphrates Railway," com-municated by Mr. Turnor, July 17, 1878 (F. O., 78/2893. See appendix).

[33] A. Turnor to Tenterden, 10 Downing Street, Whitehall, July 17, 1878 (*ibid.*).

[34] Sutherland to Layard, Private, Dunrobin Castle, August 26, 1878 (Add. MS. 39,021, fos. 317-20).

Whether or not Lord Beaconsfield did more than this is a matter of conjecture. He is credited by R. Hamilton Lang, a former consul in Cyprus and a prolific writer on that subject, with having made plans for a railway via Aleppo to Diarbekir and Kharpout "the essential element" of his scheme for the defense of Armenia. The *Times* correspondent at Berlin in 1882 reported that Beaconsfield told Bismarck at the Congress that Cyprus was meant among other things to cover the terminus of a Euphrates Valley railway. A writer in the *Quarterly Review* of 1917 asserted that Beaconsfield instructed Major Ardagh, one of the military experts with the British delegation at Berlin whose mission to Alexandria has already been noted, to trace on a map the alignment of a railway from Alexandretta to Basra.[35]

There is no doubt some truth in these stories but they prove little more than that Beaconsfield took a genuine interest in an enterprise which, if carried out, would greatly enhance the value of Cyprus in the eyes of the public and would aid the government in its task of protecting and reforming Asiatic Turkey. Apparently he was not, however, in any way instrumental in launching the actual association which was formed under the presidency of the Duke of Sutherland nor was he in other ways responsible for railway projects.

Beaconsfield, immediately after his return from Berlin when he was no doubt in a rather flushed and generous mood, gave Sutherland the impression that he was willing to support the association "actively,"[36] although he turned the proposals over to the Foreign Office for its advice. Here they received the first douche of cold sober reasoning, for Lord Salisbury wrote "This is a question for the Treasury. The railway will not

---

[35] R. Hamilton Lang, private letter of October 22, 1897 (Courtesy of Colonel J. M. Home); *Times,* June 12, 1882, quoted by Andrew, *Euphrates Valley Routes,* p. 45; and "Bagdad Railway Negotiations," *Quarterly Review,* CCXXVIII (Oct. 1917), 490. For other reported connections between the government and surveys in Asia Minor, see Hoskins, *op. cit.,* 441; Cameron, *op. cit.,* I, 2-3; and Grant and Temperley, *Europe in the Nineteenth Century* (New York, 1928), pp. 383-84.

[36] Sutherland to Layard, Private, Aug. 26, 1878 (*loc. cit.*).

pay its working expenses for 20 years. Are the treasury willing during that time to pay interest at the rate of £1,000,000 yearly?" They received a second chilling blast in the House of Lords when Lord Derby declared that without a guarantee, a Euphrates Valley railway would not pay, and a guarantee would be a dead loss to the Exchequer of a million pounds a year.[37]

After these sobering opinions, Sutherland found on July 24 that Beaconsfield, "while not expressing disapproval of the project, expected that it would have been brought before him without the demand for a guarantee from his gov't and throwing upon the Turkish Gov't the onus of making it worth the while of Capitalists, to embark their money in it." Sutherland did not despair however of getting some kind of a guarantee,[38] although the only "active" support which he received from the government for the time being was diplomatic backing at the Porte and refusal to consider any of the other schemes which were being brought to the attention of the Foreign Office.[39]

At this point the question of the railway became merged into the larger problems connected with British responsibilities under the Cyprus Convention. In the minds of Sutherland and his associates, and that meant nearly all who were ardently working for railways in Turkey, the proposal had been

---

[37] Endorsement on "Memorandum. Asia Minor and Euphrates Railway" (*loc. cit.*); and 3 Hans. CCXLI, 1794.

[38] Sutherland to Layard, Private, Stafford House, July 25, 1878 (Add. MS. 39,021, fo. 115).

[39] The most persistent petitioner for government help was Sir R. Macdonald Stephenson whose project for a railroad from Constantinople through Persia to India was turned down by the Foreign Office which informed him that the government had promised its support to Sutherland's scheme; F. O. to Stephenson, Nov. 15, 1878 (F. O., 78/2897). Correspondence between Stephenson and the Foreign Office and Layard from August 1 to Oct. 28 is to be found in F. O., 78/2894 and 2896, F. O., 195/1208, Add. MS. 39,021, fos. 154-56, and Add. MS. 39,022, fos. 41, 86, and 145-48. See also, McCoan, *Our New Protectorate*, II, 11 and 27-33. Other proposals to the government were: McBean, July 8, 1878 (F. O., 78/2892); Pocock, Aug. 1 (F. O., 78/2894); Alison, Aug. 1 (*ibid.*); and Palestine Railway, Land & Building Company, Nov. 16 (F. O., 78/2897).

linked from the first with the policy of a British protectorate over Turkey, and as Sutherland expressed it, "if [the government] means to do anything for Asia there is no time to be lost about fixing the line of railway." [40]

It was in much the same light that General Sir Lintorn Simmons addressed a memorandum to the Foreign Office on July 26. Its subject was the danger to which British interests would be exposed if Russia should extend her dominions into Asia Minor and the measures Great Britain should adopt in order to prevent it. After describing the way in which a Russian advance might endanger the Straits, Syria, and Persia and the importance of free entrance into the Black Sea for the British fleet, he suggested that other measures to be taken were: "to obtain order and security for life and property in Asia Minor and to open up the country by making such roads and communications through it as will not only serve the purposes of commerce but will be capable of being used as military roads for the movement of troops and stores to the vicinity of the frontiers and to organize the country militarily for defence by improving its financial position, by enrolling and training the inhabitants as soldiers and by constructing such defensive works as the careful examination of the country might dictate." After pointing out how a native force could best oppose the progress of Russian arms in Armenia, he concluded that "if not in sufficient strength to do this a British force landed in the Gulf of Skenderoon [*sic!*], *if a line of railway were constructed thence up to Diarbekir and Erzinghan,* would be as near to the theatre of war as any reinforcements coming from Russia and arriving there fresh without the fatigues of long marches [would] be in a favorable position to aid the forces of the country in repelling attack." [41]

Whether or not Lord Salisbury took these arguments into consideration, or was interested solely in enabling the Sultan

---

[40] Sutherland to Layard, Aug. 26, 1878 (*loc. cit.*).

[41] Simmons Memorandum on "Danger to which British Interests would be exposed if Russia were to extend her dominions in Asia Minor" (F. O., 78/2893). The italics are mine. See appendix.

to reform his Asiatic dominions and to secure financial assistance, he proposed to Northcote on August 5, that the Sultan
be asked to grant a concession for a railway from Alexandretta to Bagdad, with ten miles of land on each side, to persons whom the British government should name. Then the
English government should guarantee two and a half per cent
on 500 miles of the line at £5000 a mile.[42]   This proposal
lacked nothing in boldness because it meant an English administration of 10,000 square miles of territory in the heart of
the Sultan's Asiatic dominions, and along with other suggestions made by Salisbury at about the same time shows that
he was ready to consider if not that annexation of which members of Parliament and the press were suggesting, at least a
very real control of large areas in Asiatic Turkey.   Although
Northcote did not encourage this plan, it was undoubtedly
discussed along with even more far-reaching schemes such as
the cession to England of the revenues from the Pashaliks
through which the projected railroad was to pass.[43]

The government finally decided, however, that it could not
undertake to ask Parliament's consent to a guarantee of the
proposed railways and Lord Beaconsfield informed the Duke
of Sutherland of that fact on October 1.[44]   Affairs in the
meantime had gone none too well at the Porte.   The Turks
were in a suspicious mood toward all proposals which seemed
to give too much power into British hands and were being
encouraged in their attitude by the Russian and French Ambassadors.[45]   About the middle of September, Layard learned
that the Porte had accepted in principle Klapka's scheme for
a Bagdad railway.   He represented chiefly French capital-

---

[42] Cecil, II, 306-07.

[43] *Ibid.*, and *Times*, Dec. 17, 1878, p. 3. This article from Pesth purported to
give the terms of a concession asked for by Layard and is one of the few
references to terms to be found. Cf. McCoan, *Our New Protectorate*, II, 34-37.

[44] Sutherland to Layard, Private, Nov. 9, 1878 (Add. MS. 39,023, fo. 44).

[45] Layard to Sutherland, Private, Dec. 3, 1878, and Jan. 16, 1879 (Add. MS.
39,131, fos. 219-20 and 241); Layard, *Memoirs*, VIII (Add. MS. 38,938), fos.
19-20; and *Times*, Aug 22, p. 4, and Dec. 19, 1878, p. 9. Cf. Hajo Holborn,
Deutschland und die Türkei, 1878-1890 (Berlin, 1926), p. 70.

ists and had asked for ten kilometres of land on both sides of the line, which Layard thought would entail an inconvenient French influence in Asia Minor and Mesopotamia. Klapka, however, either through need of more financial backing or more political influence with which to obtain the actual concession, attempted to come to an arrangement with Sutherland, but without results. The latter, after discussing the situation with his associates and deciding that there was little hope of building a railway without an English guarantee or grants of land and similar concessions from the Turks which they were reluctant to give, resigned from the presidency of the company and severed connections with all railway ventures in Turkey.[46]

Although the "Association for Promoting a Railway from the Persian Gulf to Constantinople and the Mediterranean" was perpetuated under the auspices of the indefatigable W. P. Andrew, and ardent believers in its feasibility continued to urge its construction, there is no evidence that it was ever again seriously considered by the British government or given much attention by the Porte.[47] The project failed for reasons

[46] Layard to Salisbury, Private, Sept. 20 and Oct. 11, 1878 (Add. MS. 39,131, fos. 168 and 188); Sutherland to Layard, Private, Aug. 29, Nov. 25 and Dec. 16, 1878 (Add. MS. 39,021, fo. 331; 39,023, fo. 198; and 39,024, fo. 63); and W. P. Andrew to Layard, Dec. 12, 1878 (F. O., 195/1210). The Porte was besieged by requests for railway concessions in August and September; Layard to Salisbury, Private, Sept. 13, 1878 (Add. MS. 39,131, fo. 164-66); and Lhéritier, *op. cit.*, p. 241. Cf. *Times*, Aug. 6, p. 5; Aug. 13, p. 3; Aug. 22, p. 4; and Sept. 4, 1878, p. 3; and A. Romer, "Notes on Roads and Railways in Asia Minor and the Communications of England with India," Constantinople, August 12, 1878 (Add. MS. 39,054, fos. 232-39).

[47] W. P. Andrew continued to carry on the negotiations begun by Sutherland, but without success. See *Times*, Jan. 4, 1879, p. 5; and Andrew, *Euphrates Valley Railway* (1882). Except for occasional mention in the press, the grant of a concession to build the railway from Scutari to Ismid in 1880, and the efforts of Cazalet in 1882 to promote a road from Tripoli to Bagdad and Basra, the subject gradually dropped from sight. See *Times*, Feb. 12, p. 5; Aug. 23, 1879, p. 6; and April 3, 1880, p. 7; Vice-Consul Cooper to Wilson, Political No. 2, Adana, Feb. 9, 1880 (F. O., 78/3129); Cazalet, *England's Policy in the East*, p. iv; Schmidt, *op. cit.*, p. 4; Young, *op. cit.*, IV, 117-18; Egerton, *op. cit.*, p. 325; and 3 Hans. CCLXXXII (1883), 507-12.

which are obvious. The Porte was reluctant to add a British controlled railway with all the political implications which it might entail to the already established "protectorate" over Asia Minor and Mesopotamia, and the Sultan was not apparently impressed at this time by the advantages a railway might give him in linking his Empire together.[48]

But the real obstacles to the undertaking were the lack of faith in the financial returns of railways in Turkey and the inability of the British government to guarantee the project. Times were hard. Turkey was bankrupt, and the debates in Parliament both at the end of the session in August and the beginning of the next in the autumn showed that Englishmen were in no mood to tax themselves for imperialistic schemes in Asiatic Turkey where experience had already bred distrust and where hard-headed business men were unwilling to risk their money.[49] A scheme which had failed to materialize in the "wild-cat" speculation days of the 'Sixties could scarcely hope to succeed in the soberer period of the 'Seventies even though the government had inspired dreams of a new era in the Near East by its Cyprus policy.

Meanwhile Lord Salisbury and Sir Henry Layard had begun the difficult task of inaugurating reforms in Asiatic Turkey. While the announcement of the Cyprus Convention had removed some of the suspicion and distrust of England which had been created by the *Globe* revelations and England's policy at the Congress of Berlin, the Sultan and many Turks in his entourage professed to believe that England's object was the partition of Turkey and the reduction of the Sultan to

---

[48] H. von Treitschke, "Unsere Aussichten," *Preussische Jahrbücher,* XLIV (1879), 566-67; "Bagdad Railway Negotiations," *loc. cit.,* p. 493. Holborn alleges that the Turkish General Staff energetically worked for the project of a Bagdad railway at this time, *op. cit.,* p. 71.

[49] "Bagdad Railway Negotiations," *loc. cit.,* pp. 492-93; R. Hamilton Lang, "Reforms in Turkey," *Macmillan's Magazine,* XXXIX (Nov. 1878), 82-83; W. S. Blunt, "An Indo-Mediterranean Railway," *loc. cit.,* pp. 702-03; Geary, *op. cit.,* II, 287; *Times,* Aug. 30, 1878, p. 6; V. L. Cameron, "Indo-Mediterranean Railway," *Macmillan's Magazine,* XL (Sept. 1879), 414; and M. E. Grant Duff, "British Interests in the East," *Nineteenth Century,* VII (April 1880), 667.

the position of an Indian protected prince.[50] This impression was fostered by the Russian and French Ambassadors at the Porte[51] and strengthened by the expectations of the disaffected populations in Asia Minor and the discussions in the British press and Parliament of England's aims and mission in the East.

The *Times,* almost a year later and *à propos* of a speech by Lord Carnarvon calling the attention of the House of Lords to the dreams aroused in Armenia by the Cyprus Convention, declared that "it may be doubted whether the brilliant imagination of Lord Beaconsfield himself ever painted a more beautiful picture than that which passed before the eye of many a poor peasant in Asia Minor when he first heard of that convention." While this was a slightly exaggerated bit of rhetoric calculated to impress its readers with England's responsibilities, consular and newspaper reports and the words of travellers and missionaries in the East support the impression that both the Christians and Moslems in Syria and Armenia especially, were ready to welcome British domination.[52] This was not a new story in 1878, but had become the settled conviction of every Englishman who was acquainted with the East. Over and over again it had been repeated in much the same language as that of Lord Sandon, "the one same cry has always arisen from all the best in all ranks of these toiling

---

[50] Layard, *Memoirs,* VII, fos. 153 and 208; *idem,* Tel. No. 661, July 12, 1878 (F. O., 78/2907), and private letter to Salisbury, July 16 (Add. MS. 39,131, fos. 122-23). Cf. Constantinople Correspondent, *Times,* July 13, p. 7; July 22, p. 5; July 24, p. 11; and Aug. 22, p. 4.

[51] Layard to Salisbury, Private, July 26, 1878 (*loc. cit.*).

[52] *Times,* June 28, 1879, p. 11; Chermside to Hornby, Therapia, May 22, 1878 (F. O., 78/2892); Eldridge to Layard, Aleih, July 22, 1878 (*Parl. Papers,* C. 2204 (1878), No. 7); Gatheral to Layard, Angora, Sept. 14, 1878 (F. O., 195/1161); *Times,* Oct. 28, 1879, pp. 3-4; Cameron, *op. cit.,* I, 118; "Syrian Subjects of the Porte," *Blackwood's Magazine,* CXXXI (April 1882), 512; Rev. H. F. Fanshawe, *Turkish Armenia and Eastern Asia Minor* (London, 1881), p. 31; and W. M. Ramsay, *Impressions of Turkey during Twelve Years' Wanderings* (London, 1897), p. 142.

and long-suffering populations—'When are you coming?' Yes; 'When are you English coming?' " [53]

Whether or not such reports were entirely true, it was a logical step from belief in them to the position of a writer to the *Times* who urged "good and timely use of the confidence offered us"; and of Admiral Hornby who asserted that "it's a thousand pities we don't take the country in hand, muzzle the useless but oppressive pashas, and give this brave and honest people the blessings of a good government as we do in India." Others had long been advocating that a few picked Indian officials should be sent to govern Turkey.[54] From this point, the next step brought interpreters of the Cyprus Convention to conclusions that were little short of terrifying to a Sultan jealous of his independence.

Before it was officially announced, rumors had spread that Beaconsfield intended to annex the Syrian coast and that the British flag would soon fly over Jerusalem and Damascus.[55] Many hailed the Convention upon its publication as a sign that Asia Minor was to become a genuine protectorate and some commentators even declared that "Asiatic Turkey is annexed to the British Crown, to be henceforth administered by English officials as well as defended by English troops." [56] The staid and conservative *Blackwood's Magazine* joined in this

[53] 3 Hans. CCXLII, 670-71. Cf. Layard, *ante,* pp. 73-74; and appendix, No. 4a One constantly comes across the repetition of this idea in reports of consuls throughout the period from 1875-1878.

[54] "A Traveller" to the Editor, *Times,* June 24, 1878, p. 6; and Egerton, *op. cit.,* p. 277. Cf. Lord Stratford de Redcliffe, letter to the Editor, *Times,* Jan. 3, 1876, p. 6, and leading article, *ibid.,* Jan. 4, p. 9; M. E. Grant Duff to the Editor, *Times,* Sept. 11, 1876, p. 6; *Pall Mall Budget,* Oct. 7, p. 17, and Nov. 11, 1876, pp. 11-12; Rowland Blennerhassett, "The Reform of the Ottoman Empire," *Fortnightly Rev.,* XXVII (Feb. 1877), 236; *Pall Mall Gazette,* Nov. 15, 1877, p. 3; British Residents at Smyrna to Beaconsfield, Jan. 17, 1878 (F. O., 195/1161); Musafir to the Editor, *Times,* July 3, 1878, p. 10; and Malet to Layard, Constantinople, Jan. 26, 1879 (F. O., 78/2944).

[55] *Pall Mall Gazette,* June 25, 1878, pp. 10-11.

[56] *John Bull,* July 13, 1878, p. 445. Cf. George Campbell to the Editor, *Times,* July 10, p. 10; Epitomes of the *Saturday Review, Spectator* and *Economist* in *Pall Mall Gazette,* July 13, p. 3; *Times,* July 13, p. 11; and July 16, pp. 8-9.

chorus and declared: "The whole transaction, whether we regard the present virtual annexation of Cyprus, or what in all probability is the prospective annexation of Asia Minor, is a gigantic step in the development of that empire which is the inheritance of the British people. . . . The two empires of India and Asia Minor . . . will eventually be brought into closer contact, and will mutually aid each other in the development of their resources." The *Fortnightly Review* asserted that "the British protectorate over Asia Minor saps forever the independence of the Porte." [57]

Although Lord Salisbury stoutly denied that he had any intention of acquiring territory in Asia Minor, it is probably true that few Russians, Germans or Frenchmen in 1878 believed otherwise and that everyone in Asia Minor was forecasting the passage of the country into British hands.[58] While Salisbury's correspondence with Layard does not altogether bear out this opinion, except at moments of exasperation with the dilatory tactics of the Porte, he did certainly hope to see Europeans employed in the highest governmental posts in Turkey and explained that unless this were done, very little would be accomplished. "Would it be possible," he asked Layard, "to begin with some one province and appoint some Indian officer or civil servant, who would be selected with great care?" He wished to work through the Sultan, however, and realized the difficulty of persuading a sovereign to place power in the hands of men who would not be likely to let it slip back again.[59]

Layard himself was in favor of carrying out a firm and con-

---

[57] "Treaties of Peace," *Blackwood's*, CXXIV, 246; and *Fortnightly Rev.*, XXX, 307. Cf. *Blackwood's*, CXXIV, 360-61; *Edinburgh Rev.*, CXLVIII, 565; James Bryce, "The Future of Asiatic Turkey," *Fortnightly Rev.*, XXIX (June 1878), 929-30 and 933; Thomas Brassey, *Recent Letters and Speeches* (London, 1879), pp. 11-12; Cazalet, *England's Policy in the East*, pp. 23-24; *Times,* Aug. 8, 1878, p. 7.

[58] See Ramsay, *op. cit.,* pp. 141-44; Blunt, *Secret History*, pp. 24-25 and 32-33; and H. Nicolson, *Portrait of a Diplomatist* (Boston, 1930), p. 21.

[59] Salisbury to Layard, Private, June 25, 1878 (*loc. cit.*).

sistent policy in Asia Minor and thought that "we ought to make the Sultan govern his Asiatic Territories as we think fit, and this would be to his ultimate advantage as well as to our own. . . ." He recognized the "dreadful want of men" in Turkey who could be relied upon to carry out reforms in a thorough-going fashion.[60]   Nevertheless he agreed with Lord Salisbury that the "authority and influence of Great Britain at Constantinople . . . is one of the most important objects of English policy, perhaps the most vital of all," and he was keenly aware of how he might jeopardize that influence by pressing the Sultan and the Porte too strongly to do what they feared would weaken the sovereign's authority.[61]

Had reforms alone been in question, Layard might have gone to much greater lengths than he did, but there were other problems requiring immediate attention after the Congress of Berlin, which helped to complicate the task of the Ambassador.   The principal ones were the occupation of Bosnia and Herzegovina by Austria, the evacuation of Russian troops from the vicinity of Constantinople, the settlement of the Greek frontier, the institution of reforms in Crete, and agreement upon the details connected with the occupation of Cyprus such as the legal position of the Sultan's lands and the amount of money England was to pay the Porte annually. England's active interest in all these problems, either because of her desire to support Austria or through fear of Russia or public opinion at home, reacted unfavorably upon the task of reforms.   To take Bosnia as an example, England's support of Austria oftentimes seemed to confirm the belief that she was participating in the partition of Turkey and impinging upon the sovereign rights of the Sultan.   In all these matters, Layard was given entire discretion and was warned that he was not to prejudice his chances of negotiating the projects

---

[60] Layard to Lytton, Private, June 19, 1878 (Add. MS. 39,131, fos. 107-09); and *idem* to Salisbury, Aug. 20, 1878 (*ibid.*, fos. 145-47).

[61] Cecil, II, 315.

of reform by his attitude in regard to these subjects of second-ary importance for British policy.[62]

The fundamental assumption upon which Salisbury and Layard based their hope of success was that the Sultan and the Porte were sincerely desirous of reforming the empire. The method which they adopted, therefore, was to use the Sultan as a "fulcrum" upon which the lever of advice and admonition was to work in order to stir the slow-moving Turkish govern-ment into action.[63]   In view of the intrigues which Layard suspected were going on, he felt it more politic and prudent to induce the Sultan to initiate the reforms which Great Brit-ain desired than to use anything like threatening language or a menace, and this continued to be his method at the Porte so long as he saw any chance of success in it.[64]

He recognized that the Sultan was a poor enough instru-ment for the purpose in mind, partly because his good inten-tions, upon which Layard never ceased to dilate, were likely to be frustrated by his vacillation and weakness of will, and partly because his fears for his own personal safety, especially after the plot to dethrone him in May, made him extremely nervous and suspicious whenever a strong tone was adopted toward him.[65]   Therefore the inevitable corollary to the policy of making the Sultan the instrument in matters of reform was to surround him with strong men who could influence him in the right direction.   Unfortunately, in the months following the Congress of Berlin, the principal minister was Safvet Pasha, whose intentions like the Sultan's were of the best and

[62] Layard, *Mem.*, VII, fos. 223 and 245; Letter to Salisbury, July 11, 1878 (Add. MS. 39,131, fos. 116-19); and Letter to Sir H. Elliot, July 26, 1878 (*ibid.*, fos. 131-32).

[63] Salisbury to Layard, Private, May 30, 1878 (*loc. cit.*); and despatch, Dec. 4, 1878 (*Parl. Papers*, C. 2202 (1878), No. 5). Cf. *Times*, July 23, 1878, p. 9; July 25, p. 9; Aug. 1, p. 9; and Sept. 26, p. 4.

[64] Layard to Salisbury, Private, Sept. 6, 1878 (Add. MS. 39,131, fos. 161-62); and Sept. 13 (*ibid.*, fos. 164-66). Cf. leading articles, *Times*, Aug. 7, 1878, p. 9, and Aug. 9, p. 9.

[65] Layard, *Mem.*, VII, fos. 42-47; and Desp. No. 768, June 12, 1878 (F. O., 78/2791).

whose loyalty to England was unquestioned, but whose determination and influence were too weak to fit him for the task which the British Ambassador laid upon his shoulders.[66]

Nevertheless Layard persisted in the belief that England's only recourse in dealing with the Turks was the gentle art of persuasion and the inspired press swung into line with this point of view. The *Times* declared in August that it was "only a crude and untrained judgment" that supposed the Sultan's empire could be transformed into a state like India. And after the announcement of the reform program and reports of the suspicious frame of mind at the Porte, the same paper admitted that "the changing temper of an Oriental potentate is a poor foundation for a great policy of any kind. But since there is no better to be had, we must take it and do the best we can with it." [67]

By the end of July it had been agreed that the program which England should demand should be a mild and inoffensive one, involving the institution of a gendarmerie in Asiatic Turkey to be organized and commanded by Europeans, the establishment of central courts of justice likewise to be supervised by European lawyers, the reform of tax collection by abolishing tithe farming and again introducing Europeans into the system, and the appointment of strong men as governors of provinces upon definite terms of office instead of at the Sultan's pleasure.[68]   The Sultan and Safvet Pasha professed themselves to be well pleased with these proposals when they were presented early in August.   They noted especially that England had not asked for supervision of the reforms by Englishmen, a point which Layard had insisted upon in order to avoid creating the impression that Great Britain was at-

[66] Layard, *Mem.*, IV, fos. 96-97; Tel. No. 604, June 22, 1878 (F. O., 78/2907); and private letter to Salisbury, Nov. 22, 1878 (Add. MS. 39,131, fos. 212-14). Cf. leading articles, *Times,* July 10, p. 9, and July 11, 1878, p. 9.

[67] Leading articles, *Times,* Aug. 28, 1878, p. 7, and Sept. 16, p. 9. Cf. *ibid.,* Aug. 31, p. 9; Sept. 12, p. 3 (Reuter's); Sept. 16, p. 5 (Constantinople); and Sept. 18, p. 9.

[68] Salisbury to Layard, Aug. 8, 1878 (*Parl. Papers,* C. 2202, No. 1). Cf. 3 Hans. CCXLII, 666-67.

tempting to make Turkey-in-Asia a veritable protectorate. Furthermore, the Sultan and his ministers had been well prepared for the plan laid before them by conversations with Layard throughout June and July.[69]

But in spite of the professed satisfaction with the English suggestions, more than two months elapsed before the Porte accepted them, and even then it made modifications in the proposals regarding the employment of Europeans and promised to change the tax system only gradually. Layard professed that the delays had nearly exhausted his patience, but ascribed them largely to the suspicion and distrust engendered by Russia in the minds of the Sultan and the Council which had discussed the reforms. He thought, however, that the answer was on the whole acceptable and on this the British government perforce agreed with him.[70]

The obstacles to both the acceptance and the application of the reforms were indeed overwhelming. The greatest of these was the virtual bankruptcy of the Ottoman government and the inability of Great Britain to remedy this situation. The Sultan had called attention to his financial plight early in June and Layard began to emphasize it as a problem of paramount importance on July 26 when he suggested that England could obtain the gratitude and loyalty of the Sultan by helping him to obtain a loan.[71] For the remainder of the year the question of how to bolster up Turkey's sinking credit and straighten out her tangled finances remained a persistent and perplexing one.

[69] Layard to Salisbury, Aug. 21, 1878 (*Parl. Papers,* C. 2202, No. 2); Layard, *Mem.,* VII, fos. 209, 263-66, and *Mem.,* VIII, fos. 3-5; Desp. No. 768, June 12 (*loc. cit.*); letters to Salisbury, July 6 (Add. MS. 39,138, fos. 30-33), July 11, July 19, July 26, Aug. 14 and Aug. 20, 1878 (Add. MS. 39,131, fos. 116-19, 123-25, 131-32, 141-43, and 145-47).

[70] Layard to Salisbury, Desp. No. 1347, Oct. 30, 1878 (F. O., 78/2803, and extract, *Parl. Papers,* C. 2202, No. 4), and Private, Dec. 11, 1878 (Add. MS. 39,131, fos. 222-23). Cf. Layard, *Mem.,* VIII, fo. 28.

[71] Layard, Desp. No. 768, June 12 and private letter to Salisbury, July 26, 1878 (*loc. cit.*). Thereafter, Layard mentioned finances in almost every one of his weekly letters to Salisbury. See also Layard, *Mem.,* VIII, fo. 6; and Hornby to the Editor, *Times,* Sept. 24, 1878, p. 4.

The British government found, however, that there was no hope of guaranteeing a loan to Turkey because of the temper of Parliament, whose members believed that England's financial obligations were already too great and that Turkey was unworthy of confidence.[72]   Layard's almost pitiful and sometimes frantic appeals for help ended only in the advice from Salisbury that "Turkey must be her own friend in matters of finance," and the rather cynical view that perhaps bankruptcy was not a bad thing for Turkey because an absolute sovereign like the Sultan only uses credit "to build palaces and ironclads."   However true such a statement might be, Layard pointed out that Turkey could not pay policemen or judges nor relieve an over-taxed population from distress and misery unless she had the money with which to do it.[73]

Another obstacle in the way of pressure upon the Porte was the fear almost constantly present of Russia's aims in regard to Constantinople and Turkish Armenia.   Her army had not yet been removed from the vicinity of Constantinople although in September it had been withdrawn beyond the Chataldje lines and the British fleet had accordingly been sent to Artaki.[74]   Even Lord Salisbury feared in October that the Russians would not evacuate Eastern Rumelia at the stipulated time and Layard constantly reported the rumor that Russia was planning to defy the powers, and was seeking a pretext to attack Turkey again in order to advance her frontiers in Armenia.   What alarmed both Layard and Salisbury was that Russia might win the acquiescence of Austria and Germany and by means of a renewed *Dreikaiserbund* feel free to do what she pleased.   Accordingly the British government authorized Layard to inform the Sultan that "the Queen is fully resolved to insist on the evacuation of the Balkan

---

[72] Cecil, II, 305-14. Cf. *Times*, Aug. 3, p. 10, and Nov. 28, 1878, pp. 5 and 9; Barclay to the Editor, *ibid.*, Dec. 6, p. 3; and Reuter's, *ibid.*, Dec. 25, p. 3.

[73] Layard, *Mem.*, VIII, fo. 75; and private letters to Tenterden, Nov. 22, Dec. 11, Dec. 25, 1878, and Jan. 1, 1879 (F. O., 363/2). Cf. "Contemporary Life and Thought in Turkey," *Contemporary Rev.*, XXV (July 1879), 747-48.

[74] Layard, *Mem.*, VIII, fos. 7-10; and Egerton, *op. cit.*, p. 294.

Peninsula by Russia next May, in accordance with the Treaty, and if force is necessary will co-operate with him for that purpose." [75] This is the first and perhaps the last time when England explicitly and unmistakably declared her willingness to execute the defense clause in the Cyprus Convention.

When Layard was not worried over the offensive attitude of Russia toward Turkey, he was afraid that she was becoming too friendly with the Porte. At one time he believed that Lobanov's efforts to regain something of the position held by Ignatiev were succeeding so well that a secret treaty of alliance was about to be signed between the Sultan and the Tsar, although he later confessed that such a rumor must have been put about by Lobanov himself. [76] Under the circumstances, Layard felt that he could not push the Sultan too far in respect of reforms, for he might either yield to Russian threats backed by force, or seek an alliance with Russia as the lesser of two evils. [77]

Despite the difficulties encountered, Layard was able to accomplish one or two measures of minor significance. After long and arduous negotiations, the details of the Cyprus occupation were practically settled through agreements whereby Great Britain was empowered to enact laws and conventions for the government of the island, and the definite sum to be paid to Turkey was fixed. [78] He also had a hand in the pro-

[75] Salisbury to Layard, Tel., Oct. 26, 1878 (Layard, *Mem.*, VIII, fo. 33); Salisbury to Layard, Private, Sept. 18, 1878 (Add. MS. 39,138, fo. 113); Salisbury to Layard, Oct. 3, 1878 (F. O., 78/2772, and an extract in *Parl. Papers*, C. 2205 (1878), No. 11); Layard to Salisbury, private letters, Sept. 13, Oct. 11, Nov. 8, Nov. 15, 1878 (Add. MS. 39,131, fos. 164, 186, 205 and 210); Layard to Sir William White, private letters, Sept. 20, Nov. 1, and Nov. 15, 1878 (Add. MS. 38,939, fos. 79, 84 and 86); and Trotter to Salisbury, Erzeroum, Nov. 21, 1878 (F. O., 195/1211). Cf. W. N. Medlicott, "Diplomatic Relations after the Congress of Berlin," *Slavonic Rev.*, VIII (June 1929), 66-79.

[76] Layard, *Mem.*, VIII, fos. 19-20 and 65-66; *idem* to Salisbury, letters, Oct. 4, Oct. 25, Nov. 22, 1878, Jan. 15, 1879 (Add. MS. 39,131, fos. 186, 196, 212 and 239).

[77] Layard to Salisbury, Private, Sept. 20 and 27, 1878 (*loc. cit.*); and *idem* to Tenterden, Private, Jan. 15, 1879 (F. O., 363/2).

[78] *Parl. Papers*, C. 2229 (1879), Nos. 1-5.

mulgation of a constitution for Crete which was embodied in the Pact of Halepa, issued in October.[79]

Furthermore, at least one step in the direction of securing strong men for the higher positions in Asiatic Turkey was taken with the appointment of Midhat Pasha, the famous leader of the reform party and promulgator of the 1876 constitution, to be governor of Syria. When the question of Midhat's recall from exile was first mooted, both Layard and the British Government were uncertain as to what attitude they should adopt toward the man who had defied Europe at the Conference of Constantinople and about whom there were so many conflicting opinions.[80] Perhaps what turned the scales in his favor, in addition to the strong support of men like Sir Henry Elliot and his reputation as an able administrator, was his great interest in the material development of Turkey by the construction of railroads, canals and roads, and the fact that his position at Damascus would enable him to forward the schemes for railroad building which were being urged by Sutherland and supported by Layard.[81] The appointment, however, eventually proved to be a doubtful gain for the cause of reform, not only because the Sultan continued to be suspicious of Midhat and his policies, but also because he was himself the prey to the intrigues of selfish and ambitious friends.[82]

[79] Cf. William H. Dawson, *loc. cit.*, III, 237-38; and Layard, *Mem.*, VII, fos. 236-39.

[80] Salisbury, at the Congress of Berlin, thought that the return of Midhat Pasha to Turkey would then "be most dangerous and at any time not very safe." Tel. to Layard, No. 10, Berlin, June 22, 1878 (F. O., 78/2906). Layard was not at first sure whether or not to encourage the Sultan to recall him; Layard, *Mem.*, VIII, fos. 21-23; private letters to Salisbury, Sept. 13, Sept. 20, 1878 (*loc. cit.*).

[81] Layard to Salisbury, Private, October 11, 1878 (*loc. cit.*); *idem* to Tenterden, Private, Nov. 15, 1878 (F. O., 363/2); *Edinburgh Rev.*, CXLVIII, 590-91; and Zetland, II, 122. For Midhat's interest in railways, see Blunt, *Secret History*, p. 51; and *Parl. Papers*, C. 2432 (1879), pp. 64-65.

[82] Layard to Salisbury, Private, Nov. 22, 1878 (*loc. cit.*); Eldridge to Layard, No. 72, Aleih, Nov. 8, 1879 (F. O., 195/1264); and Ali Haydar Midhat Bey, *The Life of Midhat Pasha* (London, 1903), pp. 177 and 195.

To offset these meager gains and the doubtful value of the Turkish promises to accept the English program of reform, were the glaring failures of British policy in 1878. Layard could not get the organization of the gendarmerie started nor even the appointment of Baker Pasha to head this work, which had been one of his most cherished aims. Schemes for railroad building and the opening up of trade and commerce to Englishmen and the world had likewise failed even to promise realization. No progress had been made in relieving the financial situation and Layard himself later summed up the efforts of the year 1878 by saying: "The result of this deplorable state of things was that Turkey had no friend or ally left and that even the sympathies of England were being rapidly alienated from her. The year 1878 sealed the fate of the Ottoman Empire and proved to me that all hope of restoring to it even something of its former power and independence would have to be abandoned. Its fall and dismemberment were only questions of time." [83]

It is unnecessary to sketch in detail the story of the next year and a half to the fall of the Conservative government in April, 1880. The fate of British policies at Constantinople was still left largely in the hands of the Ambassador, although one measure was adopted by the British government which not only aided him in his fight for justice and order but also enhanced British influence among the Turkish people, if not at Constantinople. This was the appointment in the autumn of 1878 and the spring of 1879 of military consuls to various posts in Asia Minor and Armenia in order to watch more closely over the activities of Turkish pashas and Kurdish chiefs, to redress as far as possible the injustices which were brought to their attention and to report to the British Am-

---

[83] Layard, *Mem.*, VIII, fo. 51. He did not talk that way in his letter to Salisbury, Jan. 1, 1879 (Add. MS. 39,131, fos. 233-36). For the poor opinion of progress in reform which was held by a friend of Turkey and of the Conservative government, see R. Hamilton Lang, "Reform in Turkey," *Macmillan's Magazine*, XXXIX (Nov. 1878), 82-90; and *idem*, "Notes on Turkish Reforms," *ibid.* (Feb. 1879), 354-56.

bassador the facts upon which he based his representations to the Sultan and the Porte. The fact that these men were chosen from the army on the basis of their experience and training led to exaggerated interpretations of their mission which seem to have little foundation other than that they were excellent reconnaissance agents in a country which England might be called upon to defend.[84]

The urgent need of improvement in the diplomatic and consular service throughout the Ottoman Empire had long been recognized,[85] and a first step had been taken toward increasing the quality and usefulness of British agents in the Near East by the establishment in 1877 of a school for interpreters at Constantinople. Six young men were sent out, among whom some later achieved considerable distinction, notably Sir Adam Block and Sir Harry Eyres. Even before they had taken their examinations at the end of 1879, the interpreters were assigned to aid Major Trotter at Erzeroum and Colonel Wilson and his vice-consuls in Anatolia, and thus assisted in the task of regenerating Turkish administration.[86]

Everyone who was in a position to witness the work of the military consuls testified to their usefulness and the high re-

---

[84] "Return of Recent Consular Appointments in Asia Minor," *Parl. Papers,* C. 2456 (1879); Monypenny and Buckle, II, 1172-73; Sir Charles M. Watson, *The Life of Major-General Sir Charles William Wilson* (London, 1909), pp. 104-09; Capt. A. F. Townshend, *A Military Consul in Turkey* (London, 1910), p. 7; Blunt, *op. cit.,* p. 32; Ramsay, *op. cit.,* p. 143; and instructions, *Parl. Papers,* C. 2432, pp. 63-64 and 76; Trotter to Malet, No. 32, Diarbekir, April 24, and to Clayton, Erzeroum, July 24, 1879 (F. O., 195/1211); and Layard to Kitchener, Therapia, Aug. 23, 1879 (F. O., 195/1234).

[85] See M. E. Grant Duff, "The Pulse of Europe," *Contemporary Rev.,* XXVIII (July 1876), 348-50; *idem,* "The Situation," *Nineteenth Century,* III (March 1878), 572-74; *Pall Mall Gazette,* July 22, 1878, p. 10; 3 Hans. CCXLII, 496, 572, 577, 590 and 955-56; "Treaties of Peace," *Blackwood's Magazine,* CXXIV (Aug. 1878), 246; and Farley, *op. cit.,* p. 106. Layard complained on May 8 of the consular service and on August 21, 1878, advised that the time had come to appoint consuls in Asia Minor; private letters to Salisbury (Add. MS. 39,131, fos. 86-88 and 147-48).

[86] A. G. Hulme-Beaman, *Twenty Years in the Near East* (London, 1898); Watson, *op. cit.,* pp. 109-10; and A. Nicolson to Layard, Therapia, Oct. 18, 1879 (F. O., 78/2960).

gard with which they were held by the oppressed people of Asiatic Turkey despite the fact that they were looked upon with considerable suspicion by the Porte and were hedged about with every possible restriction. They travelled throughout the region of Anatolia and Armenia, listened to petitions, accompanied Turkish commissions which were appointed at the instance of Sir Henry Layard to investigate conditions, and reported faithfully the misdeeds of pashas and the misery of the people.[87] Indeed, they represented almost the only practical effect ever given to the desire of the British government to reform Turkey by means of European and English advisers.

Helpful as the military consuls were, however, Turkish administration could not be improved until the incompetence and wilful capriciousness of the system at the capital were cleaned out, and despite Layard's utmost efforts this condition of affairs grew rather worse than better as the months dragged on.[88] Safvet Pasha had been replaced as Grand Vizier by a Tunisian statesman, Haireddin Pasha, in December 1878, and while Layard regretted the loss of his friend, he found Haireddin to be an energetic and on the whole a satisfactory man with whom to work. Unfortunately the Ghazi, Osman Pasha, had been appointed to the War Office at the same time and proved to be a thorn in the flesh of both Haireddin and Layard because he had the ear of the Sultan and was fanatical

[87] Watson, *op. cit.*, pp. 108-15, 195, and *passim;* Ramsay, *op. cit.*, p. 145-47; Tozer, *op. cit.*, pp. 30-31; H. C. Barkley, *Ride through Asia Minor and Armenia* (London, 1891), pp. 101-02 and 280; and Sir George Arthur, *Life of Lord Kitchener* (London, 1920), I, 45-46. The correspondence between these consuls and Layard or Lord Salisbury, in 1879, is instructive of their work and methods, and is published with the omission of most of the specific references to the misdeeds of individuals, in *Parl. Papers,* C. 2432 (1879), C. 2468 and 2537 (1880).

[88] On complaints against the central government, see Trotter to Layard, Diarbekir, Dec. 28, 1878 (F. O., 195/1211); Henderson to Layard, Aleppo, July 24, 1879 (F. O., 195/1264); Biliotti to Salisbury, Carlsbad, Aug. 12, 1879 (C. 2537, No. 9); Chermside to Layard, No. 29, Adana, Nov. 29, 1879 (F. O., 195/1269); Wilson to Layard, Nos. 41 and 42, April 12, 1880 (F. O., 78/3129); and Tenterden Memorandum, May 25, 1880 (F. O., 363/5).

and opposed to all foreign interference in Turkey. He represented that clique in the Sultan's entourage which constantly supported the latter's desire to increase his own personal authority and safeguard it by the police and spy system. Under the circumstances Haireddin Pasha found it impossible to continue as Grand Vizier and resigned in July 1879 when the Sultan refused to accept his conditions that he be allowed to form his own cabinet, that Osman Pasha be removed from office and the palace, that the Sultan and others outside the ministry should not be allowed to interfere with it, and that the promised reforms be executed. At the same time the Sultan plainly indicated to Layard, who had gone to great lengths to support Haireddin most vigorously, that he intended to retain personal control of the government and its policy; and he also recalled Mahmud Nedim Pasha, the former friend of Ignatiev, from exile.[89]

Again Layard despaired of seeing "those reforms introduced into the administration which could, in my opinion, alone arrest that rapid progress of disorder and decay which unless speedily and effectively checked, could only lead to the downfall of the Ottoman Empire."[90] Nevertheless he persevered and at times resorted to a policy little short of intimidation in order to gain even the smallest triumph. A notable example of this method was the fleet scare of October 1879.

Rumors that the Russians were intending to threaten Constantinople with an armed force led the British cabinet to order the fleet once more to the vicinity of the Straits from which it had been withdrawn in April. Layard, uninformed of the object for which the fleet was again being sent to Besika Bay, was at a loss to answer the anxious questions of the Porte. Having at a previous time warned the Sultan,

---

[89] Layard, *Mem.,* VIII, fos. 45-46, 53-54, and 120-27; *idem* to Salisbury, Private, Sept. 20, and Dec. 4, 1878 (Add. MS. 39,131, fos. 168 and 220); and Desp. No. 649, July 22, 1879 (F. O., 78/2955).

[90] Layard, *Mem.,* VIII, fo. 127. Cf. *idem* to Tenterden, Private, July 22, 1879 (F. O., 363/2).

however, that unless England's advice were better followed she might have to adopt strong measures, the Ambassador used the approach of the fleet to frighten the Sultan and his ministers. The threat procured, after a year and a half of postponement, the appointment of Baker Pasha to be Inspector-General of the gendarmerie in Asia Minor; but this amounted to little because the Porte saw to it that his activities were carefully checked by Turks who were appointed to "assist" him.[91]

The Sultan was angry at Layard for his action, and, refusing to see him for a time, reproached him in no uncertain terms through the medium of the Embassy dragoman. Henceforth Layard fought a discouraging battle with the rising fanaticism of the Palace and the Porte and the shifty tactics of the Sultan. While he managed to re-establish something of the friendly relationship which he had enjoyed with the Sultan, and continued to be consulted by Turkish ministers, including even Mahmud Pasha who professed to be sincerely desirous of following the English policy, he had really lost the predominant power he formerly exercised.[92]

The failure of the great and ambitious policy envisaged by Beaconsfield, Salisbury and their advisers and adumbrated by the two articles of the Cyprus Convention was obvious. Aside from party polemics which had been raised to a fresh pitch of recrimination by the election campaign, the dry and judicious survey by Lord Tenterden of the existing state of questions arising from the Treaty of Berlin attests the meager results of two years' effort. Only three Europeans had been appointed as financial inspectors in the seven vilayets of Asiatic Turkey and only one of them, a Frenchman, was in a position of the first class. An Englishman had been appointed to a fourth post, but had refused because of his subordination

[91] Layard, *Mem.,* VIII, fos. 161-172. Cf. Cecil, II, 319-20; and "Contemporary Life and Thought in Turkey," *Contemporary Rev.,* XXXVII (Feb. 1880), 335-38.

[92] Cf. Layard, *Mem.,* VIII, fos. 167, 170-71, and 196-97; and Sir A. Sandison Memorandum, Oct. 28, 1879 (Add. MS. 39,143, fos. 110-11).

to a higher Turkish official. The judicial system had not been improved in practice because incompetent and corrupt men had been made inspectors and good men refused to serve without a guarantee of five year tenure. English officers engaged for the organization of the gendarmerie had never been employed because of Osman Pasha's opposition. Commissions appointed to investigate conditions had proved incompetent and useless and Mussulmans in the consultative assembly called at Aleppo had blocked the effective co-operation of Christians in it. While the fleet scare of October 1879 had led to some action, Tenterden concluded that the situation, particularly in Armenia, was still very serious and might lead to complications and a superintendence of administration as yet unforeseen.[93]

In summarizing the reasons for this lack of success two things must be borne in mind. First of all, time was needed in order to bring about the desired results. As Layard explained in connection with the Turkish promises to reform: "By the concessions thus made by the Porte, and solemnly sanctioned by the Sultan himself in many verbal and written communications to me, we had obtained a firm standpoint which would have enabled us, by insisting upon their fulfillment, to carry out in the end, to a very great extent, the reforms contemplated by the convention of the 4th of June and the policy of England as regards Asiatic Turkey."[94] Both Layard and Salisbury admitted that eventually some other method might have to be adopted than that which they were following and that Turkey was bound to decay and disintegrate, but they wished to hold on for a little longer until England was in a better position to protect her Indian Empire

---

[93] "Memorandum by Lord Tenterden showing the present state of the Questions arising under the Treaty of Berlin," Foreign Office, April 28, 1880 (F. O., 358/4). Cf. "Contemporary Life and Thought in Turkey," *loc. cit.*, XXXVII, 334-56; "Mysteries of Administration in Turkey," *Contemporary Rev.*, XXXVII (March 1880), 357-70; and "The Armenian Question," *ibid.* (April 1880), 533-47.

[94] Layard, *Mem.*, VIII, fos. 30-31.

and until the Christian peoples could gradually supplant the Turks without violence and bloodshed.[95]   In other words, the real difference between the Beaconsfield government and Gladstone's which succeeded it, lay not so much in the attitude toward the Porte and the Turks, but rather toward Turkey and its relation to the route to India, as Salisbury had explained to Home three years before.

In the second place, it must be remembered that the problems of Asiatic Turkey, complicated and far-reaching as they were, constituted only a few of the many demands of a far-flung empire upon the energy and power of England.   Those demands may have represented the nemesis of Beaconsfield's imperialism and in that sense be blamed upon him and his government.   It is clear, however, that the wars in South Africa and Afghanistan and the diplomatic conflict over Egypt, to name but three of these imperial problems, were crises which dissipated English strength and prevented her from fixing her undivided attention on the tasks in Asiatic Turkey where success depended upon the expenditure of both wealth and man-power.[96]

But even if the absence of other distractions had left Great Britain free to pursue the Cyprus policy, it is clear that reliance upon the Sultan to bring about reforms was one cause of delay and failure. As long as the Sultan's back was forced to the wall by the Russians, he spoke fair to the English and seemed ready to comply with all their wishes. As soon, however, as the danger from Russia was removed by the Treaty of Berlin and the Cyprus Convention, and the Sultan was once more relieved of the immediate fear of being overthrown or of seeing his dominions entirely taken from him, his attitude towards England changed, and in fact England, because of her

---

[95] For Salisbury, Layard, *Mem.*, VIII, fo. 213; for Layard, *ibid.*, fos. 248-49. Cf. *ibid.*, fos. 15 and 194-95; Tenterden Memorandum, Dec. 29, 1878 (F. O., 363/5); and Cecil, II, 320-24.

[96] Cf. Gladstone, *op. cit., Nineteenth Century*, IV, 574 and 581; *idem*, "The Country and the Government," *ibid.*, VI (Aug. 1879), 201-07; and James E. T. Rogers, "British Finance," *Contemporary Rev.*, XXXIV (Jan. 1879), 299-300.

policy, came to occupy in his mind much the same position as that which the Russians had held up to July 1878.[97]

The Sultan therefore attempted to return as quickly as possible to the position of an absolute oriental sovereign, and bit by bit through cunning and craft thwarted the policy which Layard believed he could force upon him. This was the normal policy for any man in the Sultan's position, but was even more natural of him because of his fear for his own personal safety which drove him to get rid of every able and energetic minister, to enhance the control of the police, and to rely upon sycophants and self-seekers who fed the springs of his mistrust and aided and abetted him in his oriental game of opposing the power which might endanger the system by which they throve.[98] The Sultan, then, was one of the greatest obstacles to the inauguration of reforms and the maintenance of British preponderance, and proved to be one of the greatest stumbling-blocks to the realization of the Cyprus policy in Asiatic Turkey.

The Sultan's attitude toward this policy was but one side of the inherent weakness in it. It had been pointed out in Parliament and had been proved to be too true that England by taking upon herself alone the task of protecting and reforming Turkey inevitably called down upon herself not only the forces of reaction in Turkey, but the opposition of the other interested powers. So long as England insisted upon maintaining the structure of the Ottoman Empire, she was likely to run the risk of incurring the opposition of religious fanaticism, as she did, the

---

[97] See Baker, *op. cit.*, pp. 443-46; Blunt, *op. cit.*, p. 37; Brassey, *op. cit.*, pp. 29-30; Cameron, *op. cit.*, II, 324-25; Ramsay, *op. cit.*, pp. 140-41; L. de Mas Latrie, *Chypre* (Paris, 1879), p. 82; H. von Treitschke, *loc. cit.*, pp. 566-67; Trietsch, "Zypern als Angelpunkt der englischen Islam-Politik," *Asien*, XIV (Nov. 1916), p. 33; and Hajo Holborn, *op. cit.*, pp. 8-9.

[98] Cf. Layard to Salisbury, Desp. No. 40, Jan. 7, 1880 (F. O., 78/3078); Layard to H. M.'s Principal Secretary of State for Foreign Affairs, No. 461, April 27, 1880 (F. O., 78/3085, and in extract, *Parl. Papers*, C. 2574 (1880), No. 3); and Edwin Pears, "A Programme of Reforms for Turkey," *Nineteenth Century*, VII (June 1880), 1020-39.

objection of self-seeking Turkish pashas, as she did, and also the jealousy and resistance of Russia and France who, because of their position or their traditions, were the outstanding opponents of England. While Layard's almost constant complaints of Russian and French intrigue at Constantinople and in Armenia and Syria probably present an exaggerated picture of their action, it is none the less true that as the interests of those nations were likely to be injured by England's success, so their ambassadors were eager to thwart England and advance the cause of their own countries and their own nationals.[99]

These obstacles to the attainment of England's political aims were equally effective in preventing England's economic policy. In fact a great deal of the opposition to England was more economic than political, both on the part of the Turks and of other powers. Layard complained to the Sultan toward the end of his career as Ambassador at Constantinople that whereas English capitalists were being denied the concessions which they sought in Turkey, French promoters were being received and their desires complied with.[100] Although the German government was not as yet seeking special privileges for itself or its nationals in Turkey, it was also noted that, true to the principle of preferring the weaker power to the stronger, the Sultan was turning to Germans for posts in the administration, and looking upon them with favor in connection with the economic development of his country.[101]

[99] On the question of fanaticism, see Layard, *Mem.*, VIII, fos. 175-90; Maynard to Mr. Evarts, Constantinople, Oct. 15, 1879 (*Papers Relating to the Foreign Relations of the United States*, 1879, p. 993); *Parl. Papers*, C. 2553 (1880); and Blunt, *op. cit.*, 94. France and especially her Ambassador at the Porte became as much a bugbear to Layard in 1879 and 1880 as Russia. See Layard, *Mem.*, VIII, fos. 56-58, 86, 93, 148-49, and 191-92; Layard, Desp. No. 43, Jan. 8, 1880 (F. O., 78/3078); Newton, II, 169-70, 174, 182-84, and 210; Thomas Brassey, *op. cit.*, pp. 30-31; and "Contemporary Life and Thought in Turkey," *loc. cit.*, XXXV (July 1879), 754-55.

[100] Layard to Salisbury, Desp. No. 57, Jan. 11, 1880 (F. O., 78/3079); and Layard, *Mem.*, VIII, fo. 192.

[101] Layard, *Mem.*, VIII, fos. 156-57, and 167; Ramsay, *op. cit.*, p. 151; and "The Syrian Subjects of the Porte," *Blackwood's Magazine*, CXXXI (April 1882), 508.

The whole reason for England's failures in 1878 to 1880 comes to this: The Sultan and those who shared the spoils of the old regime were not interested in reform or in any policy other than that of maintaining the system which fulfilled their selfish desires regardless of the cost to the mass of people whose welfare, after all, was more often than not an excuse offered by self-proclaimed reformers who sought gains quite as selfish as those of the Sultan and his pashas. Their method was the old and well-tried one of playing one power and one group of interests off against another and in this game they were past masters who could not be outdone easily, even by men as energetic and forceful as Layard or as wily and sharp-witted as Ignatiev.[102]

In fact in 1875 England had stood at the parting of the ways in her policy toward Turkey. Was she to bolster up the Ottoman Empire or partition it and take her share? The exigencies of imperial interests and the constellation of the foreign powers had led Beaconsfield to proclaim the traditional policy but had not prevented partition, although England's share was disguised by the Cyprus Convention and by lip-service to the old shibboleth of the independence and integrity of the Ottoman Empire. Nevertheless, men in or connected with the government like Salisbury, Home, and Layard, and capitalists and imperialists like Sutherland, Andrew, and almost every consul or Indian official in the East, had dreamed dreams of England's mission to civilize the backward regions of Turkey and thereby to strengthen and protect British imperial interests. This view formed a part of the Cyprus policy but was incompatible with that other part

---

[102] The general situation in regard to Turkey and the British policy in 1880 is very ably summed up by Layard, in his Desp. No. 461, April 27, 1880 (*loc. cit.*). Since he was of course anxious to put the best interpretation possible on affairs in order to defend himself before the Gladstone government, his tone was not as pessimistic as it later was in his memoirs. Furthermore, many of his most damning statements were omitted from the Blue Book because they concerned the Sultan or other nations. See appendix for the most significant omissions.

which made it necessary to work through the existing Turkish institutions.

Great Britain failed in the great objects which Beaconsfield and Salisbury set before her because she was compelled to adopt a compromise and the compromise would not work. What changes they might have made it is impossible to know, for the election of 1880 ended the experiment. But the fundamental problem which Beaconsfield and Salisbury tried to solve was later in part settled by the occupation of Egypt[103] and eventually by the entente with Russia, although at the cost of much bloodshed and the abandonment and disregard of Asiatic Turkey.

The development of Turkish railroads, on the other hand, was destined to be undertaken by Germany instead of England who was thrust from first place in the affairs of Asia Minor until the outcome of the World War went far to give her that predominance in the Euphrates Valley and the Near East which Beaconsfield, Salisbury, Layard and a host of others had desired in 1878. Likewise, while Cyprus did not immediately become a great stronghold nor an "emporium of trade," the recent developments in airways and the current political trends in Egypt, Palestine, and Arabia may yet render it an indisputably valuable link both in the commerce and the defense of the Empire.

[103] Cf. Headlam-Morley, *loc. cit.*, p. 207.

APPENDIX

APPENDIX

DOCUMENTS

No. 1

a. Lieutenant-Colonel Robert Home to General Sir J. L. A. Simmons, Confidential, Constantinople, 20-12-76. Rec'd 10/1/77 (F. O. 358/1).

My dear Sir Lintorn,

.   .   .   .

I have hitherto refrained from writing anything about the state of the negotiations, or on any polititical [*sic!*] subject. These things are not my métier, but at the present moment things are looking very strange indeed. The state of tension here can last but a short time longer, something must give way and that shortly. I feel sure that either before you get this letter, or immediately after, you will hear of startling events. And I greatly fear events which will not be to the advantage of England. As you know I am narrow in my ideas. My heart is not largly [*sic!*] enough to embrace all the distressed nations of Europe, as Mr. Gladstone's does. My experience of said nations, is that they are reaping a just reward of previous bad conduct, and that the only thing to do them good is to let them learn in punishment the folly of their former ways. As a rule they are a dirty ill-conditioned set of scoundrels—and I cannot embrace them. I think only of England. I care only for her interests, and I fear much her interests are likely to be jeopardised. Let us look at the position. Russia has mobilized a large proportion, two thirds, of her army. She is said to be on the eve of mobilizing the remainder. Her army of the South, she has posted with the evident intention of crossing the Pruth near Sculiani, Kischenev and Maritz or Galatz from Akerman.

Russia cannot keep her forces mobilized for any length of time and do nothing. She must use this force, or she must return to a peace footing having uselessly spent much money. Which will she do?

At the present moment the public opinion of Europe is an element that cannot be neglected. Russia a short time ago found herself to a certain extent isolated. With the view of placing herself in accord with the European powers, she will agree with the various proposals whatever they may be that the representatives of those powers may make. She will endeavor to keep some sore subject, something very difficult to swallow for Turkey in their condition, and she will endeavor to effect an agreement with all the powers that if she thus reduces some of her demands, the Powers must promise to sever diplomatic intercourse with Turkey should she refuse to accept the terms en Bloc. Meantime she will by means of her agents amongst the Turks themselves, urge the Porte to refuse these conditions. She will thus go to the Conference which meets on Saturday in full accord with all the powers, knowing that Turkey will never accept the terms proposed, and knowing well that she, Russia, has arranged this. When the Turks give their definite refusal which they will be urged to do at once, Russia will issue a manifesto to the world calling on the Great Powers to fulfill their engagements & withdraw their Ambassadors & she will cross the Pruth.

The Turks are eager for war. The tremendous strain of the corruption has driven the Moslem population to contemplate war, as preferable to peace. We have two embassies here. I sometimes see both; but the substance of what I now write, put in a clear form, I submitted some days ago to Sir H. E[lliot] and Lord S[alisbury]. The former agreed with me, I don't think the latter did.

You thus see that Turkey will be deprived in the earlier stages of the war at least of British support. She will be isolated, & Russia will have the sympathy of Europe with her, as against "these impracticable Turks." My own view is that you will see the Manifesto I have referred to either about the 5th or 7th of Jan'y & the Pruth crossing about the 7th or 9th.

Now what will happen? You may depend on it that there will be another so called Massacre of Christians; that is to say the Moslem population dread an uprising or revolt. The Christians dread a massacre & when two parties are living in juxtaposition with such views, you may depend on it that a spark, some fellow kissing a girl if even she do not object; will produce a riot & bloodshed. Next atrocity meetings, necessity of Gladstone's bag and baggage policy being carried out. I am not as you well know an alarmist. I do not expect a general Massacre of Xians, but I should be not the least surprised to see a serious emeute in this city; got up by these very agreeable Xians, with the object of plunder. Under the circumstances I have proposed, with Sir H. E.['s] sanction, a scheme for defending the Embassy buildings. If the arms which are coming from the fleet as wine cases, are got up, we can hold the place for some time. I do not dread much, but I think we should have our retreat covered. The Turks are beginning to question the policy of England. They are beginning to suspect that if their country is partitioned; England will want a slice—and that if an English army comes here, it may remain. This feeling of suspicion is very palpable. The Turk is beginning to quote our Saviour's words, "He that is not for me is against me."

These questions are being further complicated by the action of Austria. *I*, the pronoun is dashed to mark it as my opinion, *I* think Austria is playing us false. She is I am convinced urging the Turks to resist. She will then throw in her lot with Russia & seize Bosnia & Herzegovina, probably giving Cattaro to Montenegro as a sop to Russia. Andrassy is quite willing to take Bosnia, & Herzegovina; he is only coy [because?] the Magyars do not wish it & he is their Great Man, but force of circumstances, has made many a woman yield and allow what she really did not much dislike, but what she would have shrunk from seeking. Andrassy is a coy maiden. "La belle qui parle—La femme qui hesite—l'une et l'autre toujours se renden[t]."

Under the circumstances who will benefit? I have no hesitation in saying that the country that has her army ready, and her sword drawn will benefit. That country is Russia. Turkey will fight desperately. Old and Young Turkey, both will unite, & when blood is drawn & passions roused Deeds of terrible violence will be done on both sides, Deeds which will be echoed through Europe. Q[uery of] Gladstone "Was not I right, did I not say the Turks were savages, to be kicked out of Europe bag and baggage." Russian cruelties, Montenegrin atrocity, Xtian crime will be hidden—And the fair haired young Bulgarian Lady will again come to the front—With what result? When passions are roused, Imperial promises disappear, & Russia is seated here, it is a "fait accompli" & Europe will accept it—

England doubting and hesitating will look on, and the National interests will suffer. The empire will be jeopardized, because Mr. Gladstone wishes to turn Lord Beaconsfield out.—

There is a strong party I believe in England & there is certainly a strong party here, who want England to come here, & occupy Constantinople & hold it against Turks and Russians, annex it in short.—Your friend White who talks often to me on these questions wishes this. We discussed it last night, and I think he left with a different opinion.

To hold this place, you must hold 4 distinct lines. You must cover the City on the Asiatic and European sides, & you must cover the Dardanelles on both sides.— Permanent works to do this would cost 25 or 30 millions. There are in this city a million of people some the greatest scoundrels on earth (Xians) how will you keep this city in order & garrison the forts? Will 60000 men do it? And how long will England keep 60000 men here? And conterminous with a great empire, she must do so. Railways will be made through the Balkans, & from Belgrade—& Russia will besiege the place. England here would be like France in Rome. The Prestige and moral power of this place is enormous— its situation is unrivaled, its advantages no one contests. But to seize a place & then abandon it, is the severest blow the prestige of any country can have. The Prestige of England sustained a graver shock by the abandonment of Corfu than it has done for many years.—

There is another course open to us, to seize Crete, Egypt or Rhodes, or all three.

Let us discuss these points. Crete is magnificent, a splendid island, everything we could wish as to soil, climate, military situation, but it is inhabited by 200000 Greeks—Now what would happen. Greek intrigues or Russian intrigues (for after the annexation of Constantinople Greece & Russia would be one) would soon rouse up disturbance precisely as was done in Corfu. The people would take to the mountains, & plunder, English cruelty & misgovernment would be paraded to the world. Mr. Gladstone & his Homer would come to the front. He would entirely forget Herodotus' dictum, that all Cretans are liars!! & we would have Corfu over again. It is said that Bismarck wants us to take Egypt. His reason is plain, bad blood with France. If there is a good harbour at Rhodes I think I would take it only, and I shall send an officer to inspect it when I can get one to spare. If the Harbour is good it would suit, a little too much to the East-ward, soil & climate good, pop. 30,000 Roman Catholic to a great extent. This Island was for many years the seat of the titular king of Jerusalem; it then belonged to the Knights of Malta (St. John)—& on their being driven out by the Turks they went under L'Isle d'Adam to Malta. Rhodes is not Greek history & Gladstone might leave us alone. Any way the Siege of Rhodes is more modern & would be the last & most popular event. Fur-ther a good deal might be made out of our being the Natural heirs of the Knights Hospitalers the good Samaritans—and as we have got Malta so ought we to have Rhodes.

Whatever may be done. I do hope & trust H. R. H. [The Duke of Cambridge] will push on our war preparations. Whether we have war or not, a nation that has bayonets behind speaks more forcibly than if She has not. 10,000 men should be held in hand to seize Rhodes at once.— But be sure of this, that the people who wish to occupy this place, in case of a war between Russia & Turkey, without our being allies of the Turks—who wish us to fight for our own hand, & thus engage in a triangu-lar duel, are utterly wrong. If we come here, we must come as friends & allies of the Turks.

Believe me to be

Yours truly,

R. HOME

b. *Home to Simmons, Constantinople, 16-1-77. Tuesday. Rec'd 26/1/77. (F. O. 358/1).*

My dear Sir Lintorn,

My packet of papers plans and reports was perfectly ready to go this morning by the messenger when he was ordered to stop until Friday his usual day. I now add a little.

The Political state is the great excitement. Midhat Pasha has positively refused to yield, what is demanded. The Conference has cut down all the disagreeable demands to two (there were eight). These are the appoint-ment of an international committee, and the appointment of the governors of provinces. But a large number of people say that at the last moment Midhat will give way. A large number say he will not.

If he does give way Lord S. will go home and a triumph be claimed, but I can't see much triumph in it. He has acted I fear too roughly.— He went round Europe looking for allies. He found none. When he came here, he fell into Ignatieff's arms. Madame Ignatieff laid herself out to catch Lady Salisbury. They became inseparable and Lady Salisbury spoke publicly & to everyone in a very unguarded foolish way about Turks & Turkish morals & customs. When, after preliminary meetings of the Con-ference were held, & the ambassadors agreed to make certain demands, or to leave Constantinople if not granted, it was found that Ignatieff & Mid-hat were en rapport. Ignatieff declared that Midhat proposed the treaty of Unkiar Skelessi over again. Midhat swears Ignatieff proposed it.

You remember this treaty admitted Russian men of war into the

Dardanelles & Bosphorus but no others. It matters little who proposed it, but it was proposed between Midhat & Ignatieff—This induced the other [?] powers to cut down the terms & so they now stand. I feel sure that Lord Salisbury would have done much better if his wife had remained at home. The Stories of her rudeness and insolence to Madame Midhat (not one of which *I* believe) which are in circulation, & the Pictures of her in a scurrilous Turkish Punch are not pleasant. That she has talked in a very unguarded way to Madame Ignatieff & to all the world, I can bear witness to, but Madame Ignatieff has retailed the stories. She is a very pretty handsome woman who shows her neck to the old Turks & retails Lady S honest English indignation at Madame's stories of the Turks, Madame forgetting to mention her share in the matter and says "There are your friends the English."

The result of all this is that English influence is simply nil, the people like Ignatieff better than Salisbury. He rightly is our enemy; we understand him, but we can't understand our friend. Whether Lord S. goes home with the Turks adhesion to the reduced terms or no, his mission must be regarded as a failure, if the maintenance of British influence is the object aimed at. For my part I think the time has nearly come when we must strike for our hand, & I beg that you will consider my Gallipoli Secret memo. Anstey is on the Asiatic side. I go to see him in a day or two.—I feel sure that if a treaty of Unkiar Skelessi is revived, that our reply should be the seizure of the Dardanelles & Gallipoli.

I have just heard that the departure of the ambassadors is delayed until Monday next, positively the last day of the performance. I hear the Turks are cutting up about our being here now & wonder why we don't go away. So you see matters are very queer.

Russian papers I hear say that she will not attack Turkey at the bidding of Lord Salisbury. Now Lord Salisbury did say when asked what would he do if the Turks were obstinate "He would set Ignatieff & the Russians at them." So you see Ignatieff has played his game so far as destroying British influence very well.—

When Lord S came out he spoke confidentially to me on many subjects & I told him my views but I saw at once that to attempt to give military advice to the Turks under such circumstances was worse than useless. And this is the reason why I have never been able to work the Turkish war office or Turkish officers.—The great error people in England make & people do it here, Lord S did it to a great extent, they think there are three people in the game: Russians, English & Turks. Now the most powerful class here, are the Greeks & next to them the Armenians. The Greeks have been utterly ignored by Lord S and the conference & they have opposed it tooth & nail. The Armenians also a very wealthy powerful faction, consider that they have been insulted because in Asia an outrage on an Armenian is thought nothing of in Europe. If a Bulgarian is trod on all Europe is up at the bidding of Russia. The Greeks also do not desire the proposed extension of Bulgaria to Philipopilis [*sic!*] & down to Salonica. They object strongly & being very clever unscrupulous people they have brought great pressure to induce the Turks to resist. Whatever is done: Peace or war, we have lost our position in the matter. If Russia and Turkey fight we can't back Turkey & I do not see how we can fight for Turkey without fighting for the Turks. Lord Salisbury says England will never fight for the Turks, but she will fight for Turkey. I can't see unless you have a triangular duel how it is to be done.—Any way beg of His Royal Highness to watch Gallipoli. If we get that we can hold it as a Material guarantee & there is no difficulty in doing so.—I want to get charts of Rhodes & Cyprus sent out as we must see these Islands.— Telegraph to me if you want further information about Gallipoli.

Another Bad thing here has been Sir H. E. was Philo Turk, Lord S anti Turk, Lady S violent anti Turk, Miss E violent Philo Turk. The two embassies were like oil and water, the old embassy considered that they were professionals, the New Embassy amateurs who were bumptious. The old Embassy said what ignoramuses, the New Embassy said what Duffers. Ignatieff said it took me 4 minutes to set the two embassies by the ears. So much for diplomacy.

Believe me to be

Yours truly

R. Home

c. *Home to Simmons, Constantinople, 8-2-77. Rec'd 21/2/77. (F. O. 358/1).*

.   .   .   .

Why did you say to my wife that I had become a Russian? Quite the contrary I have not altered one bit since I came to this country beyond being more than ever convinced of the truth of what you wrote in your paper about the Asiatic Frontier. There were but two courses open to England.

1. To maintain Turkey. To do so she would have to fight Russia & Austria certainly with Italy in reserve. Could England & the Turks do this? She might I believe, with the expenditure of enormous treasure & blood but cui bono.

2. To leave Turkey to her fate seizing upon some place that might be of use to her, such as the Dardanelles & Cyprus—This Lord Salisbury was prepared to do. It is quite impossible to deal with a question as this has been dealt with. You cannot have your Turkey dead and alive too. You cannot destroy Turkey and maintain her. Yet this has been our policy and the result has been a miserable fiasco.

You cannot undertake such a serious matter as a war with Russia, without having a united nation. A divided nation will simply break down, for it causes the Government to take half measures.

Lord Salisbury repeatedly talked over these things & when I urged the necessity of showing a bold front to Russia & helping Turkey *at once,* he always said "I know my countrymen too well, they will not shed one drop of blood for the Turks. But they will for the country for [*sic!* of] Turkey." And when I asked "How are you going to divide them, how are you going to fight for Turkey & not for the Turks, ["] he never could answer.

No Power short of a protectorate will make the country go straight, you have no upper classes at all. No points on which the people can form. No Public Opinion. The Pashas are a Bureaucratic Oligarchy of adventurers who seek to enrich themselves and do not care one halfpenny about the Empire. If England assumed a protectorate for 10 years, she could make the country go straight, but would the Powers allow this?

I should far rather see the status quo preserved, but how is it to be preserved? Austria and Russia both being prepared to invade & occupy Turkey in a moment.

These are the difficulties, and we should look at them perfectly independent of the word "ancient allies." Why ancient allies. I don't know, as we destroyed their fleet at Navarino, and also forced the Dardanelles under Duckworth. Also we should consider the question perfectly independent of Sodom, & the religious question, and look at it as a mere question of policy. Can we maintain the independence of Turkey & the integrity of the Ottoman Empire? If we can, is it worth doing? The first is a soldier's question, the second a statesman's. If the answer be that we cannot maintain it, or that its maintenance is not worth the trouble, then the question arises, what part of the Ottoman Empire shall we take possession of, to cover and protect our interests in case of war? These questions are not religious questions neither are they sentimental questions, & should be dealt with entirely out of the region of either religion or sentiment. And the mistake that has been made in my humble opinion is that we have had no policy whatever. We have never known what we were going to do, & how we were going to do it.

And we have been unfortunate in the manner in which we tried to bring our reforms about. And unfortunate in our agents. "The army, Russia & England combined can make the Turks do anything" declared Lord Salisbury, and as I think I told you he managed to get all shades & colors of Christians except the Slavs against him.

I send you a pamphlet which is well worthy of perusal, it is I believe quite authentic. So much for general questions.

Now as to myself. I trust & hope you have been satisfied with *all* I have done or left *undone*. It was no affair of mine to deal with political questions, it was no affair of mine, if Lord S. & Sir H. E. disagreed. But my cue was to keep straight with both & to play the Amateur & the Professional Embassies, so that I should not cause a quarrel or produce any discontent or dislike. This I trust I did & I hope people are satisfied. But the most troubled waters I have ever fished in, are Turkish waters— and I shall leave the country strongly imbued with the opinion that no reforms, no constitution will make a nation or a country here. What can you do, what can you expect of a nation that governs itself in the affairs of life by the Koran? What would England be if the administration of the law was in the hands of the Parsons and the law of petty Larceny & assault was based on the New Testament? What can you expect, to descend to details, from a country where there are 3 kinds of Time, 3

Sundays in the week and 5 kinds of money. When everything is Buck-seesh [*sic!*], from the miserable Octroi sentry at the Railway to the Prime Minister? What can you expect from a country, where truth is unknown, were a lie is always told in preference to truth and when high minded English gentlemen sink gradually to take bribes like the natives? When the word Christian means a body of men not Moslems, & when the Christians of various races & creeds hate one another worse than they do the infidel? I say nothing of Vices. I believe Polygamy & Sodomy are not more fre-quent in Turkey than they are in England. For I look upon Polygamy as an institution as preferable to the Promiscuous intercourse in London, & I dare say Henderson [?] could tell tales of Sodomy quite as bad as are told here. All over the world mens passions & mens vices are much the same—and I believe the Turkish Village population as a population will compare most favorably with any population in the world. But the whole state of affairs is utterly rotten & wrong & I do not think there is recuper-ative power in the nation to put it to rights.

It wants something from the outside. Can England put things right? Undoubtedly she can. But she will not.

Can Russia put things right? Undoubtedly she cannot. But she is quite ready to try. Such is the state of affairs.

It is all very well to blame our envoys but no envoy can make matters straight, when the Trumpet gives an uncertain sound.

Blame not Sir Henry Elliot, nor Lord Salisbury. But blame the people of England who boast that they rule themselves, & that the Prime Minister is but their servant. How can he go straight if they don't know their own mind?

Such are my ideas formed after a residence in Turkey for 3 months.
Believe me to be
my dear Gen'l
Yours very truly
R. HOME

No. 2

a. Memorandum by Lieutenant-Colonel R. Home Concerning a British Occupation of Gallipoli and the Dardanelles, submitted to Lord Salis-bury at the Conference of Constantinople and forwarded to General Sir J. L. A. Simmons on January 12, 1877 (F. O. 358/2).

Should circumstances occur to induce the British Government to seek a material guarantee in the East or should on the breaking up of the Turkish Empire it become requisite to seek compensation in the Levant—

The Peninsula of Gallipoli offers some great advantages. This peninsula is about 55 miles long from the Serjan Tepa mountains to the Sedil Bakr Cape and 15 miles wide at the widest part viz: from the Dardanelles to Sarola Burna, the narrowest portion being near the village of Bulair where the peninsula is just 3 miles wide. The area may thus be put at about 500 square miles. The surface is much diversified rising in parts to the height of 1100 feet. The soil is as a rule very fertile & cultivated and the population present all signs of comfort & material prosperity. There are numerous small harbours all along the shore line of the Dardanelles that at Gallipoli being remarkably good.

If Great Britain were to seize & occupy this Peninsula fortifying it at it's narrowest point she would completely deny the use of the Dardanelles to men of war or vessels of any kind.

But although powerful batteries on the European side would effect this an enemy having advanced through Asia Minor or having landed in the Black Sea & advancing via Broussa could by placing heavy batteries on the Asiatic side command the Dardanelles to such an extent that the use of the straits might be denied to the British Fleet also.

Holding the Peninsula of Gallipoli would thus be an incomplete measure while it would completely deny the Mediterranean Sea to vessels coming from the North that is from the Black Sea & Sea of Marmora it would not open the latter sea to British Vessels at all times. The former would prevent Russian men of war from coming south the latter would prevent British men of war from going north.

It is conceived that this may be met by holding the position above Kale Sultan. This position would really give the force holding the Gallipoli Peninsula a Tête du Pont on the Asiatic side from which it might at all times sally out & prevent an enemy from constructing heavy batteries on the Asiatic side.

The following is an approximate estimate of the cost:

Defences of Bulair

1 Fort	£150,000
3 Do at 50,000	150,000
1 Do at 80,000	80,000
Barracks for troops	1,000,000
Railway from Gallipoli to Bulair 9 miles at £8000.	72,000
Store Establishment Wharves & Pier at Gallipoli	200,000
Total European side	£1,672,000

To this must be added the following:
Occupation of the heights over Kale Sultan.

4 Forts at 100,000	£400,000
Pier & stone	80,000
Barracks	150,000
Roads 30 miles at £1000	30,000
Total Asiatic side	£660,000
Remodelling defences of Dardanelles	300,000
Total	£960,000
Grand Total	£2,632,000

In war the garrison required would be about 20,000 men in peace about 4000 the cost of the work is not excessive but the annual expenditure & the difficulty of maintaining 4000 men in another foreign country would be considerable.

To meet these points it is submitted that a sufficiently large tract of country in Asia Minor should be taken possession of & that the British territory should not be terminated by the rayon of the works. Such a portion of territory on the Asiatic side would be that extending from the Gulf of Edremid to the Sea of Marmora, and on the European side the country bounded by the Kuru Dagh & Tekir Dagh mountains thus securing the very rich valley of the Kewak river. Both these countries are very rich and both are inhabited by a very mixed population Turks, Jews, Greeks & a good many Armenians.

Questions of nationality would not be burning questions with such a population and the enormous advantages of a strong just & improving Government would very soon induce the people to regard their rulers with at least liking.

One half of the taxes now extorted from these people would pay the annual cost of the whole military establishment and the native population formed into a local militia and officered by English Officers who would undertake in peace time the duty of local magistrates or Kamiakhams would be able with the help of an English contingent to maintain the works.

The moral & political advantages that would accrue from this occupation would be great. The sight of a mixed population of varied creed & race well governed & in a happy flourishing condition and the contrast that would be afforded between those under British rule and those outside its pale would be very great.

There is however the great & undoubted disadvantage that this arrangement commits the country to having a continental possession close to the frontier of what may be a great military power. The extent of the front to be defended 3 miles near Bulair & 4 miles near Kale Sultan will admit of the works for the defence of those places being made exceedingly strong; they may be kept constantly supplied from the Sea while for many years the enemy would be unable from the want of good roads & the nature of the country to bring up a heavy siege train. It may perhaps be urged that it is impossible to take possession of these places without forcing the passage of the Dardanelles. This however is not so.

There is an admirable landing for troops not far from Bulair on the Gulf of Xeros—a small force landed here & marched along the heights overlooking the European defences of the Dardanelles would effectually silence them, while a similar force landed near Kum Kale would perform a similar function as regards the Asiatic side.

In a report which Admiral the Hon'ble. Sir James Drummond K. C. B. has been good enough to give me I find the following: "At the head of the" "Gulf of Xeros there is excellent anchorage well sheltered for a very large" "fleet from all winds except West. The landing all along the coast from" "Bulair to the mouth of the river Kewak is excellent".

Should circumstances necessitate there would be no difficulty whatever in seizing the Peninsula and so turning the whole defences of the Dardanelles. Attached are exact statistics [1] of the Gallipoli Position. These statistics may be relied on. Two points are remarkable: the great wealth of the people and the effect of conscription on the Turkish Population, which is rapidly disappearing from this cause alone.

(S'd) R. HOME Lt. Col. R. E.

b. *Memorandum by General Sir J. L. A. Simmons Respecting Instructions to be Sent to Home. Confidential, 2 February 1877. For the Commander-in-Chief and the Secretary of State for War. (Extract from F. O. 358/2).*

. . . .

The importance of sending instructions to Lieut. Col. Home is greatly enhanced by the fact, that he has sent to me, in a private letter confidentially a memorandum, herewith, marked I, drawn up for Lord Salisbury, which he has requested me to lay before your Royal Highness; in which as a "suitable compensation" he draws the attention of Lord Salisbury, to the importance of the position of Gallipoli, and suggests, that Great Britain should, as a material guarantee, take possession of a large tract of country, embracing the European and Asiatic shores of the Dardanelles, and fortify positions thereon at a cost of £2,632,000; requiring a peace garrison of 4000 men, and a war garrison of 20,000 men to hold them.

It is quite evident, as stated by Lieut. Col. Home, that holding the Dardanelles, if Russia held the Bosphorus, Great Britain could prevent the ships of Russia or any other power from passing between the Black Sea and the Mediterranean—but, as the position contains no good port, some other territory would have to be seized in which to place a naval dockyard and arsenal.

It is evidently to this necessity that the examination of Cyprus and Rhodes points. This further occupation would probably involve a second fortress, and garrison; which, if, on the scale of Malta, would lead to an expenditure of probably an additional £2,000,000 and require a garrison of from 4000 to 6000 men.

The magnitude of the question cannot therefore be exaggerated, and I venture to submit, that the material guarantee, secured by the occupation of the Dardanelles in the manner contemplated, is one, which should only be entertained after the most serious consideration. It is well to say that a peace garrison of 4000 men would suffice, but, considering the distance from England, its proximity to a territory, which, under the assumed hypothesis, will be in the occupation of a continental power, possessing an enormous army, recruited by conscription, and the certainty that railroads would soon be made in connection with the strategical lines, already

---

[1] These statistics are to be found in *Reports and Memoranda*, (0631), pp. 118-19.

existing in Russia, it would not be wise ever to leave it in occupation by so small a garrison; and, in the event of a war after the construction of these railways, I doubt, however strong the position, whether 20,000 men would suffice to hold it.

There is another point in connection with it, which must not be lost sight of. As Russia, or any other power, which might hold the Bosphorus, would have under its government, people of the same nationality as the population of the territory proposed to be seized by Great Britain, there would be constant intrigues and difficulties arising, which would keep the garrison and government of this territory in a perpetual state of feverish excitement.

Considering the smallness of our army with reference to the duties now cast upon it, by the extent of the British Empire in India, and elsewhere; and the necessary augmentation this territory would entail, which, including troops for relief would not be less than 50,000 or 60,000 men, the measure would, I fear, prove an element of embarrassment by an inordinate increase of our yearly national expenditure, would be an element of weakness rather than of strength in the event of a European war, in which Great Britain might be involved, and might eventually compel the adoption of conscription in this country for the recruitment of the army.

This takes no account of the increase of H.M.'s fleets, which would be necessary.

The partition of Turkey is a question of such vast magnitude from a military point of view, that I have ventured to submit these remarks for the consideration of your Royal Highness, with reference to the instructions to be sent to Lieut. Colonel Home, which if approved to the extent indicated by him, must clearly point in the minds of any foreign powers who might become acquainted with them, to a policy of partition.

Certainly, if the Turkish Government should become aware of them, they cannot plan any other interpretation upon them, and hence, I should apprehend difficulties in the performance of these duties.

The magnitude of the responsibility involved in the questions, also points to the desirability of finding some other solution than that of an extension of Russian territory, which might force such a measure on the consideration of Her Majesty's Government.

.　.　.　.　.　.　.　.　.　.　.　.　.　.

c. Memorandum on the Dardanelles by Home, Constantinople, 3-2-77 (Extract from printed Reports and Memoranda. 0631 (War Office, 1877), pp. 130-31).

There is perhaps no portion of the Turkish Empire, the future of which is so important to Great Britain as the Dardanelles. If these Straits be held by England, or a power friendly to England, the Bosphorus is of comparatively small importance.

In peace the great corn trade of the Danube must find an exit through the Bosphorus, and English merchant ships may trade in the Black Sea as they ever have done.

During war, although the entrance into the Black Sea may be denied to British ships of war, yet all exit from that sea may be denied to Russian ships by the Power holding the Dardanelles.

Master of the Dardanelles either directly by actual occupation, or, indirectly, by the action of a friendly Power, Great Britain, so long as she maintains her naval supremacy, may, command the Sea of Marmora, and Constantinople will be under the fire of her ships, as from its situation it must be always exposed to a naval attack from the Sea of Marmora.

Master of the Bosphorus, but denied the use of the Dardanelles, the Russian Navy would really be in much the same situation that it now is.

There is, I believe, however, one case, in which the possession of the Bosphorus, militarily speaking, would give Russia considerable advantage, even should the passage of the Dardanelles be denied to her. I allude to the case when having occupied Constantinople, either directly, or by a subordinate and subservient Power, she should seize, as she undoubtedly would do, on Turkish Armenia. If, indeed, the latter event were not antecedent to the former.

Holding Armenia and the Kurdish mountains Russia could threaten the head of the Persian Gulf *via* the valleys of the Euphrates and Tigris. The best means of meeting such an attack, viz., by aiming a blow at Tiflis and the valley of the Kura River, so as to sever the Russian communications at the most vulnerable point would (were Russia in possession of the Bosphorus) be denied to England. This, perhaps, is the only military advantage Russia would gain were she seated on the Bosphorus, the Dardanelles being denied to her.

Morally and politically her gains would be very great, but it is desirable to deal here with the military question only.

The peculiar topographical nature of the Dardanelles and the Gallipoli Peninsula seem to invite their occupation by a Power strong at sea, disposing of a powerful navy and a small army.

It is quite true that, as time went on, Russia could turn the Dardanelles, as it were, by using Salonica on the Aegean Sea, or Avlona on the Adriatic, now no longer guarded by Corfu. But many years must elapse before this could be done, the occupation of Salonica as a military post would place the Russian fleet under the surveillance of England at the Dardanelles. And the occupation of Avlona on the Adriatic would bring her into collision with both Italy and Austria. These contingencies are merely alluded to here as forming a portion of the general question.

. . . .

No. 3

a. A. H. Layard to the Earl of Beaconsfield, Private and Secret, Therapia, June 20, 1877 (Layard's Letter Book, Add. MS 39,130, fos. 37-40. Cf. Monypenny and Buckle, Disraeli, II, 1014-15).

Dear Lord Beaconsfield:

I rec^d yr. letter of 6th by the Mess^r on the 16th. You may rely upon my looking upon it as a strictly personal communication of the utmost confidence. I telegraphed a reply to it on Monday last (18th) & enclose a decypher of my telegram to prevent mistakes.

You will judge of my opinion of the present state of affairs here & of the prospects of the future by my confidential despatches to Lord Derby relating to the terms of peace proposed by Prince Gorchakow & by my Tel. to you. The Chancellor may have put forward these conditions to frighten us into an attempt to impose them upon Turkey & to endeavour to use England as a cat's paw—as he has done before. He may have no serious intention of insisting upon the whole of them & may be prepared to give way as he did, thro' Ignatieff, at the Conferences, when he succeeded in making the Porte believe that the original proposals came from us, & that we were more hostile to Turkey than Russia herself. But supposing them to be the minimum demand of Russia before her armies cross the Balkans when still more onerous & fatal terms are to be required of the Turks, they w^d be tantamount, if accepted, to the immediate dismemberment & dissolution of Turkey in Europe. I have given some of my reasons for thinking so in my Despatches to Ld Derby above referred to, & I need not, therefore, repeat them here. I may be & no doubt shall be accused of exaggeration and Russophobism! But I appeal with confidence to your impartial judgment. I have endeavoured to avoid exaggeration & to deal with facts past & present. One cannot cast history aside altogether in dealing with such momentous questions, nor ought a statesman who has to deal with them to shut his eyes to past experience. As to "Russophobism" I have no hatred of Russia or Russians, but I place above any feeling for them the interests of my country, which I believe to be most seriously menaced at the present time, & wh. I further believe w^d be most gravely compromised should Russia succeed in imposing Prince Gortchakow's terms upon Turkey.

You ask me in your letter whether, in my judgement, there are no means which might lead to the maintenance generally of the "status quo" & at the same time place England in a commanding position when the conditions of peace are discussed? I answer frankly that I believe the only way of accomplishing these ends is by telling Russia distinctly & decidedly what we shall allow her to do & that we are prepared to take measures at once to prevent her doing more. But then we must make up our minds as to how far we are willing to allow Russia to go. The formation of the two Bulgarian Provinces, north & south, of the Balkans into a vasal [*sic!*] autonomous province, will, in my opinion, lead inevitably to the dismemberment of the Turkish Empire, not only in Europe but in Asia & Africa. I have given my reasons for thinking so in my official Despatches. Is H.M.G. prepared for this dismemberment & its consequences to England and to the balance of power in Europe? If not, we should tell Russia with no hesitating or uncertain voice that we will not permit the formation of an autonomous state out of the Bulgarian districts in question. Is H.M.G. prepared to see the north of Persia & the alternative road to India by the Euphrates valley fall into the hands of Russia? If not we should tell her with equal clearness & decision that we will not permit her to make territorial acquisition in Armenia. As yet as far as I can judge from the information wh. has reached me H.M.G. have only pointed out to Russia the capital points upon which England will insist, viz., That she shall not occupy Constantinople & the Straits or interfere with the Suez Canal. On these points she has no difficulty in giving assurances that some people are willing to accept as satisfactory, but both these objects may be accomplished quite consistently with those assurances. The dismemberment of Turkey in Europe & the extinction of the rule of the Sultan in that part of his Empire must sooner or later lead to the fall of Constantinople. The right of free navigation for Russian fleets thro' the Straits must give Russia the command of the Suez Canal, unless we are prepared to annex Egypt & to keep at all times a very powerful fleet between the Coast of Egypt & the entrance to the Dardanelles.

We should be ready to assist Russia in obtaining every possible guarantee for the good gov't not only of the Slav, but of all other Christian populations of Turkey—short of forming autonomous states that must be completely under Russian Controul [*sic!*], & must soon throw off their dependence upon the Sultan. Perhaps the best measures to be taken with this object w^d be such as w^d ensure the effective working of the Constitution & the Parliament. But to them Russia w^d probably not agree. She will scarcely permit Turkey to have Constitutional institutions.

Such a demonstration as the occupation by us of the Peninsula of Gallipoli as a material guarantee to be restored at the end of the war, & the sending up of our fleet to Constantinople might induce Russia to pause & to reconsider the terms that she would consent to give Turkey. But supposing that she did not, but persisted in her intention of breaking up the Ottoman Empire in spite of us what could we do further? It must be remembered that Greece will in all probability move as soon as Russia has obtained any marked success, & that it will be almost impossible to prevent a rising in Thessaly & Epirus & perhaps in part of Macedonia where there is a considerable Greek population. It is by no means certain that Albania will not rise also & that the insurrection will spread in Bosnia. There may be a general break up and anarchy.

If England were determined to deal with such a state of things in a manner adequate to the vast interests she has at stake she could, I believe, compel Russia to hold back. You are the best judge of how far public opinion in England w^d permit H.M.G. to take the decisive & energetic measures that w^d be necessary to effect this. We should have no small or easy task before us. In case we were resolved to go thro' with it there are certain measures wh. could be used against Russia.

1. To assist the Turks actively by money & officers & by troops. It would perhaps not be too late now to give them such assistance as w^d enable them to withstand the Russians even with such materials as they have, supposing no other power interfered on behalf of Russia.

2. To make use of Hungary & Gallicia to prevent the active interference of Austria in behalf of Russia, or if necessary even to incite the Hungarians & Gallician Poles to take part against Russia. If my informa-

tion is trustworthy, they are ready, especially the Hungarians, with whose national leaders the Porte is in secret communication.

3. To raise the Mahommedan States in Central Asia occupied & threatened by Russia against her. For this object we might avail ourselves of the aid of Turkey as the influence of the Sultan is great in those states. I have to a certain extent prepared the way for this, should H.M.G. be disposed to avail themselves of it, by inducing the Sultan to send an Envoy to Afghanistan to counteract the Russian policy of the Ameer & to promote that of England. The Sultan w^d at our request call upon the whole of Central Asia to rise against the Russians. Yakoob Khan the envoy of Kashgar now in England can give information as to the probable success of such an appeal to the Mahommedans of Turkestan. I am in communication on this subject with Lord Lytton.

4. We should at once inform the Hellenic Gov^t that we will not permit Greece to move against Turkey or to promote insurrections amongst the Greek populations. The presence of one or two British men of war at the Piraeus w^d keep Greece quiet & prevent her causing Turkey & ourselves serious embarrassment. At the same time we should let the Greeks know that when terms of peace are being discussed their interests shall be considered, & that any rights & privileges granted to the Slavs should be extended to them. It should be our policy to make a bulwark of the Hellenic race against the Slave [*sic!*] & to look to the Greeks as the future occupiers of such part of Southern Turkey in Europe as the Turks may not be able to retain.

The occupation of Gallipoli and the appearance of the British fleet in the Bosphorus must of course be the first steps toward carrying out such a policy as I have indicated. It w^d require some management to get the Sultan & the Porte to invite us to take them; but I think that I could contrive that they should do so. There is a strong feeling of suspicion & mistrust of England. The Turks cannot understand our policy. They are disposed to believe that altho' we will not help them we are disposed to help ourselves and are looking out for our share of the spoil. There is however a powerful party in the palace in favour of Turkey acting by herself & against foreign interference. This party is to be feared as it is one wh. might make terms with Russia without us. I have a good opinion of the Sultan, & I might, I think, do much with him, if my hands were not tied. His Ministers are weak & incompetent, those about him in the Palace for the most part corrupt & bad. I see no man fit to be Grand Vizier at such a crisis. Altho' I have no very favourable opinion of Midhat Pasha & believe him to be a dangerous Minister & one of the principal causes of the difficulties in which Turkey is placed, he may perhaps be the best man for the moment; but it w^d not be easy to get the Sultan to receive him, as he has given H.M. good cause to fear him.

In considering our policy with regard to Russia we must take into account the attitude of Germany & Austria. As far as I can judge of it here it is decidedly favourable to her, & hostile to Turkey. I was, at one time, inclined to think that Zichy was instructed to act with me & to be moderate in his dealings with the Porte. But I have now good grounds for knowing that he has been playing a double game & that Austria is taking a far more hostile tone to Turkey than any other power, altho' the Austrian Gov^t may endeavour to conceal the fact from the Hungarians. Germany, if I can trust to what falls from Prince Reuss is ready to support Russia in imposing terms upon the Porte which w^d be most dangerous to our interests. France judging from Decazes language to Lyons is wavering & undecided as to the course she will pursue.

Altho' I have ventured to write to you as to what I think might be done I hope that you will understand that I have hitherto confined myself strictly to carrying out what I understand to be the policy of H.M.G. & that while endeavouring to pave the way for a more energetic & decided policy hereafter, should such a policy be hereafter adopted, I have most carefully abstained from in any way committing H.M.G.

If you decide upon occupying the Gallipoli Peninsula it should be as a material guarantee to be given up at the end of the war & this should be fully explained to the Sultan. As Russia has, I believe, offered a territorial guarantee to Austria she could have no reasonable grounds for objecting to England having a similar guarantee. She has already proposed that our fleet should appear before Constantinople, & as you observe, we could not allow our fleet to be in the Bosphorus especially in time of war, without at the same time, securing the passage of the Dardanelles, & this could only be effected by holding the Gallipoli Peninsula.

I have suggested in a Telegram to you that an Engineer officer of ability & experience should be sent out here at once to look to the defences of Constantinople. The Buyuk Tchekmedji lines are now being completed but nothing whatever has been done, I believe, on the Gallipoli Peninsula. As soon as you decide upon its occupation, I will urge the matter strongly upon the Turks. A few English navvies w^d do the work best. I find Sir C. Dickson of much use in communicating with the Turkish Military Authorities to whom we have been able to give quietly a good deal of important information & many hints. But he has no practical experience in the construction of defensive works, not being an Engineer.

I must apologise to you for the length of this letter, wh. could only be justified by the importance of the matter to which it relates. I beg to thank you very sincerely for the approval you are kind enough to express in your letter to me of my conduct here.

(Signed) A. H. LAYARD.

b. A. H. Layard to the Earl of Beaconsfield, Secret, Constantinople, December 12, 1877 (Layard's Letter Book, Add. MS 39,130, fos. 195-99. See Beaconsfield to Layard, Nov. 22 [sic! 27], 1877, in Monypenny and Buckle, Disraeli, II, 1123-24).

Dear Lord Beaconsfield,

The last messenger brought me your message of the 27th ult. I had an opportunity on Monday last to obtain some information wh. may enable me to answer some of your enquiries. The Minister for F. A., upon whom I was calling shewed me a telegram from Musurus[1] relating his conversation with you on the subject of a loan to Turkey. He said that you had shewn an earnest desire to assist her, but that to obtain money a guarantee was required & you wished to know what kind of guarantee the Porte could give. You had hinted at some territorial cession which might be acceptable to England & for which she might be inclined to pay a sum sufficient to enable the Porte to enter with some prospect of success upon a second campaign. But you had not specified what that cession should be. You had mentioned that overtures had been made some months ago on the subject to the British Gov't. Musurus added that he had suggested an arrangement with the Turkish creditors wh. w^d reduce by one half the rate of interest paid upon the foreign debts and the sinking fund. A large portion of the guarantees assigned to the present foreign creditors would then be released & could be given for a new loan. H.M.G. might assist the Porte in making this arrangement. Such was the general substance of Musurus telegram.

I had thus occasion to ask Server Pasha[2] what he & the Gd. Vizier thought of the suggestion that, according to Musurus you had made to him. He replied that it w^d be very difficult, if not impossible, for the Sultan to cede any part of his territory for money, and, moreover, if once a territorial cession were made to one Power there was no saying what other Powers might require. He understood, he said that before he was in office some kind of suggestion had been made to the Grand Vizier about Crete, but it came from a private source, & had never been seriously entertained. He asked me whether it had come from the Embassy; I replied in the negative. He then took up Musurus idea of making an arrangement with the creditors & of freeing a part of the guarantees assigned to them, for the purpose of raising a new loan. He seemed to think that by this means & with the help of H.M.G. the Porte might get the money it required. I pointed out to him that after Mahomed Pasha's decree, amounting to a declaration of bankruptcy, & the way in which the Bondholders had been treated as regards the guarantees given to them, there was very little hope of the Porte being able to raise a loan without giving other solid guarantees, upon the punctual application of which the utmost reliance can be placed. We then discussed the possibility of an assignment by the Porte of certain monies to be collected & paid over to the Bondholders by or through the British Gov^t. These revenues might be of two kinds—territorial & fiscal. Server Pasha spoke of the possibility of giving over the administration of the island of Crete to functionaries of the British Gov^t or to persons to be appointed by it. But were this feasible & he did not say that it was, he admitted that the revenues to be derived from the island would amount to very little. At present the Porte, instead of deriving any from it is obliged to remit money

[1] Turkish Ambassador at London.
[2] Turkish Foreign Minister.

to it. Under a good administration the revenues might, no doubt, be increased. The customs of the principal ports of the Empire might unquestionably be improved if an honest & intelligent administration were substituted for the present system of fraud & corruption, and if competent foreign officers were placed over them. Upon this subject I have frequently spoken to the Grand Vizier who professes himself ready to make the necessary reforms. He would apply to H.M.G. to send capable men to undertake them, but all help of this kind has been refused by us. The matter is worthy of consideration. If Constantinople, Smyrna, Beyrout, Salonica & some other of the principal Ports were properly & honestly administered they would furnish a very much larger revenue than they do now.

My conversation with Server Pasha was strictly private & confidential & for obvious reasons I made it as general as possible. It was merely an "exchange of ideas" in diplomatic phraseology. I gathered from what fell from him that under present circ[umstance]s the Porte w^d not be likely to listen to any proposal for a cession of territory. The Sultan & the Turkish Ministers still cling to the formula of the "independence & integrity" of the Empire & they w^d think that to give up territory w^d be to renounce the latter. The subject could only be approached with the greatest caution. Their suspicions of our intentions which had been allayed if not altogether removed have been revived by the reports sent to them of Lord Derby's recent speech & of its effect upon public opinion. I believe that they have confidence in me & are inclined to listen to anything that I may say. But as you may conceive my position is a most difficult & delicate one. It is my duty to avoid, with the utmost care, committing H.M.G. or holding out hopes that may be disappointed, or may encourage the Porte in any policy which may end by being disastrous to it.

I will now endeavour to answer the questions you put to me as to what territorial concessions the Porte might make to England in return for pecuniary assistance, supposing it were willing to do so, which w^d be conducive to British interests.

You refer to a Port in the Black Sea. There is, I believe, but one, not in the possession of Russia which would be of any use to us—Batoum. In a Despatch sent home by the last Mess^r I ventured to insist upon the great importance of this place to Russia as giving her the command of Armenia & consequently of the vallies [*sic!*] of the Tigris & Euphrates. Unfortunately the English people who know little of geography, have been induced to look upon its acquisition by Russia with indifference, as if it had nothing to do with English interests. In my opinion Batoum in the hands of Russia would be most dangerous to them. Neither Batoum nor any other Port in the Black Sea would be of much use to any Power that had not the permanent command of the straits, except Russia. But the Gd Vizier has made a suggestion, which I have already brought to the notice of H.M.G. deserving, I think, your most serious consideration, viz., That Batoum should be made a free port. It is so near Poti, the terminus of the Tiflis railway that a few miles of rail would unite the two places. If Russia really desires Batoum, as she states for Commercial purposes she would obtain all that she wishes if it be declared a free port. It might be placed under the guarantee or protection of the Great Powers. Even if Russia should retain Kars, the danger to us would be greatly decreased if she did not hold Batoum also. If England were prepared to adopt a definite & energetic policy in support of British interests, she might insist upon Batoum remaining in the possession of Turkey as a free port. There would be nothing unfair or unjust in her doing so. Commercial advantages w^d be secured thereby to all the maritime powers who w^d thus have the way open to them into Central Asia, Asia Minor & Northern Persia, unless Russia were to cut it off by the annexation of the whole of Armenia. If Russia does obtain Batoum she will probably convert it into a great naval, military & trading station. The place still holds out notwithstanding the determined efforts of the Russians to take it, which afford a proof of the vast importance they attach to the Port. There is no doubt, as you observe, that our possessions of Batoum would be equally advantageous to Turkey & to ourselves. But we could not be certain of holding it unless the straits were not only absolutely free but were deprived of all defence. I am assured that Batoum cannot be taken by the Russians as long as the Turks command the sea from whence it is completely protected. The Russians are, it appears, making preparations to attack the Turkish ships now there, & it is not impossible, considering the carelessness of the Turks that they may succeed in launching torpedoes upon them. Hobart Pasha ought to be sent there at once. I am pressing this.

A commanding position in the Persian Gulf might, you suggest be a great object to us, if Armenia is lost to the Porte. I am not aware that Turkey has any such position in the Gulf. Upon that point the Indian Gov^t can, no doubt, give full information. But there is a position near the mouth of the Euphrates and at the junction of that river with the Karoon which traverses one of the richest provinces of Persia that has always appeared to me of the greatest importance to England; viz. Mohammorah. In my youth I examined that country with great care & was the first to prove the navigability of the Karoon, a river upon which an English Company w^d now open steam communication but for the refusal of the Persian Gov^t to permit them to do so. I induced Col. Taylor, then Resident at Bagdad, to send a steamer up the Karoon & I succeeded in getting, in her, within a short distance of Shuster. When people in England scoff at the idea of the vallies [*sic!*] of the Euphrates & Tigris being of any value to England as affording a means of direct communication with India they seem to "ignore" the fact that a railway might & probably will, in the course of time, (if it is allowable for any one in these days to think or speak of a "hereafter") be carried thro' the country to the East of the Tigris and Euphrates, through the Provinces of Khuzistan & Fars & ultimately through Beloochistan to Scinde. The idea is no doubt gigantic; but things apparently equally impossible have been accomplished in our time. If there be one quality greater than another which is required in a statesman it is the power of seeing into the future. Now Mohammorah would give us the command of the low country between the great and difficult range of Zagros (the Lower & Bakhteyan mountains) & the Tigris & Euphrates & consequently of any railway that might be constructed through the Province of Khuzistan. This will be seen by a glance at the map. Khuzistan is moreover a rich and valuable province. But it belongs to Persia, as does Mohammorah. To the latter place Turkey has ancient claims, which were set aside by Russia & ourselves when defining the boundaries between Turkey & Persia. The question really depends upon whether the stream which bounds the island of Mohammorah to the East is the outlet of the Karoon, or a mouth of the Shat-el-Arab (the Euphrates). Great changes have taken place in the courses of these rivers. I have little doubt that not very long ago the Karoon really flowed into the Euphrates & formed part of what is called Shat-el-Arab. It so appears on ancient maps. Had we not recognised the right of Persia to Mohammorah we might now perhaps have obtained a cession of the Porte's claims to it for a money consideration.

I do not believe that, at the present time, the Porte w^d be prepared to cede Crete, Cyprus or any other island in the Mediterranean to us. Crete has a splendid harbour, Souda, but would yield little or no revenue. Cyprus would be even of less use to us by all accounts. If we only want a good harbour one can be found in the small island of —————[1] which has been visited by some of our officers with that view. As regards the Suzerainty over Egypt that is a question of Imperial Policy upon which I do not feel myself competent to give an opinion. All I can say is, that I very much doubt whether the Porte would consent to part with it, unless Turkey were no longer in a condition to keep it, & it was practically already lost to her.

I quite agree with you in thinking that if the Porte could be enabled to enter upon a second campaign, & we could help it to get money to do so & could combine with it the presence of the English fleet in the Bosphorus & a British army Corps at Gallipoli & Derkos, the result as to after negotiations might be great. But in order to accomplish this we ought to abandon at once a hesitating and undefined policy. The Turks do not know what to make of us. We seem to them to blow hot & cold. They think that we take an interest in them & advise them for their good, but that we will abandon them at once should Russia decline to listen to us, & that we are not ready even to make an effort in support of the most vital English interests. This language has been held to me by the G^d Vizier & Server Pasha & by other Turks of high station & influence. The impression that such is the case is gaining ground & at the same time the conviction that the only course for Turkey to pursue is to throw over England altogether & to come to a separate & direct understanding with Russia. Several members of the Cabinet & influential persons about the Sultan are of this opinion. Prince Reuss[2] loses no occasion of advising this course. Whether he only expresses his personal views or those of his Gov^t I cannot positively

---

[1] Space left blank in this copy. He undoubtedly refers to Astropalia, (Stampalia) recommended by Edwards and Egerton. See *ante* p. 60.

[2] The German Ambassador at the Porte.

say, but I suspect that he would not hold such language without the authority of the Emperor or of Bismarck. The Sultan & the Grand Vizier are still opposed to entering into direct communication with Russia, without the concurrence of England, but events may compel them to give way. I have observed that recently both the G^d Vizier & Server Pasha have alluded to the surrender of the right passage thro' the straits of Russian ships of war as a concession they were quite willing to make to Russia. The Grand Vizier in speaking of the subject a day or two ago to Jocelyn hinted that he did not see why Turkey should make sacrifices to maintain a right which, after all, was of little real importance to her only because it was in the interest of England for her to do so.

The fall of Plevna has now added to the dangers which menace this country. Should the Russians be determined to carry on the campaign during the winter & to advance upon Adrianople there is now absolutely nothing to oppose them, with the overpowering forces they have at their disposal. I almost doubt whether sufficient forces could be collected at Adrianople to defend the place. There would only then remain the lines of Derkos and of Gallipoli to prevent the Russians possessing themselves of Constantinople & the Dardanelles. Austria says, & some people in England also, that it signifies little if Russia should occupy Constantinople, she will not remain there. But admitting that she would, in the end withdraw, have those who are willing to see her in temporary possession of Constantinople calculated the effect that its capture would have upon the Eastern & Mahomedan world? I cannot believe that any man who has the greatness, the interests & the honour of England at heart can contemplate such an event without the deepest anxiety & the most melancholy forebodings. I will venture to repeat what I said some months ago when Adrianople was menaced by the Russian force that crossed the Balkans. "If we desire to save Constantinople & to prevent the break up "of the Turkish Empire, not only in Europe but probably in Asia too, we "must be prepared, at all costs & hazards, to assist the Turks in defending "the lines of Gallipoli & to bring our fleet up to the Golden Horn. But "neither of these things can we do unless we are prepared to act openly "either as the enemy or ally of Turkey."

I trust that you will forgive me for writing thus frankly to you. I should not be worthy of your confidence did I do otherwise. I grieve to hear that you are suffering from your eyes & trust that this long letter & a not very legible hand writing may not try them too much.

(Signed) A. H. LAYARD.

No. 4

a.   A. H. Layard to Lord Salisbury, Confidential Despatch No. 525, Constantinople, April 24, 1878 (Extract from F. O. 78/2786).

My Lord,

The present feeling of the Mussulman populations of the Turkish Empire with regard to England is of so remarkable a character that it deserves, it appears to me, the serious consideration of Her Majesty's Government.

In my despatch No. 492 of the 15th instant I informed Your Lordship that I am constantly receiving from Mahomedan gentlemen of influence and high position offers to place large numbers of men at the disposal of Her Majesty's Government as soldiers in the event of a war between her and Russia. Petitions and memorials are coming to me from the Mussulman inhabitants of various parts of the Empire asking for the protection of England. In Egypt, Syria, Bagdad, Asia Minor and Lazestan, the same desire is felt that England should either annex those countries, or secure to them, for the future, under her immediate supervision, a good just and equal Government, such as is enjoyed by Her Majesty's Mussulman subjects in Her Indian Empire.

The determination of the Mussulman populations of Constantinople, and of other parts of Turkey, not to permit the Government to abandon what is known as the 'English policy' is so strong that if the Sultan were to show any disposition to enter into an alliance or even into intimate relations, with Russia he might very probably lose his throne. Fortunately, his own views and inclinations are, I have every reason to believe, in conformity with those of his subjects. He has dismissed Raouf Pasha from the Ministry of War because public opinion, perhaps unjustly, accused him of being 'Russian'. His conduct towards Lord A. Loftus on his late mission to St. Petersburg greatly irritated His Majesty, and was, I have reason to believe, one of the causes of his fall, as the Sultan thought that the weakness of character he had shewn on that occasion in listening to General Ignatiew might place him completely under Russian influence.

Said Pasha, the late Minister of Marine, who is looked upon as one of the most loyal advocates and supporters of the 'English policy', and was known to enjoy the complete confidence of the Sultan, told me that the day after he had been dismissed from office his house was crowded from early morning to night by Mahomedans of all classes, from the highest to the lowest, who were anxious to learn whether the change of Ministry indicated a change of policy on the part of His Majesty and of his Government. He had the greatest difficulty, he said, in persuading them that such was not the case, and that His Majesty had no intention of departing in any way from the policy that he had hitherto pursued. It was not until more than twenty four hours after the fall of Ahmed Vefyk Pasha and his colleagues that the Mussulman population of the capital was convinced that this event did not indicate the triumph of Russian influence and the defeat of that of England. Had it proved otherwise the consequences to the Sultan, considering the present temper of the people, might have been serious.

.   .   .   .

This feeling in favor of England, and of the 'English policy', extends to the functionaries of the Porte, and even to men of the highest rank and influence in the State. Sadyk Pasha, the new Prime Minister, told me that when, on accepting office, he was discussing with the Sultan the policy that he should pursue, old Mehemet Ruchdi Pasha, formerly

Grand Vizier and a man of great influence with His Majesty and with the people, observed that 'he ought to sleep at the British Embassy and' 'never take a step without consulting the British Ambassador'!

There may be some exaggeration in the statements that are made to me as to the feeling towards England that I have described; but they come to me from so many independent sources, and from so many parts of the Empire, that I am convinced that they are well founded. This feeling does not arise solely from the belief that through the help of England Turkey may recover some of the territories that she has lost by her fatal war with Russia, and that she may be restored to her former position in Europe. This expectation may, no doubt, have something to do with it; but as far as I can judge it mainly arises from the conviction of the Turks that the Government of their country has been radically bad, that the men to whom it has been confided are for the most part incompetent, without patriotism and corrupt, and that if a complete reform in the administration be not speedily carried out the ruin of the Empire must ensue. They believe that this reform, which they all most ardently desire, can be best brought about by England, that she would effect it disinterestedly and in the interests of Turkey and of the Mussulmans as well as of the Christians, and that she is influenced by no special predilection in favor of any particular race or creed, but that she is prepared to obtain just, impartial and equal government for all. They consequently believe that if England is averse to annexing any portion of the Turkish Empire, the next best thing for her to do would be to make use of her influence to reform and direct the administration, and virtually to take the Government into her own hands.

. . . . [1]

b. *A. H. Layard to Lord Salisbury, Private, Therapia, May 15, 1878*
    (Layard's Letter Book, Add. MS 39,131, fos. 90-93. Extract).

. . . .

Asiatic Turkey must be differently governed from European Turkey. The former requires a good and just Government, but, at the same time, a strong one. Such a Government as we have in India. Autonomy for Armenia is an absurdity & probably a Russian intrigue. The Armenians of Armenia are utterly incapable of self government. They are not the Armenian Bankers of Constantinople. The problem to be solved in Asia Minor & in Mesopotamia & indeed in Syria is how the peaceful & industrious populations, Christians & Mussulmans can be protected from the barbarous and lawless tribes that inhabit those countries. This can only be done by a strong hand & by military force. An autonomous Armenia would not hold its own against the Kurds for a month, and would call for Russian help. A thoroughly just & impartial administration is absolutely necessary for the protection of the Christians. It would be for England to introduce & carry out such an administration & this should be made one of the conditions of our alliance with the Turks. India would

---

[1] See further quotation and summary of this despatch *ante* pp. 74-75.

furnish us with a number of able administrators, acquainted with the feelings & wants of Orientals; the Porte could furnish the material strength in the way of troops which, under our direction & controul [*sic*], could ensure the necessary protection to the populations & in the course of time compel the Kurds, Arabs & other wild tribes to renounce their lawless habits, & to turn to peaceful pursuits.

Order & tranquility would soon lead to a vast development of the agricultural & other resources of Asiatic Turkey. Even under the bad administration hitherto existing, the exports have greatly increased & a considerable commerce with England was rapidly being established. The interior of Asia Minor has been opened up to our trade & the navigation of the Euphrates & Tigris by an English Company has proved so successful that other steamers are now required for the carrying trade.

It appears to me that an alternative route to India & our Colonies is absolutely necessary & that route can alone be carried through Northern Syria & the valley of the Tigris-Euphrates. This must sooner or later become one of the great highways to India, first in connection with the Persian Gulf and Indian Ocean; hereafter in connection with a line of rail through Southern Persia and Beloochistan. Many years may elapse before this is complete & direct-railway communication between England & India by this latter route, but it must come in the end. It seems to me therefore of the utmost importance that we should maintain our influence & controul [*sic!*] over the countries through which it is to pass. The Turks are quite ready, if they could find the means to construct a railway through Asia Minor to Baghdad, which could be united to the coast of Northern Syria by a branch.

As regards the "Port in the Levant" which would best suit us I hesitate to give an opinion. The question must be decided upon military and naval as well as upon political considerations. High authorities advocate Mitylene as a fine island with two excellent harbours near the entrance to the Dardanelles & in a position which would enable the British Fleet to command the Eastern end of the Mediterranean. Others suggest Crete; but there appears to me to be a strong objection to the possession of that island in consequence of the Greek population which would constantly be kept in a state of agitation through Greek intrigue. No such objection exists to Mitylene. There are other islands in the Archipelago which have been pointed out as affording a good naval station. A Port on the Northern Coast of Syria such as Alexandretta or Suedia which would command the terminus of the railway through Mesopotamia might be of great advantage to England. The position would be a central & good one politically, as affording access to Asia Minor & the valley of the Tigris-Euphrates.

To resume, our programme should be:

i.   The Balkans, as a frontier for Turkey in Europe
ii. An alliance between Turkey & Greece
iii. An administration under European supervision which will ensure just and equal government to all the populations under Turkish rule in Europe.

iv. A defensive alliance with Turkey to defend her Asiatic possessions against Russia on condition that we should be allowed some direct controul [*sic!*] over their administration, without in any way touching the absolute sovereignty of the Sultan.

v. The acquisition of a Port in the Levant which would give England a direct material interest in the maintenance of the Turkish Dominion in Asia & would enable her to exercise the necessary influence & controul [*sic!*] over the reform of Turkish rule.

Such, if I rightly understand your letter, are your general views. They certainly agree with my own. Indeed I may say that in my policy here I have throughout steadily kept these objects in view. I think that we may induce the Sultan & the Porte to consent to them. If they do not, I am of your opinion that nothing is in store for this Empire but rapid disintegration & "Russification". Whenever you think the time come to act you have only to give me instructions. They will be carried out to the best of my ability & with all the energy at my command.

No. 5

Extracts from the Salisbury-Shuvalov Memoranda of May 30 and 31, 1878, and Correspondence Respecting Them. (F. O. 65/1022).

Memorandum No. 1, May 30, 1878.

. . . .

7. Les promesses pour l'Arménie stipulés par le Traité Préliminaire de San Stefano ne doivent pas être faites exclusivement à la Russie mais à l'Angleterre aussi.

. . . .

9. En ce qui concerne l'indemnité de guerre, Sa Majesté l'Empereur n'a jamais eu l'intention de la convertir en annexions territoriales et il ne se refuse pas à donner des assurances à cet égard. . . .

10. Quant à la vallée d'Alashkert et la ville de Bayazid, cette vallée étant la grande route du transit pour la Perse et ayant une immense valeur aux yeux des Turcs, Sa Majesté l'Empereur consent à leur restituer, mais il a demandé et obtenu en échange l'abandon à la Perse du petit territoire de Khotour, que les Commissions des deux Cours médiatrices ont trouvé juste de restituer au Shah.

11. Le Gouvernement de Sa Majesté Britannique croirait devoir constater son profond regret pour le cas où la Russie insisterait définitivement sur la rétrocession de la Bessarabie. . . .

En consentant à ne pas contester le désir de l'Empereur de Russie d'acquérir le port de Batoum et de garder ses conquêtes en Arménie, le Gouvernement de Sa Majesté ne se cache pas qu'il soit probable que de graves dangers menaçant la tranquillité des populations de la Turquie en Asie puissent résulter dans l'avenir de cette extension de la frontière Russe. Mais le Gouvernement de Sa Majesté est d'avis que le devoir de sauvegarder l'Empire Ottoman de ce danger, qui dorénavant reposera d'une mesure spéciale sur l'Angleterre, pourra s'effectuer sans que l'Europe éprouve les calamités d'une nouvelle guerre. En même temps le Gouvernement de la Reine prend acte de l'assurance donnée par Sa Majesté Impériale que dans l'avenir la frontière de la Russie ne sera plus étendu du côté de la Turquie d'Asie. Le Gouvernement de Sa Majesté étant par conséquent d'opinion que les modifications du Traité de San Stefano agréées dans ce Memorandum suffisent à mitiger les objections qu'il trouve au Traité dans sa forme actuelle, s'engage à ne pas contester les Articles du Traité Préliminaire de San Stefano qui ne sont pas modifiés par les dix points précédents, si, après que ces Articles auront été dûment discutés au Congrès, la Russie persiste à les maintenir.

.   .   .   .

Memorandum No. 2, May 30, 1878

.   .   .   .

(e)   Le Gouvernement Anglais se réserve de discuter au Congrès toute question touchant aux Détroits. Mais l'Ambassadeur de Russie à Londres prend acte de la communication verbale qu'il a faite au Principal Secrétaire d'État, à savoir que le Cabinet Impérial s'en tient à la Déclaration de Lord Derby du 6 Mai 1877, et notamment:—

"The existing arrangements made under European sanction, which regulate the navigation of the Bosphorus, and the Dardanelles, appear to them (the British Government) wise and salutary, and there would be, in their judgment, serious objections to their alteration in any material particular."

Et le Plénipotentiaire Russe insistera au Congrès sur le *status quo.*

.   .   .   .

Memorandum No. 3, May 31, 1878

Sa Majesté l'Empereur de Russie, ayant consenti à restituer à Sa Majesté le Sultan la vallée d'Alaschkert et la ville de Bayazid, et n'ayant pas l'intention d'étendre ses conquêtes en Asie au delà de Kars, Batoum, et des limites posées par le Traité Préliminaire de San Stefano, et rectifiées par la retrocession susmentionnée, le Gouvernement Impérial ne se refuse pas à conclure avec le Gouvernement Britannique un engagement secret à l'effet de la rassurer à cet égard.

Salisbury to Shuvalov, F. O., May 30, 1878. (Draft).

Dear Count Schouvaloff,

Some ambiguity may arise with respect to the precise bearing of the first Memorandum upon the reservations contained in the second, and it being inconvenient to wait till the sanction of the Imperial Government can be obtained to a change in the language used, I desire to note that in signing the Memoranda as they stand, I reserve to the Government of Great Britain, while I recognize in that of Russia, entire liberty of action at the Congress in respect to the matters mentioned in the second Memorandum.

(Signed) SALISBURY.

Shuvalov to Salisbury, Londres, le 18/30 Mai 1878.

M. le Marquis,

Le memorandum confidentiel No. 1 mentionne les assurances que Sa

Majesté l'Empéreur de Russie a donné de ne pas étendre les frontières de son Empire au côté de la Turquie d'Asie. L'engagement à cet égard, qui sera signé entres les Représentants des deux Gouvernements, constitue, ainsi que cela a été convenue entre nous, un acte secret. Je tiens donc à constater qu'en tout cas, et même si le memorandum susmentionné venait à être livré à la publicité, l'acte même de l'engagement tel qu'il se trouve relaté dans le memorandum secret et confidentiel No. 3, ne saurait être rendu public sans le consentement du Cabinet Impérial.

(Signed) SCHOUVALOFF.

No. 6.

"Batoum. Declaration as to Passage of Straits." Congress of Berlin, 1878 (F. O. 78/2911).

L'Angleterre apprend avec le plus profond regret la décision définitive de la Russie d'acquérir et de garder Batoum en dépit des mauvais résultats que cette mesure doit produire.

Dans le cas où Batoum serait fortifié par la Russie ou serait employé comme station navale, on ne pourrait le considérer autrement qu'une menace de fait sinon d'intention contre le Bosphore et les possessions de la Porte dans la Mer Noire.

Quoique le Gouvernement de sa Majesté n'envisige pas l'acquisition de ce port par la Russie comme justifiant par elle-même des mesures hostiles, si cette acquisition est prise en rapport avec les autres changements auxquels le Congrès a donné son assentiment, elle entraînera des dangers contre lesquels il est de devoir de l'Angleterre de se prémunir, et qui lui imposeront la nécessité d'une vigilance permanente. Dans ces circonstances elle doit considérer qu'une obligation quelconque prise par elle envers les Puissances Européennes de ne pas entrer dans les détroits restrindrait outre mesure la liberté d'action que ces conditions nouvelles peuvent lui rendre nécessaire. Elle est toute prête à reconnaître le droit qu'a le Sultan, quand il agit de son propre gré, de fermer les détroits. Elle prendre volontiers l'engagement envers Sa Majesté de respecter sa décision lorsqu'elle sera ainsi donnée, et réservera sa pleine liberté et celle des autres Puissances de maintenir comme alliés du Sultan cette décision si on y porte atteinte.

Mais les arrangements qui ont été fait en 1871 pour le maintien du Traité de Paris n'ont pas suffisamment pourvu à un état de choses où le Sultan ne serait pas à même d'exercer une volonté indépendante et d'appeler les flottes de ces alliés quand le Bosphore serait menacé.

L'expérience a démontré que le même danger qui rendrait cet appel nécessaire pourrait également empêcher le Sultan d'user de son droit de peur d'offenser la Puissance qui le menace.

Si, dans une tel cas, l'Angleterre n'était pas liée par des engagements envers les autres Puissances, elle serait libre, sans même que le Sultan y ait donné son assentiment, de lui venir en aide, mais le fait d'un tel engagement ne permettrait pas à l'Angleterre de prendre cette mesure sans enfreindre ses obligations envers les autres Puissances.

La stipulation de l'Article 2 du traité de 1871 devient surannée en tant que toutes les stipulations essentielles du Traité de Paris auxquelles elle se rattache sont abrogées par le Congrès.

Le nouvel état de choses dans la Mer Noire, qui résulte de l'annexion de Batoum, exige que l'Angleterre soit libre d'un engagement quelconque qui pourrait l'empêcher d'adopter en cas de besoin les mesures de précaution nécessaire.

Je déclare donc de la part du Gouvernement de Sa Majesté qu'en acceptant le renouvellement des stipulations du Traité de 1841 confirmées par le Traité de 1856 avec une disposition semblable à celle de l'article 2 du Traité de 1871, Sa Majesté s'engage seulement envers le Sultan et nullement envers aucune autre Puissance, et que Sa Majesté ne prend aucune obligation envers une autre Puissance quelconque qui l'empêcherait, s'il semblait nécessaire à Sa Majesté, de donner l'ordre à sa flotte d'entrer dans les détroits dans le cas que l'indépendance du Sultan serait menacée.

No. 7

"Memorandum. Asia Minor and Euphrates Railway" and List of Members Submitted to the Foreign Office, July 17, 1878 (F. O. 78/2893).

It would appear from the recent Treaty between England and Turkey that the interests of the two countries were closely allied and that the main objects to be kept in view are the strengthening the Gov't of the Sultan in his Asiatic dominions and securing our communications with India.

The safety and prosperity of the Sultan's dominions in Asia, rich in agricultural and mineral products, would, it is considered, be best promoted by the introduction of improved means of communication and especially by the construction of a Railway from *Constantinople* to *Ismidt, Angora, Sivas, Diabikir, Mosul* and *Bagdad* [1] to the head of the *Persian Gulf,* the through line *being in railway connexion with Alexandretta* or *some other Port on the Mediterranean;* thus having its three termini resting on the sea as a basis of operations.

The lines would traverse a region which once comprised some of the most flourishing kingdoms of the ancient world and is still comparatively populous and only requires the application of modern science and skill to awaken the dormant energies of the people and draw forth the latent resources of the soil and by creating new markets for our home manufacturers revive our drooping commerce; infuse new life into Turkey by European emigration, capital and enterprise, drawing India at the same time nearer to the centre of our Power.

This design would give England with the recent addition of Cyprus the first strategic position in the world enabling her army in India to co-operate with that in England with the rapidity and force of an irresistible power in defence of a country in whose progress and consolidation England is vitally concerned, securing at the same time in the most effectual manner our communications with our Indian Empire.

[1] [Marginal] *"Note.* already in regular steam communication with all the principal ports in India and by the Suez Canal with England."

This great scheme would involve in its completion the construction of about 2500 miles of railway and the expenditure of from £20,000,000 to £25,000,000; but a section might in the first instance be constructed for a moderate outlay connecting a commercial centre with a Port of shipment and the extension be carried out should the result be sufficiently encouraging.

Good commercial relations already exist with England and India and some portion of the route and a moderate return might fairly be expected on the capital expended.

In short what is essential to give public confidence is to ascertain whether the design to connect the shores of the *Bosphorus* and the *Mediterranean* with the Head of the *Persian Gulf* is one that Her Majesty's Ministers would take into their favourable consideration with the view of extending to it their countenance and co-operation with such moderate pecuniary support as might be necessary to enable the capital to be raised for the construction of a carefully selected section of the undertaking.

In conclusion attention is drawn to the opinions expressed by the Select Committee of the House of Commons in their Report of July 1872.

"They (the Committee) are not aware of the period within which "the system of railways connecting *Kurrachee* with *Peshawur* may "be expected to be completed; but whenever this shall have been "done, there can be no doubt that a route by way of the *Persian* "*Gulf* and *Kurachee* [*sic!*] will afford means of communication be-"tween *England* and the *Punjaub,* and north-west frontier of *British* "*India,* superior to those afforded by way of *Suez* and *Bombay.*"

"Speaking generally, your committee are of opinion that the two "routes by the *Red Sea* and by the *Persian Gulf,* might be maintained "and used simultaneously; that at certain seasons and for certain pur-"poses the advantage would lie with the one, and at other seasons and "for other purposes it would lie with the other; that it may fairly "be expected that in process of time traffic enough for the support "of both would develop itself, but that this result must not be ex-"pected too soon; that the political and commercial advantages of "establishing a second route would at any time be considerable, and "might, under possible circumstances, be exceedingly great; and that "it would be worth the while of the English Gov't to make an effort "to secure them, considering the moderate pecuniary risk which they "would incur. They believe that this may best be done by opening "communications with the Government of Turkey in the sense indi-"cated by the semi-official correspondence to which they have already "drawn attention."

List of Members: President—The Duke of Sutherland [1]
Chairman—W. P. Andrew, Esq. [1]
Vice Chairman—Sir Arnold Kemball [1]
General Committee—

Lord Blantyre [1]	Sir Douglas Forsyth
Lord Kinnaird	Maj. Gen. Sir F. Goldsmid

Sir H. Drummond Wolff, M.P.[1]
Sir Henry Green [1]
Hobart Pasha
Mr. H. Chaplin, M.P.[1]
Mr. James Fleming
Mr. John Fowler
Mr. Telford Macneil [1]
Sir John Macneil
Capt. Macneil
Mr. F. Greenwood [1]
Mr. A. Borthwick [1]
Mr. I. Zohrab
Mr. Wrench
Alderman Wm. McArthur, M.P.
Mr. J. Staniforth [1]
Mr. Arthur J. Otway, M.P.

Col. Malcolm Green
Gen. F. Marshall
Mr. V. Barrington Kennett
Sir H. W. Tyler
Mr. James Macdonald
Baron G. de Worms [1]
Mr. Wm. Mackinnon
Mr. E. B. Lashwick
Gen. Saunders Abbott
Mr. Edw. Thornton
Captain Felix Jones
Mr. J. Bramly Moore
Mr. G. Brand
Mr. W. I. Ainsworth
Admiral Charlewood
Lord Shaftesbury

No. 8

Memorandum by J. L. A. Simmons, July 26, 1878 (F. O. 78/2893).

The danger to British interests of Russia being allowed to extend her dominions in Asia Minor arise from the following causes.

1. The force ordinarily maintained by Russia in her Transcaucasian dominions is about 200,000 men, who are mostly recruited in her European provinces besides a militia. As these troops have to maintain order in the country South of the Caucasus a very considerable proportion are not available for war beyond the frontiers.

In the event of war therefore reinforcements when necessary have to be sent from the provinces north of the Caucasus as was done last year, which can only be effected by the Black Sea, by the Dariel Pass 8200 feet above the Sea which traverses the Caucasus from Vladikavkas to Tiflis or by the Caspian Sea or the road skirting its shores.

It is of consequence therefore that Russia should not acquire a populous territory in Asia Minor in which an army could be recruited and maintained and by which future conquests would be facilitated; also a territory capable of furnishing supplies for an army near what would be the theatre of operations in the event of an attack upon Asiatic Turkey.

2. Within a few miles of Erzeroum which is 6000 feet above the sea the Sources of rivers are found which flow into the Black Sea, into the Caspian and by the Euphrates into the Persian Gulf. The proximity of Russia to this elevated region places her in a highly favorable position for extending her conquests westwards and spreading over Asia Minor as well as down the valleys of the Tigris and Euphrates to the Persian Gulf of which unless opposed by some stronger power than Turkey alone she would eventually become mistress.

[1] Members of the Executive Committee of which Sir Henry Green and Mr. Wright were joint secretaries.

3. By obtaining possession of the Turkish provinces adjoining Persia, Russia would acquire the means of applying pressure on the whole of the northern & western frontiers of Persia which would be irresistible and render the latter power a passive if not an active ally in the extension of her influence and territory towards India.

In speaking lately to a high Persian diplomatist relative to the Anglo-Turkish convention of the 4th June he expressed himself in the highest terms as to the result it would have in Persia by placing that country in a favorable position both as regards trade and the influences which might be brought to bear for the improvement and civilization of that country. His expressions as to the supineness of Great Britain in the past as regards her influence in Persia were equally strong and the satisfaction amounting to delight evinced by him point strongly to the apprehension under which he was that Persia might pass entirely under the influence of Russia.

4. By the eventual and almost certain extension of her influence and power, if not of her conquests, in Asia Minor, Russia might obtain practical possession of Turkish territory down to the Gulf of Skenderoon and along the shores of the Mediterranean, and if once there it would be difficult to arrest her progress to the Straits of the Dardanelles and the Bosphorus when the Black Sea would be closed against the ships of war of other powers & her position in Asia Minor would be consolidated and the flow of British commerce into the rich countries lying between the Black & Mediterranean seas might be prejudiced.

5. If the power of Russia were consolidated in Asia Minor either directly by conquest or indirectly by the country passing under her protection she would obtain the power of raising and provisioning armies which by the aid of conscription would become so powerful that no European power dependent upon the sea for its communications could expect to maintain an army in the field at such a distance from home sufficiently strong to resist further conquests.

Syria would then, under this supposition, come under the control of the Power that had obtained possession of the resources of Asia Minor and eventually the Suez Canal & Egypt might feel its influence.

6. It results from the above considerations that if the progress of Russia through Asia to the Dardanelles and the Mediterranean is to be checked at all it must be before she has acquired the means of forming and maintaining larger armies than she at present possesses to the South of the Caucasus.

The best method and in fact so far as I can see the only probability of effecting this object is to resist all progress or attempt at extension beyond her present limits which cannot reasonably be expected to be done by Turkey unaided by some other power or powers. In fact whether the Anglo-Turkish convention existed or not, it is more than probable that Great Britain in the event of Russia again attacking Turkey in Asia Minor would be compelled to take measures and even go to war to prevent the extension of Russia on this side.

7. The military means by which Russia is to be resisted require careful

consideration. There can be no doubt that the first thing is to secure the Dardanelles & Bosphorus from attack on the European side because unless the free entrance of H.M.'s ships into the Black Sea is secured the most vulnerable point in the dominions of the Czar viz: his Transcaucasian possessions will be guarded against attack, the best route by which reinforcements can be brought to the theatre of war in Asia Minor by the Black Sea would remain open to Russia, and the defence of Asia Minor against further aggression will become almost impossible.

8.   The other measures to be taken are to obtain order and security for life and property in Asia Minor and to open up the country by making such roads and communications through it as will not only serve the purposes of commerce but will be capable of being used as military roads for the movement of troops and stores to the vicinity of the frontiers and to organize the country militarily for defence by improving its financial position, by enrolling and training the inhabitants as soldiers and by constructing such defensive works as the careful examination of the country might dictate.

8. [*sic!*]   If the entrance into the Black Sea were absolutely secured and the native population organized in sufficient strength to oppose the progress of Russian arms in the elevated region of Armenia a force by threatening invasion up the valley of the Rion would jeopardize the whole of the Russian possessions to the South of the Caucasus or if not in sufficient strength to do this a British force landed in the Gulf of Skenderoon, if a line of railway were constructed thence up to Diarbekir and Erzinghan, would be as near to the theatre of war as any reinforcements coming from Russia and arriving there fresh without the fatigue of long marches be in a favorable position to aid the forces of the country in repelling attack.

J. L. A. SIMMONS.

26 July 1878

No. 9

Sir A. H. Layard to Her Majesty's Principal Secretary of State for Foreign Affairs, Despatch No. 461, Secret, Constantinople, April 27, 1880 (Extracts from F. O. 78/3085 and Parl. Papers, C.2574, No. 3. In the following copy the omissions from the printed copy are indicated by brackets).

It is my duty to submit to your Lordship the present state of our relations with the Porte, and the actual condition of Turkey. [Before doing so I would venture to call Your Lordship's attention to my very confidential despatch to Lord Salisbury, No. 40 of the 7th of January last. In that despatch I have described how the Sultan has succeeded in obtaining absolute power, and complete control over all public affairs. I am bound to state my belief that His Majesty is animated by good intentions and that he is desirous of promoting the prosperity of his Empire and the welfare of his subjects. He is, moreover, a Sovereign of much intelligence, and of considerable knowledge for a Prince educated in the Imperial Palace.

Unfortunately the events which brought him to the throne, and those which followed after his accession to it, were such as would have affected the nerves and character of a man of a much stronger constitution than Sultan Abdul Hamid. The dethronement and suicide of his Uncle Abdul Aziz; the insanity and deposition of his brother Sultan Murad; the assassination of his principal Ministers; the disastrous war with Russia; and the presence of the enemy at the very gates of his capital, rapidly succeeded each other. These events, and others, have produced their effects in developing that tendency to mental alienation which appears to be hereditary in his family. In the present Sultan it shows itself in an exaggerated fear for his personal safety, which leads him to suspect the existence of constant conspiracies against his life. Soon after the failure of Ali Suavi's plot to replace Sultan Murad on the throne,[1] His Majesty showed decided signs of mental alienation, under which he was labouring when I saw him more than once in his harem. Since that time he has never been beyond the walls of his extensive garden, except to attend a mosque on Fridays at one of its gates. He is a man of active and frugal habits, and attends closely to business.

[The Sultan's constitutional infirmity has enabled a number of fanatical, corrupt, and unprincipled persons to obtain an unfortunate ascendency over his mind. He has been led to believe that, in consequence of the supposed influence over the army of Osman Pasha, the hero of Plevna, a bigoted Mussulman, very ignorant, and much opposed to Europeans and European innovations, he is necessary to his personal safety. His Majesty has, consequently, retained him, through all changes of Government, and notwithstanding his recognized incapacity as an administrator, of which His Majesty is fully aware, as Minister of War and Marshal of the Palace. Thinking to conciliate his Mussulman subjects, His Majesty has installed in the Palace several fanatical Sheikhs whom he is in the habit of consulting and who have inspired him with extravagant ideas of his sacred position as Caliph of Islam, with the fear of offending the Mussulmans by showing too much favour to the Christians. To their evil advice may be attributed, to a great extent, the hesitation of the Sultan in carrying out such of the stipulations of the Treaty of Berlin as may bring him into collision with his Mussulman subjects, or compel him to surrender any part of them to Christian rule. Hafiz Pasha, the Minister of Police, maintains his ascendancy over His Majesty, and his place, by the vigilance and ability he displays in detecting imaginary conspiracies against His Majesty's person and throne. A number of innocent persons, many of high rank including some of the leading Ulemas have been falsely accused by this man, and have been summarily arrested, imprisoned, and sent to exile. Some according to general rumour, have even disappeared altogether. These arbitrary proceedings have added greatly to the Sultan's unpopularity.

[There are several officers of the Palace, such as the Second Chamberlain, Osman Bey, the Chief Eunuch, Bahram Ager, the Band Master, Nedjib Pasha, and others, who, having constant access to His Majesty,

---

[1] The plot of May, 1878, at the time of negotiations for the Cyprus Convention.

exercise a considerable influence over him. They are all notoriously corrupt, and in the habit of receiving bribes from those who seek for appointments, or have business to transact with the Palace and the Porte. They form what is usually known as 'the Palace Party.' One or two of them are supposed, probably on good grounds, to be in the pay of the Russian Embassy.] As all the power in the State is now in the hands of the Sultan, who has the complete control over public affairs, it is very important that Her Majesty's Government should be made acquainted with His Majesty's political views. I have seen much of His Majesty, and have been invariably treated by him with marked favour and kindness. I believe him to be grateful to me for the services that I have been able, on many occasions to render him. Nevertheless, I have not concealed my opinions from him, but have warned him, over and over again, of the dangers to which he is exposing himself and his Empire by the course which he has of late pursued, in language which has rarely, if ever, been addressed to a Sovereign. He has received my advice and my warnings in good part. At one time he acted to a certain extent upon them. Of late he has been less inclined to do so. The persons about him, [to whom I have referred,] have succeeded in inspiring him with a profound distrust and suspicion of England. They have induced him to believe that her occupation of Cyprus, the nomination of English military Consuls in Asia Minor, the interest she shows in the Armenian population, and her peremptory demands for the introduction of reforms into Asiatic Turkey, are so many proofs of a design of annexing his Asiatic territories. [He has even told me that England had been accused to him of wishing to acquire the Hedjaz, as by possessing the Holy Cities of Mecca and Medina, she could more easily maintain her rule over her vast Mussulman population in India. These suspicions have, no doubt, been encouraged by Russia, and, I have reason to believe, by the French Embassy here.] The irritation against England now felt by the Sultan, and to some extent by his people, was first excited by her proposing at the Congress of Berlin the Austrian occupation of Bosnia and Herzegovina. It was greatly increased by the [sudden] orders given to the fleet in October last to proceed to Turkish waters. [By an unfortunate oversight [1] I was not informed of the decision taken by Her Majesty's Government, and only learnt it by a telegram from Admiral Hornby and through the Press. It was nearly a week before I received any official intimation on the subject. I consequently was at a loss to give the explanations required by the Sultan of the sudden determination of Her Majesty's Government to send the Fleet to Besika Bay.] Public rumour attributed it to a resolution, on their part, to compel the Porte, by a hostile demonstration to put into execution the promised reforms in Asia Minor. [I had every reason to believe that such was the case, as I had been instructed to warn the Sultan that the return to office of Mahomed Nedim Pasha would lead to a change in the policy of Her Majesty's Government, and he had just been brought to Constantinople from exile and named Min-

---

[1] [Marginal Note in pencil] "This was not the case. Sir H. Layard has had what really took place explained to him repeatedly. T[enterden]."

ister of the Interior.] The Sultan was greatly alarmed, [and, at one moment, was threatened with a return of the attack of mental excitement that he had experienced after the Ali Suavi affair. Prince Lobanoff availed himself of the opportunity to excite the anger of His Majesty against England, of whose influence Russia was at that time very jealous. Communications constantly passed between the Prince and the Palace, and he went himself to Livadia to see His Emperor. Namyk Pasha was also, about that time, sent on a mission to His Imperial Majesty, the object of which was concealed from the Grand Vizier and the Turkish Minister for Foreign Affairs. It has been suspected, indeed assumed, that a secret Treaty was then entered into by the Sultan with Russia. I have not been able to obtain any evidence to lead me to believe that such was the case. That the representations of Prince Lobanoff, and messages which the Sultan received from the Emperor, greatly increased his growing mistrust of England, and effected a change in his sentiments and policy as regards her, there is, I think, ample proof. It is by no means impossible that some secret understanding was come to with Russia, although it may not have taken the form of a written engagement.] Nevertheless, it is my conviction that, if the Sultan has a leaning to any European Power, it is towards England. He has a [kind of] personal attachment to the Queen and the members of the Royal Family, to whom he expresses much gratitude for the kindness experienced from them when in England with his Uncle, Abdul Aziz. He is convinced that, in his own interests and in those of his Empire, he ought to conciliate England. [I believe him to have, at the bottom of his heart, an intense hatred of Russia, on account of the disasters and sufferings which the late war has brought upon his country, and especially upon his Mussulman subjects, of the humiliation to which it has exposed him, and of the loss of so considerable a portion of his dominions. This feeling it would be exceedingly difficult for him to get over, but he may succeed in concealing it, and he may even listen to her counsels, as her agents well know how to work upon his suspicious nature.

[The Sultan has no love for Austria, to whom he attributes the late disastrous war. He will not easily forgive her for having encouraged the insurrection in Bosnia and Herzegovina for the purpose, he is convinced, of officially annexing those Provinces, and for having permitted the Montenegrins to obtain guns and arms through Dalmatia. His Majesty was so incensed against Count Zichy, whom he accused of having deceived him, by promising that Austria would prevent Servia from attacking Turkey, that he treated the Austrian Ambassador with a marked coldness, if not discourtesy, very foreign to his habits. His Majesty has lately seen the impolicy of thus offending a nation which has, on the whole, been friendly to Turkey, and may be of use to her hereafter. He has received the new Austrian Minister with much attention, and an exchange of compliments and expressions of good will have passed between His Majesty and the Emperor. His Majesty has more than once told me that he was desirous of entering into a Convention with Austria, by which she should guarantee to him his European possessions, as England had guaranteed to him his Asiatic territories by the Convention of the 4th June. There is reason to believe that, had His Majesty acted promptly and loyally in executing the Treaty of Berlin as regards the surrender to Austria of Bosnia and Herzegovina, and had not rejected the secret Article of the Convention concluded by his Minister for Foreign Affairs with Count Zichy for the Austrian occupation of Novi Bazar, he might have obtained some such guarantee.

[The relations between Germany and this country have not yet been of such a nature as to lead the Sultan to believe that she has any direct interest, or wishes to exercise any special influence, in it, or that she will interfere in its affairs. He has, I fancy, a general idea that if she did, she would support the policy of Russia. His Majesty's relations with the German Ambassador have always been of a very friendly character, and he has frequently expressed to me his esteem for Count Hatzfeldt.

[The influence of France has, of late, been exercised against England, and may have been even more mischievous to her interests than that of Russia. This may mainly be attributed to the character of Monsieur Fournier, the French Ambassador, whose extreme suspicion and jealousy of England and excessive susceptibility and irritability of temper, have led him to oppose her on every possible occasion. He is convinced that England is preparing to annex the Sultan's Asiatic territories, and that, with this object, she is endeavouring to destroy what he claims to be the legitimate influence of France in Syria. I would direct Your Lordship's attention to my despatch to Lord Salisbury, No. 43 Secret of January 8, in which I gave the substance of a letter, or despatch, alleged to have been written by Monsieur Fournier, and shown to me by Mahmoud Nedim Pasha. Whether this document be authentic or not, it describes very accurately the opinions that have been expressed, to my knowledge, by Monsieur Fournier, and the policy which he has pursued here. Despatches from Her Majesty's Consuls at Aleppo and Jerusalem, and from the British Vice-Consul at Mossul, will show the use that the French Government is now making of the Roman Catholic clergy in the Levant to extend French influence, and to destroy the ancient rights and privileges of other Christian Communities, and the exaggerated pretensions which France is now putting forward to protect Roman Catholic Establishments, and even all Ottoman subjects who profess the Roman Catholic faith. The Sultan and the Porte are perhaps, more disposed to listen to the advice of France than that of Russia, especially as regards the course they should pursue with respect to England. They believe that the former may be a disinterested friend, while they cannot but suspect the intentions of the latter, and attribute her counsels to hostility to England, and to a design to create a misunderstanding between her and Turkey. Monsieur Fournier has found a valuable support, in his endeavours to counteract the influence of England in the Palace, and at the Porte, and to thwart her policy, in Commandant Dreyssé, the Sultan's French Aide-de-Camp, and Monsieur Tarin, the French legal adviser of the Turkish Government. The former, who is very hostile to England, has succeeded in obtaining the Sultan's confidence, and is in the habit of seeing His Majesty at all times. Monsieur Tarin is employed in the most important public affairs, and, as most state documents in French pass through his hands, or, when coming from the Porte, are actually prepared by him, he is fully informed of all that passes and exercises no inconsiderable influence over diplomatic negotiations. He is a very able, but a thoroughly corrupt and unscrupulous man, and is in the regular pay of the French Embassy.

[Antagonism between the English and French Embassies in the East is greatly to be deplored. The Porte has long learnt how to make use of any differences which may exist between the European Powers, and especially between England and France. It has been my earnest desire to work cordially with my French colleague, and to come to a thorough understanding with him, upon all matters connected with this country. But I regret to say that I have found it impossible to do so, in consequence of Monsieur Fournier's excitable and suspicious temperament. To escape a quarrel, I have avoided as much as possible the discussion of political questions with him. Our personal relations have, however, been of a very friendly character. These details may appear trivial, but a knowledge of them is necessary in order to understand the state of affairs in Constantinople, where the most important questions, and the most vital interests are too frequently sacrificed to intrigues and personal considerations and to the conflict of rival influences.]

It is very difficult to judge of public opinion in this vast Empire made up of divers races and creeds. In our sense of the word, it does not probably exist. Such as it is, it may, I think, be considered favourable to England. The Mussulman populations everywhere, and the Christian Communities in Asiatic Turkey, with the exception perhaps of the Roman Catholics, turn to her for protection against misgovernment and oppression, and rely upon her influence and aid to obtain reforms which can alone bring them justice, rest, and prosperity. The Armenians, encouraged by the Cyprus Convention, to look to her for the immediate introduction of those reforms, begin to be disappointed at not seeing them already put into execution. Judging from the reports of our Consular officers at Erzeroum, Van, and Diarbekir, Russia is taking advantage of this feeling to induce the Armenian populations of those districts to turn to her for help and protection, and to prepare the way for future interference in Asiatic Turkey, and further annexations of territory.

.   .   .   .   1

In conclusion: the most enlightened and patriotic Turkish statesmen and functionaries, and the most intelligent Turks, are fully alive to the dangers which threaten the Empire, and are prepared for the adoption of decisive and radical measures to avert them. . . . I share their views to a great extent. [Unfortunately there are apparently no men in Turkey capable of imposing these measures upon the Sultan. It can only be done by a popular movement under some leader of influence, energy and determination, or by the combined action of the Great Powers, if such combination be possible.] A commencement might be made by calling upon the Porte to put into execution Midhat Pasha's Constitution, which was formally communicated to the Powers on its promulgation. The defects which, it is admitted, it contains might be remedied.

[1]

. . . .

[1] The remainder of the despatch is printed in the Blue Book in a substantially complete form which clearly indicates the lack of success attending the British attempts at reform.

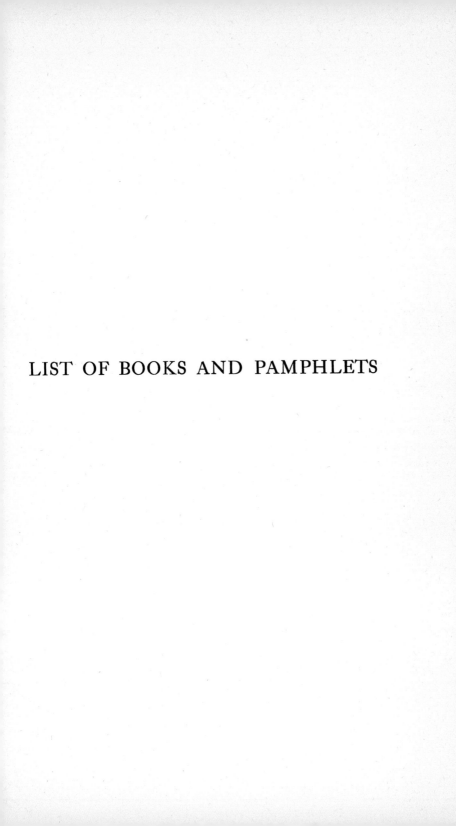

LIST OF BOOKS AND PAMPHLETS

LIST OF BOOKS AND PAMPHLETS

The following list does not pretend to be exhaustive nor even complete for this work, but is appended for the convenience of the reader, and except for the pamphlets includes only those works cited more than once. The abbreviation "Add. MS." in the footnotes refers throughout to the *Layard Papers* in the British Museum; and "F.O." refers to the Foreign Office papers in the Public Record Office.

Documents, Memoirs, and Biographies

Bareilles, Bertrand, ed., *Le Rapport Secret sur le Congrès de Berlin, Addressé à la S. Porte* par Carathéodory Pacha. Paris, 1919.

Blunt, Wilfred Scawen, *Secret History of the English Occupation of Egypt: Being a Personal Narrative of Events*. London, 1907.

Buckle, George Earle, ed., *The Letters of Queen Victoria*. Second Series. 3 v. London, 1926-28.

Cecil, Lady Gwendolen, *Life of Robert Marquis of Salisbury*. 2 v. London, 1922.

Documents Diplomatiques Français. 1re Série (1871-1900). 3 v. Paris, 1929-31.

Egerton, Mrs. Fred, *Admiral of the Fleet Sir Geoffrey Phipps Hornby*. Edinburgh and London, 1896.

Elliot, Sir Henry George, *Some Revolutions and Other Diplomatic Experiences*. Edited by His Daughter (Gertrude Elliot). London, 1922.

Gathorne-Hardy, Alfred E., ed., *Gathorne Hardy, First Earl of Cranbrook, a Memoir with Extracts from His Diary and Correspondence*. 2 v. London and New York, 1910.

Grosse Politik der Europäischen Kabinette, 1871-1914. J. Lepsius, A. Mendelssohn-Bartholdy, F. Thimme, eds. 40 v. Berlin, 1922-27.

Gwynn, Stephen, and Tuckwell, G. M., *Life of Sir Charles W. Dilke*. 2 v. New York, 1917.

Hardinge, Sir Arthur, *Life of Henry Howard Molyneux Herbert, Fourth Earl of Carnarvon, 1831-1890*. 3 v. Oxford, 1925.

Hohenlohe-Schillingsfürst, Prince Chlodwig von, *Memoirs*. Friedrich Curtius, ed. 2 v. New York, 1906.

Lang, Andrew, *Life, Letters, and Diaries of Sir Stafford Northcote, First Earl of Iddesleigh*. 2 v. 2nd Edition. London, 1890.

[Layard, Austen Henry], "The Early Life of Lord Beaconsfield," *Quarterly Review*, CLXVIII (January, 1899), 1-42.

Monypenny, William Flavelle, and Buckle, George Earle, *Life of Benjamin Disraeli, Earl of Beaconsfield*. New and Revised Ed. 2 v. New York, 1929.

Newton, Lord, *Lord Lyons, A Record of British Diplomacy.* 2 v. London, 1913.

Radowitz, Joseph Maria von, *Aufzeichnungen und Erinnerungen aus dem Leben des Botschafters.* Hajo Holborn, ed. 2 v. Stuttgart, 1925.

Raschdau, L., "Aus dem Literärischen Nachlass des Unterstaatssekretärs Dr. Busch," *Deutsche Rundschau,* CXLI (1909), 12,207, and 361.

Reid, T. Wemyss, "Lord Derby at the Foreign Office, 1876-78," *Macmillan's Magazine,* XL (1879), 180-92.

Seton-Watson, R. W., ed., "Unprinted Documents. Russo-British Relations during the Eastern Crisis," *Slavonic Review,* III (1924-25), IV (1925-26), and V (1926-27).

Watson, Colonel Sir Charles M., *Life of Major-General Sir Charles William Wilson.* London, 1909.

Wertheimer, Eduard von, *Graf Julius Andrassy, sine Leben und seine Zeit.* 3 v. Stuttgart, 1910-13.

Zetland, Marquis of, ed., *Letters of Disraeli to Lady Bradford and Lady Chesterfield.* 2 v. London, 1929.

Contemporary Books and Pamphlets on the Eastern Question, Asia Minor, and Cyprus

Andrew, William Patrick, *The Euphrates Valley Route to India.* London, 1872.

　　The Euphrates Valley Route to India in Connection with the Central Asian Question. London, [1873].

　　Euphrates Valley Routes to India in Connection with the Central Asian and Egyptian Questions. 2nd Edition with Map and Appendix. London, 1882. (95 p.)

　　India and Her Neighbors. London, 1878.

Argyll, Duke of, *The Eastern Question.* 2 v. London, 1879.

Armenians and the Eastern Question. A Series of Letters by an Armenian on Armenia and the Armenians. London, 1878. (72 p.)

Austin, Alfred, *England's Policy and Peril.* London, 1877. (32 p.)

Austin, C. E., *Undeveloped Resources of Turkey in Asia, with Notes on the Railway to India.* London, 1878. (Map, v, 123 p.)

Baker, Sir Samuel White, *Cyprus as I Saw It in 1879.* London, 1879.

Barkley, Henry C. *A Ride through Asia Minor and Armenia.* London, 1891.

Birkbeck, John, Jr., *Present Position of the Eastern Question.* London, 1879. (63 p.)

Blunt, Lady Anne, *Bedouin Tribes of the Euphrates.* W. S. Blunt, ed. London, 1879. (Postscript by W.S.B. on Euphrates Railway.)

Borthwick, Algernon, *An Address on the Eastern Question.* London, 1878. (43 p.)

Brassey, Thomas, *Recent Letters and Speeches.* London, 1879. (76 p.)

Bryce, James, *Transcaucasia and Ararat.* London, 1877.

Burnaby, Captain Fred, *On Horseback through Asia Minor.* 2 v. 6th Edition. London, 1877.

Cameron, Verney Lovett, *Our Future Highway*. 2 v. London, 1880.
   Notre Future Route de l'Inde. Paris, 1883.
Campbell, W. F., (Baron Stratheden and Campbell), *Policy of Great Britain in the War between Russia and the Porte, Speeches* . . . London, 1877. (32 p.)
   The Policy of Great Britain in the War between Russia and the Porte. Speech at the Liberal Association, Harwich, November 5, 1877. Memorial Presented by the Deputation to the Foreign Office, November 28, 1877. London, 1878. (23 p.)
Cazalet, Edward, *The Berlin Congress and the Anglo-Turkish Convention*. London, 1878. (Map, 32 p.)
   The Eastern Question, an Address to Working Men. 2nd Edition. London, 1878. (Letters and Map on the Euphrates Valley Railway. 64 p.)
   England's Policy in the East, Our Relations with Russia and the Future of Syria. 2nd Edition. London, 1879. (32 p.)
Chéon, *L'Ile de Chypre et la République Française au Congrès de Berlin*. Paris, 1878.
Clayden, P. W., *England under Lord Beaconsfield*. 2nd Edition. London, 1880.
Collen, Capt. Edwin H. H., *Report on Cyprus, Based on Information Obtained Chiefly from Consular Reports, Foreign Office, 1845-1877*. (Intelligence Branch, Q.M-G's Dept., Horse Guards, 18th May 1878). (14 p.)
Cowper, B. Harris, *Cyprus, Its Past, Present and Future*. London, 1878. (31 p.)
Cyprus (Handbooks Prepared under the Direction of the Historical Section of the Foreign Office, No. 65). London, 1920.
Cyprus and Asiatic Turkey, A Handy General Description of Our New Eastern Protectorate. London, 1878. (x, 238 p.)
Cyprus, its Value and Importance to England. Manchester, n.d. (Map, 32 p.)
Cyprus, Syria, and Palestine, the Future Emporium of British Trade in Asia. By a Consul-General. London, 1878. (40 p. See Ex-Consul-General)
Dalrymple, George Elphinstone, *The Syrian Great Eastern Railway to India, by an Entirely New Route*. London, 1878. (26 p.)
Dardanelles for England, the True Solution of the Eastern Question. London, 1876. (28 p.)
Davis, Rev. E. J., *Life in Asiatic Turkey*. London, 1879.
Dunsany (E. Plunkett), *Gaul or Teuton?* London, 1873. (309 p.)
Eastern Question, Russian Policy in the East, Will of Peter the Great. . . . 6th and Enlarged Edition. London, 1878. (64 p.)
Eastern Question and the Armenians. London, April, 1878. (18 p.)
England in Egypt, the Highway to India. A Proposal Submitted to the People of England by an Englishman. London, 1877. (16 p.)

Ex-Consul-General, *Occupation of Cyprus, Immediate and Probable Effects.* London, 1878. (16 p. Author says he wrote *Cyprus, Syria, and Palestine.*)

Fall of Turkey. London, 1875. (21 p.)

Farley, J. Lewis, *Egypt, Cyprus and Asiatic Turkey.* London, 1878. (xvi, 263 p.)

Folliot de Crenneville, Victor Graf, *Die Insel Cypern in ihrer heutigen Gestalt, ihren ethnographischen und wirtschaftlichen Verhältnissen.* Wien, 1879. (49 p.)

Gammon, F. I., *Cyprus, its History and Prospects.* London, 1878. (Map, 32 p. "25th Thousand")

Geary, Grattan, *Through Asiatic Turkey, Narrative of a Journey from Bombay to the Bosphorus.* 2 v. London, 1878.

Gladstone, W. E., *Lessons in Massacre.* London, 1877. (80 p.)

Glover, Rev. Richard M. A., *Cyprus, the Christian History of Our New Colonial Gem.* London, 1878. (20 p.)

Haughton, B., *A Railway to India.* A Paper Read before the Civil and Mechanical Engineer's Society at No. 7 Westminster Chambers, on the 27th February, 1879. (Privately Printed), (10 p.)

[Hippeau, Edmond], *Le Congrès en miniature par un Diplomate.* Paris, 1878. (78 p.)

Historica, *The Imperial Triumvirate, A Warning and an Exposure of Ambitious and Unscrupulous Designs.* London, 1877. (7 p.)

Johnstone, H. A. Munro Butler, *The Eastern Question.* (For Private Circulation Only, 1875). (50 p.)

Kuhn von Kuhnenfeld, Baron F. M. L., *The Strategical Importance of the Euphrates Valley Railway.* Captain C. W. Wilson, tr., 2nd Edition. London, 1873. (22 p.)

Lang, R. Hamilton, *Cyprus, its History, its Present Resources, and Future Prospects.* London, 1878. (xi, 370 p.)

Lake, John Joseph, *Ceded Cyprus, its History, Condition, Products, and Prospects.* London, 1878.

[Layard, Austen Henry], "The Eastern Question and the Conference," *Quarterly Review,* CXLIII (January, 1877), 276-320.

Löher, Franz von, and Joyner, Mrs. A. Batson, *Cyprus, Historical and Descriptive.* Adapted from the German . . . with much additional matter. London, 1878. (Maps; xvi, 308 p.)

McCoan, J. Carlile, *Our New Protectorate, Turkey in Asia.* 2 v. London, 1879. (Map)

Martin, Admiral Sir William Fanshawe, *Cyprus as a Naval Station and a Place of Arms.* London, 1879. (12 p.)

Mas Laitrie, L. de, *L'Ile de Chypre, sa situation Présente et ses Souvenirs du Moyen-Age.* Paris, 1879. (Map, 432 p.)

Paridant van der Cammen, Edmond, *Étude sur l'Ile de Chypre Considérée au Point de Vue d'une Colonisation Européenne.* Aerschot and Brussels, 1874. (Map, 113 p.)

Pim, Captain Bedford, *The Eastern Question, Past, Present and Future.* 3rd Edition with Addenda. London, 1877 and 1878. (Map, 48, 72 p.)

Pressel, Wilhelm von, *Les Chemins de Fer en Turquie d'Asie. Projet d'un Réseau Complet.* Zurich, 1902. (90 p.)

Ramsay, W. M., *Impressions of Turkey during Twelve Years' Wanderings.* London, 1897.

Revelations from the Seat of War. 3rd Revised Edition. London, 1878. (95 p.)

Robinson, Philip, *Cyprus and Sokotra.* London, 1878. (Maps, 50 p.)

Robinson, Walter, *The Straits of the Dardanelles and the Bosphorus.* London, 1878. (55 p.)

Savile, Capt. A. R., *Cyprus.* (Compiled in the Intelligence Branch, Q.M-G's Department, Horse Guards.) London, August, 1878. (71 p.)

Schweiger-Lerchenfeld, Baron A. von, *Der Orient.* Pest, 1882.

Scott-Stevenson, Esme, *Our Home in Cyprus.* London, 1880. (Map, 332 p.)

Theta, *The Secret of Cyprus and Our Eastern Protectorate.* London, [1878]. (8 p.)

Tozer, Rev. Henry Fanshawe, *Turkish Armenia and Eastern Asia Minor.* London, 1881.

Walters, H. L., *An Open Letter Addressed to the English Nation from Berlin.* London, 1878. (25 p.)

Wolf, Lucien, *The Russian Conspiracy or Russian Monopoly in Opposition to British Interests in the East.* London, 1877. (x, 35 p.)

Wyman, Frederick F., *The War, a Summary and Compilation of All Historical and Current Information and Matters of Interest in Connection with the Present War and the Eastern Question.* 2nd Edition. Calcutta, 1877. (vii, 103, xv p.)

Recent Studies

"Bagdad Railway Negotations," *Quarterly Review,* CCXXVIII (October, 1917), 487-528.

Blaisdell, Donald C., *European Financial Control in the Ottoman Empire.* New York, 1929.

Dawson, William Harbutt, "Forward Policy and Reaction, 1874-1880," *Cambridge History of British Foreign Policy,* III (New York, 1923), Ch. II.

Du Velay, A., *Essai sur l'Histoire Financière de la Turquie depuis le Règne du Sultan Mahmoud II jusqu'à Nos Jours.* Paris, 1903.

Hanotaux, Gabriel, *Histoire de la France Contemporaine.* 4 v. Paris, 1903-08.

Headlam-Morley, Sir James, *Studies in Diplomatic History.* London, 1930.

Holborn, Hajo, *Deutschland und die Türkei, 1878-1890.* Berlin, 1926.

Hoskins, Halford Lancaster, *British Routes to India.* New York and London, 1928.

Jenks, L. H., *The Migration of British Capital to 1875.* New York, 1927.

Langer, William L., *European Alliances and Alignments, 1871-1890.* New York, 1931.

Lee, Dwight E., "A Memorandum Concerning Cyprus, 1878," *Journal of Modern History,* III (June, 1931), 235-41.

Lhéritier, Michel, "Le Sens de l'Occupation de Chypre, d'Après des Documents Nouveaux," *Mélanges Offert à S. Lambros.* Athens, 1933.

Liebold, Rudolf, *Die Stellung Englands in der Russisch-Türkischen Krise von 1875-78.* Wilkau, 1930.

Orr, Capt. C. W. J., *Cyprus under British Rule.* London, 1918.

Schmidt, Hermann, *Das Eisenbahnwesen in der Asiatischen Türkei.* Berlin, 1914.

Temperley, Harold, "Disraeli and Cyprus," *English Historical Review,* XLVI (April, 1931), 274-79.

"Further Evidence on Disraeli and Cyprus," *Ibid.,* (July, 1931), 457-60.

Thompson, George Carslake, *Public Opinion and Lord Beaconsfield, 1875-1880.* 2 v. London, 1886.

Tyler, Mason Whiting, *The European Powers and the Near East, 1875-1908.* (Research Publications of the University of Minnesota. Studies in the Social Sciences, No. 17). Minneapolis, 1925.

Young, George, *Corps de Droit Ottoman.* 7 v. Oxford, 1906.

INDEX

INDEX

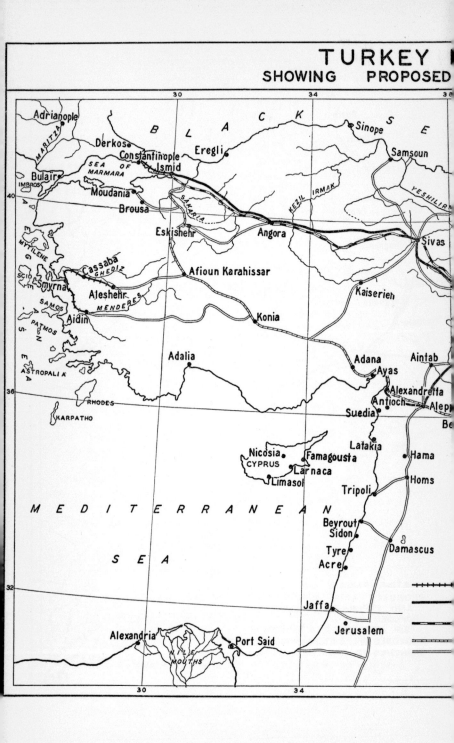

TURKEY

SHOWING PROPOSED